"Transformation: what it is, why it matters, how to achieve it, and meaningfully evaluate it. That's the territory of this book. Systems understandings can propel transformation, but to do so must cut through the cacophonous demands for more rigorous methods to pursue the challenge of engaging in more rigorous thinking. Drawing on ancient and enduring wisdom, this book illuminates the pathway to sustainability where what is at stake is nothing less than the future of humanity on Earth."

Michael Q. Patton, *founder of Utilization-Focused Evaluation, author of* Blue Marble Evaluation *and former president of the American Evaluation Association*

"Coll's groundbreaking book builds a solid bridge for you to connect the inexplicable and impenetrable world of Eastern philosophies with the wicked and vexatious challenges of sustainable management. From Chapter Five, you can ride on his Zen Business Wheel to roam back inside the mysterious domain of Taoism and Buddhism and forward to apply its wisdoms to your triple business bottom lines, principles, and practices. With this new book, you no longer will feel that sustainable management is akin to teenage sex: everyone talks about doing it; everyone thinks everyone else is doing it; but no one is doing it well."

Yuwei Shi, *Academic Director, Blue Pioneers Program at University of California, Santa Cruz*

"This book argues that emerging economies contribute to global economic growth, bringing a wealth of wisdom that is essential to fix capitalism. From a business and holistic management perspective, Coll's new book explores a novel interpretation and enlightening application of Eastern systemic philosophies to build a more conscious, harmonious, regenerative and inclusive economy in turbulent times."

Lourdes Casanova, *Director of Emerging Markets Institute at Cornell University, S.C. Johnson School of Management*

Buddhist and Taoist Systems Thinking

Buddhist and Taoist Systems Thinking explores a radical new conception of business and management. It is grounded on the reconnection of humans with nature as the new competitive advantage for living organizations and entrepreneurs that aspire to regenerate the economy and drive a positive impact on the planet, in the context of the Anthropocene. Organizations today struggle in finding a balance between maximizing profits and generating value for their stakeholders, the environment and the society at large. This happens in a paradigm shift characterized by unprecedented levels of exponential change and the emergence of disruptive technologies. Adaptability, thus, is becoming the new business imperative. How can, then, entrepreneurs and organizations constantly adapt and, at the same time, design the sustainable futures they'd like?

This book uniquely explores the benefits of applying Buddhist and Taoist Systems Thinking to sustainable management. Grounded in Taoist and Zen Buddhist philosophies, it offers a modern scientific perspective fundamentally based on the concepts of bio-logical adaptability and lifefulness amidst complexity and constant change. The book introduces the new concept of the Gaia organization as a living organism that consciously helps perpetuate the conditions for life on the planet. It is subject to the natural laws of transformation and the principles of oneness, emptiness, impermanence, balance, self-regulation and harmonization. Readers will find applied Eastern systems theories such as the Yin-Yang and the Five Elements operationalized through practical methodologies and tools such as T-Qualia and the Zen Business model. They are aimed at guiding Gaia organizations and entrepreneurs in leading sustainable transformations and qualifying economic growth.

The book offers a vital toolkit for purpose-driven practitioners, management researchers, students, social entrepreneurs, evaluators and change-makers to reinvent, create and mindfully manage sustainable and agile organizations that drive systemic transformation.

Josep M. Coll is a professor of Strategy, Sustainability and Innovation at EADA Business School, visiting professor at Yonsei University in South Korea, and research associate at Maastricht School of Management. He works as an independent consultant for a wide range of private and public organizations, such as the European Commission and the United Nations. In the United Nations system, he co-led the first corporate developmental evaluation and adaptive management movement in UNFPA. He regularly speaks internationally on sustainable transformation and coaches organizations, managers and entrepreneurs in transitioning to the new sustainable, regenerative and inclusive business paradigm.

Systems Thinking

Series editor:
Gerald Midgley
University of Hull, U.K.

Systems Thinking theory and practice is gaining ground in the worlds of social policy and management.

The Routledge *Systems Thinking* series is designed to make this complex subject as easy for busy practitioners and researchers to understand as possible. It provides range of reference books, textbooks and research books on a range of themes in systems thinking, from theoretical introductions to the systems thinking approach and its history, through practical guides to the implementation of systems thinking in the world, through to in depth case studies that are significant for their profound impact.

This series is an essential reference point for anyone looking for innovative ways to effect systemic change, or engaging with complex problems.

Managing Creativity
A Systems Thinking Journey
José-Rodrigo Córdoba-Pachón

Systems Thinking in a Turbulent World
A Search for New Perspectives
Anthony Hodgson

The Hidden Power of Systems Thinking
Governance in a Climate Emergency
Ray Ison and Ed Straw

Buddhist and Taoist Systems Thinking
The Natural Path to Sustainable Transformation
Josep M. Coll

For more information about this series, please visit: www.routledge.com/ Systems-Thinking/book-series/STHINK

Buddhist and Taoist Systems Thinking

The Natural Path to Sustainable Transformation

Josep M. Coll

Routledge
Taylor & Francis Group

LONDON AND NEW YORK

First published 2022
by Routledge
2 Park Square, Milton Park, Abingdon, Oxon OX14 4RN

and by Routledge
605 Third Avenue, New York, NY 10158

Routledge is an imprint of the Taylor & Francis Group, an informa business

© 2022 Josep M. Coll

British Library Cataloguing-in-Publication Data
A catalogue record for this book is available from the British Library

Library of Congress Cataloging-in-Publication Data
Names: Coll, Josep M., author.
Title: Buddhist and Taoist systems thinking : the natural path to sustainable transformation / Josep M. Coll.
Description: 1 Edition. | New York: Routledge, 2021. |
Series: Systems thinking | Includes bibliographical references and index.
Identifiers: LCCN 2020057508 (print) | LCCN 2020057509 (ebook) Subjects:
LCSH: Sustainable development–Religious aspects–Buddhism. |
Sustainable development–Religious aspects–Taoism. |
Management–Environmental aspects. | Organizational change. |
Gaia hypothesis. | System theory.
Classification: LCC HC79.E5 C59855 2021 (print) | LCC HC79.E5 (ebook) |
DDC 338.9/270882–dc23
LC record available at https://lccn.loc.gov/2020057508
LC ebook record available at https://lccn.loc.gov/2020057509

ISBN: 978-1-032-00972-8 (hbk)
ISBN: 978-0-367-47896-4 (pbk)
ISBN: 978-1-003-03721-7 (ebk)

Typeset in CelestePro
by Deanta Global Publishing Services, Chennai, India

To Siam and Suri, with love

To Suk Man Yu, in memoriam

To the future generations, with hope

Contents

Illustrations

Figures

Tables

Acknowledgements

Writing a book is like growing a Chinese bamboo tree. You sow and water the seed. You irrigate and nurture it for days and months and years but nothing happens apparently. Finally, around the fifth year approximately, something astonishing awaits. The tree starts to grow, and it does so for around thirty metres in only a few weeks. What happened during these five years? The tree spent this time developing a complex root system with expanding connections, thus building a strong yet unseen foundation to sustain the outward growth that is bound to come.

In a similar fashion, writing a book is like nurturing the bamboo tree. The seed of a book is an idea, and once you plant it in your mind you start nurturing it. The fertile soil is your experience, the water is your curiosity and the perseverance is your passion. For some time, your mind makes the necessary connections to expanding and developing your idea into a system of knowledge that sustains the content of the book. And finally, this content is literally written in far less time. But for seeing the final piece growing, the tree needs sunshine. For a book, sunshine is equivalent to the help, support and inspiration of the people that care for and resonate with the message and spirit of the book.

My heartfelt thanks to my wife Suri and my son Siam. They have always believed in my ideas, creating the conditions and the space for my writing, which, in the middle of the Covid crisis, was very challenging. And, most of all, they created an atmosphere of love, encouragement and inspiration that has nurtured my body, my mind and my soul in high spirits for the entire journey.

Special thanks go to my friend, colleague and partner, Jordi del Bas, 'el Mestre'. His profound knowledge and commentaries have enormously enriched the content of this book, and our passionate discussions around fundamental ideas have always been inspiring, joyful and insightful.

I'm very grateful to Josep Manuel Brañas, for two things. First, because he recommended me to go to Asia, in particular to South Korea, which marked a turning point in my life. Second, for believing in me and in my work, for making me aware of this book's potential and for encouraging me to expand my horizons.

My sincere thanks to Janet Shin, who kindly introduced me to the fascinating world of Taoist metaphysics. She generously shared her deep knowledge and wisdom with me, and encouraged me to develop my own path in bridging metaphysics with management. This book is, in a way, a result of that.

Thanks so much to Lito Lesta, friend and partner at the Zen Business, for his long-time support and feedback. His emotion and vibration have been a source of inspiration and energy during the process of writing the book.

Many thanks to Michael Quinn Patton for his "'utilization-focused'" feedback in reviewing the book. His words have deeply encouraged me to share this book, and his books on evaluation have deeply inspired my work.

Thank you so much to Lama Wangchen from Barcelona's House of Tibet, Sergio Restrepo from Casa Luker, Àngel Garrido from Voxel, Piero Caterino from MeteOro Design, Pablo Vidueira from the Global Alliance, grandmaster Raymond Lo, Lourdes Casanova from Cornell University, Yuwei Shi from University of California, Laila Baker from the United Nations, Dae-Ryun Chang and Jung-Hoon Lee from Yonsei University, Hee-Dong Yang from Ewha University and Carles Navarro from BASF for their dedicated contributions to the book.

I've always believed that a sustainable economy needs arts to communicate key messages that with science alone are very difficult to convey. Thanks to artist Daniel Berdala for believing in the importance of bridging arts and business, as it is exemplified in his wonderful portray of the Gaia organization.

The knowledge of this book does not come out of the blue. I have enormously enjoyed dancing with great universal thinkers and authors such as Lao Tzu, Buddha Gautama, Alan Watts, Fritjof Capra, Joanna Macy, Lynn Margulis, Otto Scharmer and many more, whose books have always awakened insights and deep reflections to help me grow.

I'm very grateful to Ramon Noguera and Jordi Díaz, academic director and dean of EADA Business School, respectively, for their leadership in embedding the Zen Business model and the pioneering masters in sustainability and innovation that I created as core curriculum of the school, with excellent results.

The editing of a book requires great teamwork. I'm grateful to the series editor Gerald Midgley, Guy Loft, Alex Atkinson and the rest of the team at Routledge for their careful dedication to this book.

Last, but not least, I want to extend my gratitude to my students and clients, all over the world, for being a true source of learning. My interactions with them have been key in sparking my motivation, expanding my knowledge and reaffirming my commitment to contribute to a happier and sustainable society.

Introduction

The consciousness gap

The history of civilization is the story of the ascent of humankind. An ascent full of light and shadows. At their best, humans have taken advantage of their distinctive capacities to think and create to build complex global, social, techno-economic, political and cultural systems that have guided unprecedented levels of social progress and economic development. At their worst, human intelligence has been used to cause damage, suffering, conflict and divide across the world.

The latest sufferings are related to the degradation that human behaviour is causing to the environment and to humankind. The negative impact of humans on the planet have led to the Anthropocene, the human-made era that is provoking rapid geological, ecological, biological and socioeconomic changes on the planet. The deterioration of our natural systems has been alarmingly accelerated since the advent of a global extractive economic system that trades natural and human resources for profit.

This system is blinded by an economy based on the premises of infinite economic growth and endless needs. With the exponential growth of technologies and human population, the negative consequences of such economic system have become ecologically, socially and economically unsustainable. Ignorance of these consequences—or of the causes behind them—has enlarged the human–nature divide. We have basically forgotten that we are part of nature, that we are actually nature.

I am sure you have at some point wondered why structural global challenges such as poverty, inequality, environmental degradation, economic instability, unemployment, chronic and infectious diseases, drug addiction, terrorism and war, for example, persist over time despite the brilliance of human intelligence, technological know-how and economic means that have been directed at eradicating them.

The unintended consequences of our economic system are happening at a time characterized by enormous and increasing complexity. The management field states that we are living in a VUCA (volatile, uncertain, complex

1

and ambiguous) world, a world where events occur and decisions need to be taken amid growing volatility, uncertainty, complexity and ambiguity. The Covid-19 crisis is a vivid portrait of this fragile world: an exponential VUCA or turbulent world, where disruptive events emerge out of the blue, constantly challenging the status quo.

Have you found yourself in a situation where you had to make a quick, real-time decision without having any evidence to support it? Or, even worse, have you found yourself in a situation where you had contradictory evidence and yet you had to make a decision? That is often the situation for those who work in managing business and sustainability. So, how do we prepare for such a world?

This book is for seekers, for people in search of ideas, concepts and solutions to make this world, our beautiful planet, a better place to live, in peaceful harmony among humans and other sentient beings. Seekers are driven by an inner curiosity to learn and experiment with new things. This curiosity brings along with it a subtle sense of discomfort that makes seekers constantly challenge their status quo, ask questions and reflect upon life.

The 1960s saw the emergence of a scientific interdisciplinary field—coming from physical and life sciences—to study the inherent complexity of life, called general systems theory or systems science. Back then, it was a breakthrough. Today, it is still so. Systems science offers a new paradigm of holistic—or systems—thinking to precisely capture and understand the dynamics of complexity in order to find answers to complex global challenges. This thinking is based on the concept of system, which environmental scientist and systems thinker Donella Meadows defined as "an interconnected set of elements that is coherently organized in a way that achieves something".[1] A galaxy, the Earth, a city, an organization, a forest, a tree, a person ... They are all systems. A system can be embedded in other systems, such as people that work for an organization, or the trees of a forest. The whole system is larger than the sum of its parts, and it has its own structure and patterns of behaviour, mutually influenced by external and internal factors from other systems.

This type of thinking emerges as an alternative to the traditional—and predominant—linear thinking that has long characterized the functioning of the world's economic system. It is the kind of thinking we have been exposed to, based on the reductionist division of the world into small and comprehensible units.[2] The traditional economic system uses the logic–rational analysis, the ability to trace direct linear paths of cause and effect in order to find solutions that allow us to control our "reality".

However, and despite its relevant contributions to management science, there are two problems with systems theory. The first problem is about oversimplification. The danger of system as a concept is that, as complexity theorist Edgar Morin describes, "its holism becomes a new kind of reductionism by reducing everything to the whole". We definitely need to simplify reality in order to organize it and make agile decisions, but without falling into the generalization of complex reality. System is a root-word for complexity, a concept that should illuminate and not hide all the interdependent connections between elements and among systems.

The second problem is that systems science does not take into consideration the subjective experience of the observer for healing and transforming the system. As part of the system, the degree of perception and level of consciousness of the person who observes, studies, tries to understand and acts upon the system has a direct influence to transform it for the better or for the worse. Reality, and, therefore, systems, is a function of how we perceive and see the world. It is directly conditioned about our expectations, fears and motivations. The assumptions and mental models we hold about the world influence this reality.

I think that the study and, above all, the application, of systems thinking require the recognition and integration of the perception of the observer (the agent) into the process of knowing. As systems scientist Anthony Hodgson suggests, we need to rehabilitate the observer as a first step to heal our fragmented world.[3] My point is very pragmatic: the observer's level of awareness and consciousness directly influences the system. It does so because our level of consciousness and awareness directly influences how we think, behave and act in the systems we belong to and participate in. The observer is also an agent, a change-maker that transforms the system. If you see the world as if you are part of it, you are likely to treat it better and that affects how the systems operate.

The absence of the observer in systems theory and in management science overall (including the management of sustainability) is what I call the *consciousness gap*. Bridging this gap is precisely the focus of this book. Systems science has primarily developed in the West, especially in the United States. Although it represented an attempt to break from the deter ministic paradigm, it did not include an Eastern perspective in the process of knowing. In this context, the consciousness gap carries an implicit sub-gap: the East–West knowledge gap.

The East–West knowledge gap assumes that most management concepts, theories and models are created in the West, especially in the United States. Who has not studied Michael Porter's competitive strategy and five forces? Peter Drucker's management principles? Philip Kotler's marketing fundamentals and 4Ps? Clayton Christensen's innovation theories? Or Osterwalder and Pigneur's business model canvas? The business and management world is mostly influenced by ideas grounded in Western-thinking cultures and frameworks.

I have no problem at all with Western-based theories and the fact that the West is a powerhouse in management thinking. On the contrary, I learn a great deal from these theories. But the deeper I go into studying the consciousness gap, the more I think that we have ignored a wealth of wisdom based on the natural study of human nature and consciousness. A wealth of wisdom that originated in the East. This is the case of Buddhism and Taoism, two philosophical streams that have empirically studied the liberation of human suffering in light of the fundamental nature of the universe.

We are facing global Anthropogenic problems for which management and systems science as we know them are not enough. And that is because they cannot capture the essence of some of these problems that are not only complex and systemic, but also a product of our consciousness. The Western lens is not enough for us to help capture them, understand them, and act upon them. I think that Eastern knowledge is what is missing, so that systems and management thinking get the upgrade needed for these disciplines to help us in the current world we live in. That is why this book is of the essence. We have the possibility to review, illuminate and update management science and practice with Eastern-based complementary approaches that are grounded in the conscious exploration and transformation of the self.

I have long been fascinated by the enquiry into human nature. I was attracted to the study of perennial philosophies rooted in indigenous knowledge that have long enquired about that nature, in a context in which the premise of humans as nature is considered a universal law. My learning journey brought me to South Korea, where I started practising Zen Buddhism and studying the hidden jewels of Taoist philosophy and metaphysics while working as a consultant and lecturer on international business and economic development.

It is extraordinary how, millennia ago, Buddhism and Taoism developed such an advanced systems' view of life by studying and observing nature. The fundamental principles of these life philosophies have now been discovered by modern science, especially in the fields of quantum physics and neuroscience. These recent discoveries reveal the major innovations of such Eastern-based empirical methods of enquiry into human and universal consciousness. Renowned physician and systems theorist Fritjof Capra, in his seminal book *The Tao of Physics* provides an insightful exploration of the parallels between these indigenous philosophies and modern physics. Can you imagine the potential benefits of applying these universal principles to organizational learning and sustainable transformation? This book explores such potential.

As a westerner educated under the Newtonian/Cartesian scientific paradigm, studying Buddhism and Taoism was a breakthrough for me. For some time, I explored these two fields of enquiry—business and

Buddhism–Taoism—separately. How could I make sense of combining my spiritual pursuit with my professional passion? They seemed at odds with one another. This nonetheless, the more I deepened my study and practice, the closer they were becoming. I finally realized that the real value was in bridging both apparently opposite but complementary disciplines: applying Buddhism and Taoism to sustainable business management. The result is a radical new conception of business and management, which is the subject of this book.

Buddhism and Taoism are essentially ways of liberation. Centuries ago, in a period called the Axial Age,[4] these two philosophical streams emerged—both in the East—as methods to free individuals from suffering; a kind of suffering that is inherent to the cycle of living, called the cycle of birth and death, or *samsara*. His Holiness the Dalai Lama, in his book a *Call for Revolution*, affirms that the aim of his spiritual quest is to free himself of the fundamental ignorance that has led to the notion that there is a division between people and the natural world, which is at the root of all our suffering. To escape from this suffering, Buddhism and Taoism both offer a process of self-awareness grounded in the personal experience of human nature in relation to universal nature. This experience directly influences our level of perception, consciousness, thinking and behaviour.

More than two thousand years later, the face of the world has completely changed. It is much more complex. But suffering remains in our lives. This time, it is not only about our individual suffering, but also about the suffering we are causing to our planet, and, ultimately, to ourselves. This suffering is mostly caused by an extractive economic system that takes nature as a mere resource that can be exploited mercilessly. We need a new software of the mind that can allow us to free ourselves from this *samsaric* state of the world.

In this context, Buddhism and Taoism are more relevant than ever. They offer a systems view of life based on the interdependent nature linking all living phenomena. In this regard, individual liberation or freedom is empty from a separate self. So, it is full of everything. This is what Zen master Thich Nhat Hahn calls interbeing. Applying this idea of interdependence represents an opportunity to expand our mental boundaries towards personal and organizational development in the service of people and the planet.

Applying interdependence with wisdom, compassion and humility, three fundamental principles that converge in Buddhism and Taoism, provides a path to liberate this economic system from *samsara*, in a way that allows us to reconcile with our own nature, bridging the human–nature divide. In doing so, these Eastern philosophies reveal the self and the organization as living systems, constantly changing and adapting in flow with the natural path of transformation.

I write this book as a curious human being in search of transitioning ways to a new sustainable paradigm. I know I'm a son of the old extractive business paradigm who is realizing that he is also an architect of the new. I take with passion my bridging role, of integrator between the East and the West, between human and nature, between business and society. I'm well aware of the limitations of writing about Buddhism and Taoism. These are philosophies that can only be genuinely understood by experience. As Alan Watts puts it, Zen (the symbiotic philosophy resulting from the interaction between Buddhism and Taoism) "deals with the domain of experience that can't be talked about".[5] But I hope this book at least triggers an intellectual experience that sparks your interest to practise what resonates with you. Following a fundamental principle in Zen, let me warn you: do not believe anything that is written in this book, validate it with your own experience.

In this context, I do not pretend to write a scholarly treatise on Buddhism and Taoism. My focus hinges upon the application of Buddhist and Taoist systems thinking to organizational learning, adaptation and sustainable transformation in the face of the emerging problems of our world. I understand Buddhism and Taoism as a universal asset available to humankind that transcends all kinds of geographical, mental and identity borders. This book provides a renewed interpretation of Buddhist and Taoist systems thinking in light of the challenges of the twenty-first century.

The first challenge addressed in this book is related to finding new strategies and solutions to managing the sustainable transformations required in our organizations and the economic system at large. Can we create profitable businesses inspired by nature, that create life and take care of life? How can that be done? We all have seen companies that aggressively focus on profits while externalizing social and economic costs: how can we identify these unbalances and solve them? The second challenge, and related to the first, is to find new adaptive strategies and management approaches that can allow people and organizations to adapt, anticipate, transform and navigate across the VUCA world.

Contextualized in the transition to a sustainability driven business paradigm (described in Chapter 1), this book introduces new approaches grounded in Buddhist and Taoist systems thinking. These include the application of Taoist principles into organizational development and adaptability (described in Chapter 2); the Yin–Yang creative tensions (described in Chapter 3); the T-Qualia as an experiential model of learning for transformation (described in Chapter 4); the Zen Business as a bio-logical model of sustainable organizational design and transformation (described in Chapter 5); the principles-driven Gaia organization and entrepreneur that illustrate the practices of the Zen Business model (described in Chapters 6 and 7, respectively); an analytical framework for managing abundance in the present times (described in Chapter 8); and the concept of business mindfulness as an analytical framework to guide the evaluation of the impact of the trans-formation (described in Chapter 9).

The concepts, frameworks and tools presented across the nine chapters have two objectives. The first is to provide *simplexity*, that is, to clarify complex problems and shed light on the complexities that frame our challenges in a simple manner. The second is to help organizations and entrepreneurs understand the mechanisms and dynamics that generate those problems as the basis for designing and applying solutions.

The novel contribution of this book is, therefore, to apply, for the first time, Buddhist and Taoist systems thinking to a nature-based, biological approach to manage sustainable transformation. Buddhism and Taoism have long been applied to other disciplines, such as medicine, geobiology, architecture, and martial arts, but not to business and management yet.

Joanna Macy, a pioneer scholar in studying the parallels between Buddhism and general systems theory, affirms that "encounters between modern Western thought and ancient Asian philosophies figure among the more fruitful feature of the twentieth century".[6] However, the business and management field has yet to discover the value and recognize the utility, from a systems perspective, of the Eastern approach to the process of learning, knowing, behaving and, overall, designing and managing organizations.

I believe there is so much we can learn from the systemic thinking ingrained in Buddhism and Taoism. Despite the catastrophic and sometimes apocalyptic news associated with the Anthropogenic challenges of our time, this book is about potential. Frankly speaking, I do not know whether we have time to save the planet. But this is not the point of this book. I grew up watching the insightful documentaries of Félix Rodríguez de la Fuente, a renowned naturalist and environmental broadcaster who said, "it is too arrogant pretending to save nature; the really sensible thing to do is to let ourselves be saved by nature".

Taking a planetary time-whole perspective, humans are quasi-new on Earth. I assume that the planet as a self-regulating living system can manage without us. So, I will not bother you with a self-guilt sense of urgency such as "do this or the planet is gone" type of narrative. I leave this assumption to open interpretation. I'd like you to enjoy this journey with no strings attached. The book is written with hope, which, as Vaclav Havel once said, "is not the conviction that something will turn out well, but the certainty that something makes sense regardless of how it turns out".[7]

After more than 20 years as a manager, executive, researcher, consultant, evaluator and entrepreneur, studying and working in more than forty countries, I have realized the potential of business as a positive and transformational force if consciously and purposefully directed towards solving the pressing global challenges of our world. However, to fully realize this potential, the paradigm of sustainability requires a profound transformation of the way we think. This book explores this transformation by reformulating our own conscious participation in shaping the reality we want.

The focus of interbeing and living in harmony with nature opens the door to a life of possibility, of opportunity, of lifefulness, geared towards nurturing and creating life. Applying harmony to the organization is the opportunity to build conscious businesses that qualify economic growth, regenerate ecological and human systems and drive the transformation towards the new sustainable business paradigm.

In this spirit, the book is written for purpose-driven practitioners, business and management researchers, business executives, consultants, students, social entrepreneurs, evaluators and change-makers looking for new effective ways to reinvent, create and mindfully manage sustainable and agile organizations that drive systemic transformation.

Notes

1   Meadows, D. (2015). *Thinking in Systems: A Primer*. Chelsea Green.
2   Edgar Morin calls this reductionist, linear type of thinking blind intelligence. Morin E. (1985) Blind intelligence. In: Shoham S.G., Rosenstiel F. (eds) *And He Loved Big Brother*. Palgrave Macmillan, London.
3   Hodgson, A. (2020). *Systems Thinking for a Turbulent World*. Routledge.
4   Philosopher Karl Jaspers coined the period comprised between 800 BCE to 200 BCE as the Axial Age

>   because it was a gigantic axis around which the future promise of humanity revolved. Everything we need to know about happiness and fulfillment, peace and prosperity, love and family, creativity and art, good governance and sustainable civilization can be learned in the Axial Age.

5   Watts, A. (2017). *Out of Your Mind*. Sounds True.
6   Macy, J. (1991). *Mutual Causality in Buddhism and General Systems Theory*. State University of New York Press.
7   Havel, V. (1991). *Disturbing the Peace*. Vintage.

References

Capra, F. (1975). *The Tao of Physics*. Shambala.
Dalai Lama (2018). *A Call for Revolution*. Random House UK.
Havel, V. (1991). *Disturbing the Peace: A Conversation with Karel Huizdala*. Vintage.
Hodgson, A. (2020). *Systems Thinking for a Turbulent World*. Routledge.
Macy, J. (1991). *Mutual Causality in Buddhism and General Systems Theory*. State University of New York Press.
Meadows, D. (2015). *Thinking in Systems: A Primer*. Chelsea Green.
Watts, A. (2017). *Out of Your Mind*. Sounds True.

Chapter 1

The emergence of the new business paradigm

From the ego-system to the eco-system

A human-made world: how have we ended up here?

Humans are exponentially undermining the planet at unprecedented rates, far faster than the geological speed driven by natural processes. Probably, as World Wildlife Fund Chief Executive Tanya Steel affirms, we are the first generation to know we are destroying our planet and the last one that can do anything about it. Environmental emergencies such as climate change, global warming, biodiversity loss, dying oceans, carbon pollution and food insecurity are evidence that the Earth and its ecosystems are seriously damaged.[1]

"Welcome to the Anthropocene", the human-made geological era.[2] It was in May 2011 when the *Economist* chose this title for its cover. A liberal economic magazine, for the first time, warned about the environmental consequences of a nature extractive economic system. Although the concept was not new, the publication was a hallmark that helped in raising public awareness on the economic externalities behind the disconnect between humans and nature.

The fact that nature-shaped humans are, paradoxically, shaping nature is the biggest problem of our time. And it comes with a sense of urgency. Human evolution no longer moves at biological speed but, rather, at much faster technological speed. Exponential impact on the Earth's ecosystems manifested especially after the Second World War. That time is known as the Great Acceleration.[3] It was characterized by intense industrial, technological and commercial activity as a consequence of globalization. The Great Acceleration fuelled hitherto unseen high levels of economic and population growth, democracy, life expectancy, schooling rates, and the birth of the welfare state in times of overall peace and stability. But this process of acceleration also came with a high ecological cost.

The flaw of the Anthropocene as a concept is time. The suffix –cene denotes an epoch, or era, which is normally associated with a long period of time. And timing, nonetheless, is a scarce resource. Through the lens of historical time, the correlation between human agency and ecological degradation is just an event, but one with enormous consequences for the planet. There is a growing scientific stream affirming that the Earth is nearing a point of no return. One study[4] concludes that the threshold is getting closer unless the use of renewable energies starts growing at a rate of 2% a year before then.

Dealing with this uncertain urgency adds to the increasing complexity of managing adaptive systems that integrate human and natural components. With technology arbitrating between humans and nature, it is almost questionable whether the Anthropocene will last as a geological epoch. But that's not the main point. The real issue is about change and systems transformation, before time dictates its final verdict.

The *Economist* precisely pointed to that issue. The British magazine posited that "humans have changed the way the world works. Now they have to change the way they think about it, too". This statement implicitly raises two related critical questions. First, how did it happen? And second, what kind of new thinking does humankind now require?

Exploring these two questions is the subject of this chapter.

The genesis of the modern economic system: the quest for growth

Our current social system is grounded on free market economics, an idea first conceptualized in the eighteenth century by Adam Smith. The British philosopher believed that a new social organization of work was needed. He proposed an economy focused on efficient cycles of production—supply—and consumption—demand—arbitrated by self-regulatory markets and the division of labour. As a moral philosopher, Smith's theory of change rested on the idea that an invisible hand would suffice for driving positive unintended social benefits as a result of individuals' self-interested actions.

Zooming in on this theory of change, we can see how the invisible hand refers to the effects of competition. Free markets incentivize competition in the marketplace, which spurs innovation. Innovation drives entrepreneurs' interests. Entrepreneurs take risks by allocating and managing resources needed to deliver value to the population—through the offering of new or better products and services or by making processes more efficient—in exchange for a financial profit. Part of this value is captured by the population in the capacity of individuals to act as producers and consumers. As consumers, our choices are expanded by means of reduced prices, increased quantity, access to and variety of offerings, or increased quality.

The reinforcement of the production–consumption cycle generates economic growth. Part of this growth reverts back to the risk-takers in the form of accumulation of capital.[5] Part of this growth creates jobs and pays for workers' wages. And part of this growth goes to public administrations in the form of taxes aimed at financing the welfare state (taxes on profits, wages, capital and consumption).

The benefit of economic growth was the promise that growth would improve living conditions globally. Three centuries later, has this prophecy been fulfilled? The answer largely depends on how you scope the term "living conditions globally". Certainly, during the past two centuries, progress is undeniable. The proportion of people living in extreme poverty has enormously decreased, the global level of literacy has rampantly increased, as well as the proportion of people with basic education. Global health has improved, as measured by the reduction in child mortality and the huge increase in life expectancy. Political freedom has also improved, measured by the size of the population living in state democracies. As a result of all this progress, the world's population has seen an unprecedented exponential growth. It has increased sevenfold over the past two centuries.[6]

This is a huge success of modern civilization, if we look at it retrospectively, but a success that comes at a price, if we take a forward outlook. The binomial correlation between economic and population growth are two of the root causes that explain the human–nature disconnect and, therefore, the anthropogenic challenges that threaten natural ecosystems today.

The quest for growth has left a huge imprint on the underlying structures of the current capitalist system. Free market economics is a social technology—godfathered by Mr Smith—that has shaped a mental model that believes in economic growth as a way of liberation. A kind of Holy Grail. Growth, as a personal and collective value, is understood as the recipe to solve our problems and the assumed stairway to happiness.

The world of Adam Smith and the Industrial age

The classical economic theories that still underpin the modern socioeconomic system, its patterns, underlying structures and mental models, were built in a much different context than nowadays. Poverty was the main economic status of a large illiterate majority, without access to education, in a sparsely populated planet. Society was structured according to a feudal-based patriarchal system based on land holdings, labour exploitation, and taxation over an agriculture-based economy. Landlords exercised an enormous control over the plebeians. Europe was becoming the global superpower by reaping the benefits of science and colonization. This context shaped the perception of reality, and in that reality the quest for growth was the perceived solution to the problems of that era.

The worldview and values system that characterized the modern industrial age were designed in the sixteenth and seventeenth centuries. The industrial revolution came as a result of a system transformation instigated by the scientific revolution that hinged upon science as the main way of knowing. A series of outstanding developments in the fields of mathematics, physics, astronomy, biology and chemistry transformed the views of society about nature. Iconic scientists such as Copernicus, Kepler, Galileo, Bacon, Descartes and Newton developed a scientific method based on empiricism and rationalism. The way to explore the world and the universe was through dividing nature into single parts that were analysed as isolated entities—a thought process called silo-thinking. It was assumed that the sum of the parts would make up the whole.

Therefore, reductionism, linearity, rationality, measurement and man's domination over nature[7] became key scientific principles that shaped the world of thought, behaviour and technology until today. The world was seen as a machine. This mechanistic worldview had implications not only in science but also to all domains of life, including the way of understanding the functions of ecology, society, the economy, organizations and individuals as fragmented and isolated entities.

Against this backdrop, the mechanistic worldview was also embedded in organizational praxis. Corporate organizations are the most relevant socio-economic institutions in the capitalist system. Economic growth is channelled and achieved through entrepreneurial organizations that attract and manage resources—land, capital, labour, and technology—to maximize outputs and bring them to the market in exchange for revenue. The private corporation is the cornerstone of the social organization of life.

Organizational theory and behaviour was a field of management developed in the late nineteenth and early twentieth centuries in the midst of the Industrial Revolution. Of special influence was the work of Frederick Taylor,[8] who developed the concept of scientific management. The main objective of this concept was to improve economic efficiency through productivity gains as the means to maximize shareholder value. Scientific management implied the application of scientific principles to business organization and management. This management approach led to the development of Fordism and the assembly line for mass production, standardization and economies of scale, industrial re-engineering, logistics and operations management, lean manufacturing and Six Sigma, among other popular efficiency-based models.

The rationale of the corporation was to maximize corporate growth in the frame of the organization-as-a-machine metaphor. According to this view, humans are a resource—labour—that needs to be productive in order to become more efficient. This implies a maximization of the output per working hour. In the same vein, land and nature became natural resources that could be extracted from and exploited in order to maximize output along the value chain. The integration of labour and natural resources as fictitious commodities into the market mechanism resulted in the subjugation of "the substance of society itself to the laws of the market", in words of the Hungarian economist Karl Polanyi.[9] Free market economics implied the subjugation of social and political systems to the self-regulatory market mechanism. Therefore, the increasing power of the market is inversely correlated with a dismissed power of politics. States are deprived of their major regulatory functions and, instead, forced to abide by the rules of the market. The rise of the corporation brought the loss of conscious human control.

Control became, indeed, a central aspect in organizational management; a kind of control that allowed the corporation to regularly monitor the economic performance of the organization-as-a-machine through measurable financial analysis, risk management, labour productivity and sales forecasting. Measurement systems were based on key quantitative performance indicators that filled the dashboards of strategic management goals. Measurement then became central to the development of management science. Peter Drucker, the management guru, once even said, "if you can't measure it, you can't manage it".

The *homo egonomicus* and the blind economy

The *homo economicus* is a concept introduced by the economist John Stuart Mill. This concept explains the pattern of human behaviour proper of the free market economics-based system. It conceives the economic man as a rational person, who maximizes his individual utility, trying to obtain the greatest benefits for him with minimal effort.[10]

The assumptions underlying *homo economicus* pinpoint that individuals have perfect information about reality,[11] are driven by self-interest and calculate and ponder the possibilities with total rationality to achieve their own prosperity. This theory of change rests on the idea that the sum of individual prosperities would be equal to the prosperity of society as a whole.

The heart of the problem here is that *homo economicus* only bases its decisions on the extent to which they affect its function of personal utility. Therefore, it is denied that the individual considers in his decisions the welfare of others and that of the planet itself. In systemic terms, the decision-making process does not factor in the relationships between the individual and the systems in which he belongs and interacts: socioeconomic and natural systems.

This narcissistic conception of the *homo economicus* is the root cause of the human–nature disconnect. More than a *homo economicus*, he behaves like a *homo egonomicus*. Management focuses on what can be measured, and what matters ends up hinging on what can be measured. Prevailing values systems and principles define the behavioural patterns of humans and social constructs, including the economy. And free market economics engendered an egocentric economic agent that satisfies his needs through the private accumulation of capital and material properties.

The whole spectrum of human systems—economic, social and political—and their institutions were built upon the underlying assumptions and mental models of *homo egonomicus*. According to the Austrian neurologist Sigmund Freud, ego is the psychological component of the personality that is represented by our conscious decision-making process.[12] When such an individual egocentric decision-making process is applied to the collective socioeconomic system, then the whole system behaves as *homo egonomicus*. The system reflects a level of awareness that operates under the principles of the *egonomic* system, or ego system. The behavioural patterns of the ego system sustained unprecedented levels of economic development and progress that were relevant for almost two centuries. The tradeoff was, over time, the making up of a blind economy that generated high social and environmental externalities, as exemplified by the anthropogenic challenges.

Shifting the mindset: the context–behaviour decoupling

The blind economy has become a great burden for achieving sustainable development and prosperity while leaving no one behind. Reductionist thinking towards measuring and quantifying any economic exchange simplified a reality that is much more complex. It is as if *homo egonomicus* had sold his soul to the devil, dragged by his hedonistic drive. He is driven towards, and addicted to, the short-term gratification of his individual preferences.

The consequences of this addiction are ubiquitous. Universities and business schools educate future leaders on the basis of profit maximization, consumerism, competition, private ownership, social status and short-termism. These have become principles that are put into practice by corporations and business organizations. Public administrations operate to enforce these rules of the game, incentivize private agency and feed the power dynamics of the system. Serial entrepreneurs have become the new social heroes and role models. And civil society is becoming powerless and numb.

Against this panorama, there is a relatively minor but emerging stream of business and thought leaders, environmental activists, social entrepreneurs, economists and scholars from different fields that advocate for a shift in the way capitalism is understood and practised. These leaders represent a shift in consciousness that aims at humanizing the economy and unleashing the power of business to build a happier and sustainable world.

This notwithstanding, the first reaction when people realize and become aware of the pains of the Anthropocene is an upsurge of anger and frustration. The way we respond to these afflictions is twofold. First, we try to find guilt outside ourselves, by blaming the system or someone else (such as the powerful elites). Second, we channel anger into a creative energy that focuses on finding alternative solutions to changing the world.

This approach is flawed for two reasons. First, because personalizing blame does not address the root causes and can create more resistance to change. This response is typical of a reductionist view of the issue of responsibility that reinforces the divide between good and bad. In systems thinking, where everything is connected, alternatively, there is nobody to blame as everybody shares a sense of responsibility, as we are all part of the system. There are no good or bad but people with different perceptions and roles. Anger directed at the supposed guilty is replaced with a sense of compassion towards individuals of the system that have acted within the system's boundaries, patterns of behaviour, and mental models. Replacing blame with responsibility provides a sense of relief and peace of mind that directly influence our capacity to perceive reality from a compassionate state of mind, filled with love and empathy towards others. Operating from this mindset is key for expanding our level of awareness—consciousness— of the real issues that need to be changed in order to improve the system. It is a critical part of the creative process.

The second reason why this approach is flawed is the potential unintended consequences for aspirational change agents. People that become aware of the Anthropocene and decide to make a change often focus on changing the outside world without changing their mental models and behavioural patterns first. They still continue to operate from the same patterns which, if not addressed systemically, can produce quick fixes in the short term—temporary solutions that fail to address underlying problems—but can also make matters worse in the long run.

Focusing on change without addressing the underlying problems happened to me when, after a trip to Tanzania, I saw and felt extreme poverty first-hand. I came back home and I wanted to change the situation. I developed a project and raised funding for it. I felt great and fulfilled. I went back to Tanzania and successfully implemented the project to turn an underdeveloped area severely affected by drought and climate change into an innovation hub for regional development. But, as time went by, funds diminished and local people felt frustrated and disempowered. The project generated a big mismatch in expectations and delivery and a great deal of frustration.

The first takeaway I learned is that the observer's behaviour was decoupled from the local system's context. Before designing or implementing any intervention, the observer or the intervener should thoroughly understand the context that defines, frames and scopes the system and its boundaries. This helps to sense the underlying structures that influence the events, problems and challenges, a process that is critical for developing a tailored intervention in the system from a compassionate and eco-systemic state of mind. When context and behaviour are decoupled, change agents risk jeopardizing the intervention in the long run. The problem is that they still operate from the ego-system, which prevents them from making a positive impact in the eco-system.

Addressing the context–behaviour decoupling

Overcoming the context–behaviour decoupling requires two interrelated processes. First, we need to suspend our judgement, which is a cognitive process and a rational state of mind in which one withholds judgement. This process is particularly necessary before drawing moral or ethical conclusions that could influence our perception of reality and, therefore, our decision-making without a reasoned understanding of the context. Second, and as a result of the former, we need to understand the situational factors that influenced the patterns of behaviour of change agents at that time. Applying systems thinking tools is a helpful way to contextualize a system and its problems. Tools such as the iceberg model for root cause analysis, feedback loop mapping for understanding causal relationships between factors and drawing systems archetypes for synthesizing the system behaviour can be particularly useful.[13]

To genuinely understand our modern socioeconomic system, the capitalist system, and its change agent typology, or *homo egonomicus*, we need to situate ourselves in the context and the empirical mindset of the eighteenth century. The modern socioeconomic system was a conception of the world characteristic of pre-industrial societies, built out of scarcity, with great deficits in food, health and culture. Patterns of behaviour were aimed at satisfying basic needs such as eating, knowing and healing, and the way to do it was to make the economy grow. In the world of Adam Smith, the accumulation of capital was still very rudimentary and natural resources seemed inexhaustible, which socially justified the emergence of an ideology based on degenerative growth. The extractive industrial paradigm was useful and effective in achieving unprecedented economic and social progress and prosperity for a large majority. Acknowledging its achievements is the first step towards calibrating the right thinking with the right action.

The emergence of a new business paradigm

In the twenty-first century, the world has exponentially grown in population, wealth, knowledge, technology, life expectancy and, therefore, complexity. Awareness of the Anthropocene has become the new contextual principle. It is as if the rules of the game had profoundly changed if we were still playing with yesterday's logic. Therefore, the fundamental question is: what is the right thinking required to address the current challenges?

This Anthropogenic level of awareness is already provoking the system to react, becoming the first and foremost driver of change. It seems as if the Earth had reached such a peak in its ability to sustain life that it is starting to emit signals of extreme deterioration or dissolution. This awareness is permeating into different stakeholders at different levels—political, economy and business, social and educational—that operate within the capitalist system's boundaries.

At a political level, the most significant initiative is the inclusion of sustainable development as the flagship of the United Nations which underpins the Global Agenda 2030 and the Sustainable Development Goals (SDGs). State and non-state actors localize their own national, regional and local development agendas based on the SDGs.

At a private sector level, the business world is emitting more voices asking for a shift in leading and managing purpose-driven organizations. Businesses aspire to transcend the profit maximization mantra by orientating goals toward satisfying the triple bottom line of benefits—people, profit, planet. Business-based movements and initiatives such as the UN Global Compact, the B-Corp Impact Assessment, Conscious Capitalism, the Economy of the Common Good or the Business Roundtable are emerging manifestations of a system that aspires to rethink and transform capitalism. Impact investing, often referred to as ESG (Environment, Society and Governance investing), is also gaining traction in a corporate world still dominated by short-term pressures on shareholder value maximization.

The weight of the social economy, often called the Third Sector, is, overall, gaining traction in terms of economic weight and job creation. Cooperatives, the pioneers in setting an alternative form of social corporate governance and the rise of social business and entrepreneurship, especially in developing countries, exemplify the claim for redefining how business can potentially create social, environmental and economic value alike.

At a social level, youth activism has emerged as a global phenomenon, putting the climate emergency under the spotlight. Greta Thunberg has become an icon and a role model for millions of activists who follow the climate strike movement, Fridays for Future. As consumers, people are consciously becoming more willing to buy brands that offer ecological or social benefits in their value proposition. Market research consultancies have already become aware of these trends, as is reflected in the emergence of the *lohas*, a customer segment describing a lifestyle of health and sustainability.[14] In the search for employment, people are more drawn to work for purpose-driven companies that seek to create a positive impact. These new attitudes have captured the attention of the media, which is increasingly echoing the call for rethinking capitalism.

At an educational level, business schools and college faculties of business and economics are increasingly introducing courses and designing new programmes that satisfy the demand for educating future business leaders in sustainability and responsible management. I myself had the privilege to create one of the first international Master programmes entirely built for educating and empowering change makers to advance the transition towards the new business paradigm, with a great response by the market.[15] A network of institutions have launched the Positive Impact Rating, the first rating focused on highlighting business schools that have a perceived positive impact on society.[16]

The new business paradigm manifests more explicitly and exponentially since the Great Recession of 2007–2008. The first truly global economic crisis unveiled the mental models—values and beliefs—behind *homo egonomicus* and the impact of the blind economy. The coronavirus outbreak did not only make explicit the fragility of a global system fully interdependent on social productivity and consumerism, but also brought to light the real elephant in the room, that is, the divide between the ecological and economic systems. The coronavirus also showed that a virus is a gateway to reshaping the system and, as such, an opportunity to rethink it from the inside out, thus provoking an uplift in the global level of awareness.

The developmental nature of the new business paradigm

The new business paradigm is not a stand-alone phenomenon that just appears all of a sudden. Rather, it is a shift in consciousness that emerges as a result of a series of events that bring new information into the economic system. The counter-cultural movement of May 1968 protested against casino capitalism, hyper-consumerism, American imperialism and the role of traditional institutions in perpetuating the power dynamics of the system. The public debt crisis of the 1980s showed the paternalistic approach of a development cooperation system biased towards developed countries' self-interests. The 1997 Asian financial crisis suffered the consequences of local financial markets largely dependent on global capital inflows and currency fluctuations of a speculative nature. The Great Recession of 2008 did not only bring the whole global financial system to the point of collapse, but also unveiled the crisis of the prevailing *homo egonomicus* value system. The Covid-19 crisis reminded us of the need to finally face the real elephant in the room and not only to apply quick fixes that still prolong the agony of the system.

The above crises, to name some of the most relevant, sent a wake-up call to society. The message was already latent, but crises hit the system in a way that directly alters the lifestyle and tests the values of the masses. This alteration reflects the theory that after the chaos, order emerges. This new order is not gradual or sequential. The new order emerges in discontinuous, revolutionary breaks called paradigm shifts. Fritjof Capra, building upon the work of Thomas Kuhn, introduced the concept of social paradigm, defining it as "a constellation of concepts, values, perceptions, and practices shared by a community, which forms a particular vision of reality that is the basis of the way the community organizes itself".[17]

Leveraging on Kuhn and Capra's perspective, I define a business paradigm as a constellation of perceptions, values, principles and practices shared by a business ecosystem, which shapes a particular vision of reality that is the basis of how the organization operates and generates value. The emerging new business paradigm shifts the ego-systemic view of *homo economicus* towards an eco-systemic understanding of business and the role it plays as a social, ecological and economic agent. This new business paradigm is sensed and conceptualized in four interrelated dimensions, as illustrated in Figure 1.1.

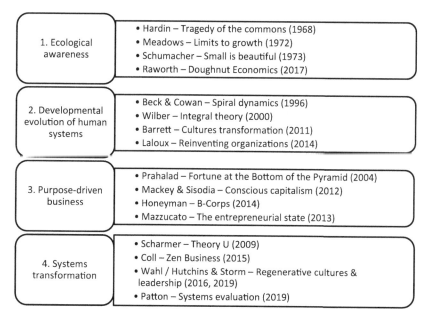

Figure 1.1 The four dimensions driving the emergence and development of the new business paradigm

The first dimension is a developed economic sense of ecological aware-ness. Environmental scientists such as Hardin (1968) and Meadows (1972) studied the divide between ecological and economic systems. Their respec-tive works, *Tragedy of the Commons* and *Limits to Growth*, already outline the ecological externalities and boundaries of the capitalist system. The economist Schumacher (1973) provides a brilliant treatise in his widely acclaimed *Small is Beautiful* on the need to design an eco-friendly economy that he named Buddhist economics. This was a first attempt to acknowledge and apply the nature-wise Buddhist principles into economic science. More recently, Oxford economist Raworth (2017) developed *Doughnut Economics* as a visual sustainable development framework to guide a regenerative economy built upon the concepts of planetary and social boundaries.

The second dimension studies the developmental evolution of human systems, which includes the interrelationships among individuals, their cul-tures, and societies. Beck and Cowan (1996) developed the AQAL framework in their seminal work *Spiral Dynamics*. The framework explains the eight-stage evolutionary development of systems based on changes in values and behaviours, called memes. Wilber (2000), building upon them, developed the *Integral Theory* as a holistic framework that captures the four domains, or quadrants, of consciousness: interior–individual, exterior–individual, interior–collective and exterior–collective. Laloux (2014) applied Beck and Cowan's and Wilber's theories to a management taxonomy that explains and categorizes the different evolutionary stages of organizational cultures for reinventing organizations. Barrett (2013), building upon Maslow's hier-archy of needs, developed the seven levels of consciousness model as a framework for guiding business organizations to transforming their cul-ture from survival to service to society and the planet.

The third dimension focuses on the opportunity to reconceive corpora-tions as sustainability change agents as they put a greater focus on pur-pose than on profit. Prahalad (2004) introduced the concept of corporations making a fortune at the bottom of the pyramid by tailoring their offerings to the needs of underserved markets in developing countries. Coen Gilbert created the B Lab for B-Corps, a certification for companies that meet high standards of verified social and environmental performance, public trans-parency and legal accountability. Honeyman (2014) developed a handbook to guide aspiring companies through the process of becoming a B-Corp, already a global movement. Mackey and Sisodia (2013) popularized the concept of conscious capitalism that has also become a global movement. Building upon the core foundations of capitalism, it advocates the need for corporations to serve all principal stakeholders. Conscious capitalism rests on the application of four guiding tenets: operating from a higher pur-pose, embedding a stakeholder orientation, the development of conscious leadership and a conscious culture. In this third dimension, I also include

Mazzucato's (2013) claim that the entrepreneurial state, in its role of an initial risk-taker, spurs innovation and purpose-driven economic growth. This perspective introduces the important role of the public sector in framing and redesigning an economic system that fosters a regenerative economy hinging upon a public–private coordinated process of value creation.

The fourth dimension addresses systems transformation. Scharmer (2009) developed a holistic change management and transformation method called Theory U. This theory is first based on the process of letting go of past egocentric patterns as a prerequisite for, second, unleashing the creative potential in individuals and organizations for performing from a sensed awareness of the eco-systemic whole. I created the Zen Business model (Coll 2015), a bio-dynamic method of holistic value creation based on the application of Taoist systems thinking theories to organizational design and development. Wahl (2016) and Hutchins and Storm (2019) applied the concept of regeneration to culture and leadership, respectively. This is a step forward in the design of life-affirming systems that promote continuous renewal and restoration of natural resources, in a context of people and place mutual reciprocity. Patton (2019) created the Blue Marble Evaluation, a utilization-focused, developmental and principles-focused approach to evaluating systems transformation. This approach stresses the need for, and highlights the value of, evaluation as a transdisciplinary practice engaged in global change interventions that work toward building a sustainable future.

The principles of the new business paradigm

The above four dimensions are emerging symptoms of the system's appetite for evolution. This appetite will be tested by our ability to get rid of the ego-system and, instead, operate from the eco-system. This ability can be guided by the new codification that emerges out of the four dimensions. If a few privileged individuals mainly codified the current business paradigm around 240 years ago, the new business paradigm emerges as a collective effort of multiple contributions from different disciplines worldwide. These contributions have common patterns of aspirational behaviour—here called principles—that shape the new business mindset. I have synthesized these features in terms of dualistic principles—X versus Y—that characterize the behaviour of the new versus the old paradigm (Table 1.1).

These principles illustrate the present understanding of the dominant business paradigm in our current economic system in contrast with the new business paradigm that is emerging. By illuminating the new paradigm from the old (the current paradigm), the aim of these principles is to understand the paradigm shift, and to guide the behaviour of entrepreneurs and organizations towards the eco-systemic new paradigm.

Table 1.1 The principles of the new business paradigm

Component	EGO-system	versus	ECO-system
Purpose	Profitability	vs	Sustainability
Beneficiaries	Shareholders	vs	Stakeholders
Thinking	Reductionist	vs	Systemic
Organization	Mechanistic	vs	Living
Context	Simplicity	vs	Complexity
Market approach	Competition	vs	Collaboration
Time orientation	Short-term	vs	Long-term
Leadership	Transactional	vs	Transformational
Structure	Hierarchy	vs	Networks
Power	Centralized	vs	Distributed
Innovation approach	Product-focused	vs	Culture-focused
Operations	Linear	vs	Circular
Production	Offshoring	vs	Reshoring
Finance	Speculation	vs	Impact—ESG
Performance	Productivity (results)	vs	Learning (impact)
Control	Predictability	vs	Adaptability
Education	Factor endowment	vs	Talent development
Information	Secrecy	vs	Transparency
Culture	Homogeneity	vs	Diversity
Growth	Quantitative	vs	Qualitative

- *Profitability versus sustainability*: within the current capitalist system, the purpose of businesses is to maximize the shareholders financial value. Milton Friedman, an influential figure of the current business paradigm (the "old" paradigm), vividly expressed this dominant assumption, as "the social responsibility of business is to increase its profits".[18] In the new business paradigm, however, business is primarily understood as a force to drive sustainable change, as an economic agent that serves societal and environmental purposes.

- *Shareholders versus stakeholders*: profitability-as-purpose is mostly targeted to serve shareholders' interest in maximizing the economic return on their investments. The new business paradigm, nonetheless, calls on organizations to rather shift the primary focus on beneficiaries to stakeholders. The new paradigm leads businesses to create shared value by balancing and, overall, optimizing the different interests of employees, suppliers, customers, government, shareholders and the environment alike.

- *Reductionist versus systemic*: the conventional thinking in the business-as-usual paradigm hinges upon a reductionist view of the business as an isolated economic entity where problems and their causes are easily traceable. This is reflected internally, where silo-based thinking permeates different business units, and externally, where the organizational impacts on society or the environment are externalities. This is progressively replaced in the new business paradigm by a systemic notion of a business as part of an eco-system whose behaviour is interdependent and a function of other systems' behaviours and relationships.

- *Mechanistic versus living*: in the new business paradigm, the mechanistic metaphor "the organization as a machine" is replaced by "the organization as a living system". In biology, living systems are open self-organizing life forms that interact with their environment. Businesses are people-centred organizations whose performance is influenced by internal and external factors, in the same way that the organization itself influences its internal and external stakeholders.

- *Simplicity versus complexity*: the context in the new business paradigm is characterized by an extraordinary interdependence among players and systems, the increasing dynamic—and often unpredictable—shifts that occur over time, and the exponential speed of change. Organizations operate in increasingly complex environments that transcend the linear business logic of turning inputs into outputs that are traded in a market in exchange for a profit.

- *Competition versus collaboration*: the market approach of the new business paradigm reconnects the organization with its fundamental essence: a collaborative agent that co-creates and delivers value in an eco-system in relation to, and collaboration with, other organizations and stakeholders. The zero-sum logic of the old business paradigm is replaced by a win–win approach that serves sustainability over—but including—profitability purposes. Competitors are seen as learning levers and innovation sources instead of threatening predators.

- *Short-term versus long-term*: the short-term pressures on maximizing shareholder-driven profitability gives way to a longer time required to create and deliver sustainable benefits to society and the environment. This implies, on the one hand, understanding that the conversion rate of turning the investment into social, environmental and economic value—the triple bottom line of benefits—requires the adoption of a longer time orientation. On the other hand, this shift represents a strategic opportunity to identify and adapt to trends and anticipate future business opportunities.

- *Transactional versus transformational*: while the leadership style of the old business paradigm is focused on achieving goals by enforcing contractual procedures in explicit command and control behaviours, the new business paradigm requires transformational leadership to empower people to achieve organizational purpose and vision. Leaders are proactive and empathetic with people's contexts. Leaders focus on inspiring others through communication and teamwork, implementing a management approach characterized by trust and delegation.

- *Hierarchy versus networks*: in the new business paradigm, the practice of transformational leadership requires organizations to shift their rigid hierarchical structures based on classical organizational charts (typical of the old paradigm) into flexible networks of agile, results-driven and self-managing teams. These networks are highly interactive within and outside the organization but require higher levels of awareness, individual responsibility and agency.

- *Centralized versus distributed*: hierarchies are corporate tools that ensure power is centralized in the hands of the top management and the executive board, which are the custodians of shareholders' interests. In the new business paradigm, networks are an open innovation approach to unleash and foster the creativity of all stakeholders in the service of the organizational purpose. People empowerment implies a gradual decentralization and redistribution of power across all levels that can only be facilitated by transformational leaders.

- *Product-focused versus culture-focused*: companies transitioning from the old to the new business paradigm invest in developing an innovative approach concerning all areas across the value creation process, transcending the traditional product-focused innovation. For the organization, this implies a continuous effort in creating and nurturing a corporate culture of innovation. This culture of innovation also includes developing real problem-based products and services. And it also focuses on designing relevant business models, in delivering time-to-market solutions, in process optimization, and in setting an optimal balance between internal and external open innovation sources.

- *Linear versus circular supply chains*: operations that are traditionally based on an extractive linear sequence from suppliers, manufacturers, distributors and, finally, users merge into a generative circular supply chain in the new business paradigm. This approach is aimed at reducing waste and pollution, reusing and recycling products and materials used and regenerating natural systems. Embedding circularity is an application of systems thinking, as it requires the inclusion of sustainability principles in all design processes, products' life-cycle assessments and reverse logistics.

- *Offshoring versus reshoring*: offshoring, or transferring the process of manufacturing goods overseas to reduce the manufacturing and labour costs, but at a high ecological cost, lies at the heart of the global capitalist system. This is progressively replaced by the opposite trend of reshoring, which is returning the production back to the company's original proximities. Companies seek to reduce their environmental footprint, secure quality in the process and reduce the risks of operating in distant markets.

- *Speculation versus impact*: investment-led growth amid a deregulated global financial market has been—and still is—a huge feature of the economic system. Too often, this system gives incentives to invest in speculative finance with the promise of attaining higher returns at the expense of assuming a higher risk: an instrument with high negative externalities. Conversely, in the new business paradigm, sustainable finance and impact investing is sought as a tool to mobilize resources for sustainability purposes, seeking a social and environmental return on the investment, besides the financial.

- *Productivity versus learning*: most organizations equate performance with productivity as a measure of the efficiency of the company in converting inputs into outputs. The search for efficiency emphasizes investments in technology rather than people. In the new business paradigm, the organization shifts the focus to expanding the learning capabilities of its members, which, in turn, results in greater creativity and better results.

- *Predictability versus adaptability*: a learning organization[19] of the new business paradigm aims at continuously adapting to emerging contexts and environments. The control focus is no longer to stick, and try to comply, with strategic goals and implementation plans—an approach more suitable for stable environments, a feature of the old paradigm. Rather, organizations in the new paradigm seek to develop the skills required to understand the new context, identify the drivers of change and adapt to the new situations with agility.

- *Factor endowment versus talent development*: in the old paradigm, education is subjected to the tenets of the economic system in the way it seeks to train and develop people to endow the system with another factor of production—human resources. This vision is progressively replaced in the new paradigm by developing the talent in organizations as an opportunity to express that talent creatively in autotelic jobs that create higher levels of satisfaction, meaning and employee well-being.

- *Secrecy versus transparency*: corporate information has long been treasured as a secret ingredient available for strategic decision-making in the hands of the executive committee and the advisory board. However, in the new business paradigm, stakeholders demand more transparency in order to regain customers' and civil society's trust. These demands include the disclosure of public information, such as internal audits, financial statements, sustainability reports, impact assessments, and supply chain traceability reports, among others.

- *Homogeneity versus diversity*: diversity is not only challenging the long-standing assumption that homogenous organizations were more efficient and easier to manage, but proving that it is an asset instead. The balanced management of diversity and inclusion in terms of gender, race or age enriches the corporate culture with tangible benefits in employee engagement, creativity, productivity and overall performance.

- *Quantifying versus qualifying*: corporate growth is a backbone of the economic system, and it will still be. But with a relevant twist. While corporations, nation-states and even individuals have become obsessed with quantifying economic growth as the measure of success, the new business paradigm is shifting towards qualifying economic growth. This new approach implies qualifying new metrics of success—managing and measuring intangibles—such as health, well-being, relationships, leisure, personal development, and community and environmental welfare.

Transitioning to the new business paradigm is probably the biggest challenge of our time. We are sons of the old business paradigm and architects of the new. This transition will require, on the one hand, challenging our own assumptions of the system, of ourselves and of our organizations in the context of the twenty-first century; and, on the other hand, reshaping a regenerative socioeconomic system by design: what MIT professor Otto Scharmer calls "letting go and letting come". In this interregnum, when the old is dying and the new is not yet fully born, Buddhist and Taoist systems thinking offer a way of liberation that can guide us in this endeavour.

Notes

1 The book *The Anthropocene as a Geological Time Unit*, published by Cambridge University Press in 2019 provides a wealth of scientific evidence detailing the correlations between human agency and its ecological impacts, in comparison to other major global transitions in Earth history.
2 A concept introduced by the Nobel Prize Winner Paul Crutzen in 2000.
3 In 2004, IGBP synthesis, Global Change and the Earth System published the great acceleration indicators, showing the correlation between socioeconomic and Earth system trends since the Second World War. They are updated and reassessed in collaboration with the Stockholm Resilience Centre.
4 Aengenheyster, M., Feng, Q. Y., van der Ploeg, F., & Dijkstra, H.A. (2018). The point of no return for climate action: effects of climate uncertainty and risk tolerance, *Earth Systems Dynamics*, 9, 1085–1095.
5 Picketty, T. (2017). *Capital in the Twenty-first Century*. Harvard University Press.
6 This data draws from "Our world in data", the online publication managed from a research group at Oxford University and *Factfulness*, the Hans Rosling book published shortly after his death.
7 Francis Bacon conceptualized this principle in Novam Organum (Aph. 59): "let the human race recover that right over nature which belongs to it by divine request".
8 Taylor, F. (2003). *Scientific Management*. Routledge.
9 Polanyi, K. (2002). *The Great Transformation*. Beacon Press.
10 Mill's assumptions are already embedded in the free market economics of Adam Smith, David Hume and Jeremy Bentham during the eighteenth century. And they were followed by their contemporaries and exponents of neo-classical economics in the twentieth century, such as Friedrick Hayek and Milton Fridman and the School of Chicago until today.
11 In those times, the Newtonian ideal of the science of universal gravitational law was embedded into management as an ideal balance in the economy, established by the market, that guarantees perfect equilibrium.
12 Freud, S. (2012). *A General Introduction to Psychoanalysis*. Wordsworth Editions.
13 David Stroh explains these tools in application to social change in his book, *Systems Thinking for Social Change: A practical guide to solving complex problems, avoiding unintended consequences and achieving lasting results* (Chelsea Green, 2015).
14 Firms such as Euromonitor (*Ethical Living*, 2017) and Nielsen (*The Global, Socially Conscious Consumer*, 2012) have echoed sustainable consumption trends.
15 For more information about the programme: www.eada.edu/en/programmes/full-time-masters/master-sustainable-business-innovation.
16 See www.positiveimpactrating.org/pir2020.
17 Capra, F. & Luisi, P.L. (2014). *The Systems View of Life: A unifying vision*. Cambridge University Press.

18 This is the title of Friedman's article published in September 1970 by the *New York Times*.

19 According to Peter Senge, a learning organization is an organization "where people continually expand their capacity to create the results they truly desire, where new and expansive patterns of thinking are nurtured, where collective aspiration is set free, and where people are continually learning how to learn together" (*The Fifth Discipline*, Doubleday, 1990).

References

Aengenheyster, M., Feng, Q.Y., van der Ploeg, F., & Dijkstra, H.A. The point of no return for climate action: effects of climate uncertainty and risk tolerance, *Earth Systems Dynamics*, 9, 1085–1095.

Barrett, R. (2013). *The Values-driven Organization: Cultural health and employee well-being as a pathway to sustainable performance*. Routledge.

Beck, D.E. & Cowan, C.C. (1996). *Spiral Dynamics: Mastering values, leadership and change*. Blackwell.

Capra, F. & Luisi, P.L. (2014). *The Systems View of Life: A unifying vision*. Cambridge University Press.

Coll, J.M. (2015). *Zen Business: los beneficios de aplicar la armonía en la empresa*. Profit Editorial.

Freud, S. (2012). *A General Introduction to Psychoanalysis*. Wordsworth Editions.

Hardin, G. (1968). The tragedy of the commons. *Science*, 162(3859), 1243–1248.

Honeyman, R. (2014). *The B Corp Handbook: How to use business as a force for good*. Berrett-Koehler.

Hutchins, G. & Storm, L. (2019). *Regenerative Leadership: The DNA of life-affirming 21st century organizations*. Wordsworth.

Laloux, F. (2014). *Reinventing Organizations: A guide to creating organizations inspired by the next stage of human consciousness*. Nelson Parker.

Mackey, J. & Sisodia, R. (2013). *Conscious Capitalism: Liberating the heroic spirit of business*. Harvard Business Review Press.

Mazzucato, M. (2013). *The Entrepreneurial State: Debunking public versus private sector myths*. Penguin.

Meadows, D. et al. (1972). *The Limits to Growth: A report for the Club of Rome's Project on the predicament of humankind*. New York: Universe Books.

Patton, M.Q. (2019). *Blue Marble Evaluation: Premises and principles*. Guilford Press.

Polanyi, K. (2002). *The Great Transformation*. Beacon Press.

Prahalad, C.K. (2004). *The Fortune at the Bottom of the Pyramid: Eradicating poverty through profits*. FT Press.

Raworth, K. (2017). *Doughnut Economics: Seven ways to think like a 21st-century economist*. Random House UK.

Rosling, H. (2018). *Factfulness*. Hodder and Stoughton.

Scharmer, O. (2009). *U-Theory: Leading from the future as it emerges*. Berrett-Koehler Publishers.

Schumacher, E.F. (1973). *Small is Beautiful: A study of economics as if people mattered*. Blond & Briggs.

Senge, P. (1990). *The Fifth Discipline*. Doubleday.

Stroh, D. (2015). *Systems Thinking for Social Change: A practical guide to solving complex problems, avoiding unintended consequences and achieving lasting results*. Chelsea Green.

Taylor, F. (2003). *Scientific Management*. Routledge.

Wahl, D. C. (2016). *Designing Regenerative Cultures*. Triarchy Press.

Wilber, K. (2000). *A Theory of Everything: An integral vision for business, politics, science and spirituality*. Shambala.

Zalasiewicz, J., Waters, C. N., Williams, M., & Summerhays, C. (2019). *The Anthropocene as a Geological Time Unit: A guide to the scientific evidence and current debate*. Cambridge University Press.

Chapter 2

TAO 4.0

Adaptive thinking amidst exponential change and complexity

The human–nature disconnect is the fundamental cause that explains the behaviour of our extractive economic system. Nature domination and over-exploitation have become implicit assumptions of the way humans socially organize their work, and lives. At this point, the million-dollar question is, how do we reconnect? Reconnecting implies changing the mental models and underlying structures that drive the ego-based behaviours of individuals, organizations and socioeconomic and political systems. Reconnecting also implies daring to stop the music when the party is still booming.

But, prior to that, we should feel the need to stop the music. And this is a matter of perception. We do have an intellectual understanding of nature, but so often we do not feel we are part of it. It is in the feeling of nature that we get close to what we are as human beings. It is in this context that we can have a deep ecological awareness of all processes interdependent on life. Life is not about having, not even about being. It is nothing but about interbeing. And we can only perceive the eco-system when we experience the whole, when we are just one. Here and now, in the fullness of the present moment.

But how do we learn to perceive the eco-system? How can we feel the whole and the interconnections between humans and nature when we deal with the challenges of a *homo egonomicus* that is struggling with the complexities of the Anthropocene and the fourth industrial revolution? Jacob Bronowski, one of the first scientists to advocate a human-centric approach to science, stated that overcoming the crisis of perception should rest on the ability of humans to receive and translate their experience of the outside world.

This is actually the primary goal of systems thinkers. They aim at perceiving and grasping the interdependencies between systems—the relationships, patterns and networks that explain their behaviour—and be able to synthetize these insights within the realm of the personal experience of the whole.

The earliest systems thinkers

Taoism is the first body of knowledge that explicitly articulated a systems view of life, the human being and the universe centred on the human–nature interdependence. Nature is understood as the set of interactions between the natural phenomena that make up the planet and the universe. In fact, the human being is considered a "small universe" that lives between Heaven and Earth. As such, a human being contains all the information of the universe. This was confirmed by a scientific study that affirms humans are made of stardust, according to a research commissioned by a team of astronomers from the Sloan Digital Sky Survey in New Mexico. Humans and their galaxy have about 97% of the same kind of atoms, which form the foundational chemical elements of life: carbon, hydrogen, nitrogen, oxygen, phosphorus and sulfur.

Alan Watts and Fritjof Capra, renowned authors in bridging Eastern and Western thought, acknowledge the natural philosophy of Taoism. Watts expresses this idea ontologically: "you are the big bang. You are the original force of the universe manifesting as whoever you are in the moment".[1] From an epistemological point of view, Capra describes Taoism as a natural way or a natural process that connects with "an ultimate reality which underlies and unifies the multiple things and events we observe".[2]

The Taoists developed a pioneering scientific approach to study nature and its processes. This approach was articulated through the so-called School of Naturalists, or the School of Yin and Yang, the development of which is attributed to the scholar Zou Yan during the 4th and 3rd centuries BC. With this approach, the Taoists developed an empirical research method based on direct observation, which involves the experimental analysis of the functioning of nature or the universe. This approach conceives the observation and analysis of the context, patterns, networks and relationships between natural phenomena. The relationship between nature and the human being as part of nature is, therefore, an object of this observation.

The earliest natural scientists were systems thinkers. Taoist-based researchers approached the study of natural phenomena as interactive participants—or participators—in the process of human–nature observation, and, *ergo*, transformation. This process of knowing acknowledges the mutual influence between the observer and the observed, or between the knower and the (un)known. It parallels one of the main principles that was, thousands of years later, conceptualized in quantum physics: the observer becomes a participator. As Capra explains, "the scientist cannot play the role of a detached objective observer, but becomes involved in the world he observes to the extent that he influences the properties of the observed objects".[3]

The systems thinker as participator and change agent

The dynamic interaction between the observer and the observed has huge implications for science, technology and organizational development. In most organizational change processes, consultants and evaluators are often considered independent. It is assumed that they study the organization with objectivity and, therefore, their intervention is free of their own cognitive conditioning. An intervention, according to organizational and systems theorist Gerald Midgley, "is a purposeful action by a human agent to create change".[4] Everything then—projects, programmes, initiatives, activities, actions or events—is an intervention. Therefore, change interventions are only meaningful in the context of the interaction between the organizational processes to be changed and the consultant and other participators, including the boundaries of the system that is intervened.

As quantum theorist Werner Heisenberg explained, "what we observe is not nature itself, but nature exposed to our method of questioning".[5] The success of the intervention will largely depend on how the consultant enquires about these interactions, which will be the result of the organic interplay between the behaviours of the consultant and the organization, as happens in any interaction between living systems. The consultant decides how they are going to set up the intervention and this arrangement will determine, to some extent, the properties of the change management project. At the same time, the evolving properties of the organization will influence how the consultant reacts and adapts to the ongoing results and changes in context. Against this backdrop, organizations might hire consultants not only for their professional expertise, but on the basis of their fitness with the organizational purpose and on their ability to organically engage, change and developmentally adapt and evolve with the intervention.

The interdependent nature between the subject and the object is also relevant for scientific and technological development. The mechanistic approach to science assumes that the scientist is value-neutral, that his motivations do not—and must not—influence and interfere with the process of observation. There is no ethical debate at the stage of development. The ethical discourse is, therefore, postponed to the technological application of the invention. Great minds participated in the development of the nuclear bomb, yet the ethical debate arose after the bombings. A systems approach to science acknowledges the importance of embedding human values from the early stages of the process of research, design and development. This is the reason why innovation projects and programmes should be purpose-driven.

The power of Tao under complexity

How could some people discover key universal principles, millennia ago, that modern science is still discovering in the present day? This is an extraordinarily amazing mystery. My premise is that those people had a much more developed system of perception—which is to say, of knowledge—based on the direct experience and connection with the Tao.

Taoism is essentially a way of liberation, like Buddhism. Its fundamental concept is the Tao, the natural way. Applied to management, the Tao is the natural path towards sustainable transformation. It is a natural path in the sense that it is embedded in universal principles that illustrate and explain the biological nature of life and the universe. Therefore, managing organizations as living systems through the application of Tao principles (they are explained in the following sections) provides a guiding framework to manage organizations in alignment with nature, taking care of it and nurturing it. Doing business that respects and takes care of nature is precisely the fundamental idea behind sustainable transformation.

Tao's relevance today, in the complex context of the Anthropocene, relies on a renewed interpretation of its systems view of life. From a managerial point of view, it is understood as a way to transcend the behavioural patterns of the current business paradigm and, therefore, as an aspirational way to attain the new business paradigm. For an organization, this new business paradigm is what *satori*—or enlightenment—is for a Zen practitioner. Attaining enlightenment is to acknowledge one has been liberated and set free from suffering or from Anthropogenic problems, which is the same thing.

As soon as you have the goal to achieve the new business paradigm, things get harsh. Once the new business paradigm is an expected result, the organization automatically sets a strategic and operational plan to get there. Executives manage and control the organization to achieve results, and if they are not met, frustration arises. The control that leads to frustration is precisely the main driver of suffering. Organizational management hinges upon control. It is a management function aimed at achieving defined results within an established timeline. Control conditions the way organizations are managed for results; they spend most of their time setting standards, measuring actual performance and taking corrective action.

The problem arises when the context grows in complexity. Organizations struggle to adapt to uncertain external and internal pressures of change[6] that challenge their own survival and thriving processes. The Covid-19 crisis is a vivid example. It was the main driver that accelerated the digital transformation in many organizations. That change in context was far more effective in catalysing change than previous strategic planning.

As change grows in complexity in a VUCA world, strategic planning is less effective and far more costly. Planning is less effective because it takes time to plan and implement what you plan, and during this time the context may have changed substantially, making your action plan less relevant for its intended purpose. Planning is also more costly because, if it is less effective than desired, the organization is likely to lose money or make other plans that require additional investment. As a consequence, strategic planning is often a barrier that prevents organizations from learning and adapting. It is a barrier because planning is not responsive to sudden changes in context or the late arrival of new information. The focus of planning is making sure that what has been planned is done; therefore, it does not enable an environment where the organization is attentive and proactive to unexpected changes.

When command and control is no longer effective, frustration levels ramp up automatically in a kind of vicious circle that places the organization under a toxic state of stress, affecting stakeholders along the value chain. The organization is trapped in *samsara*, the Buddhist concept that illustrates the cycle of birth and death that revolves around the inherent suffering in, or dissatisfaction with, life. This is the problem of cybernetics, the science of control, a field of study tightly related to systems theory. Any system approaching full self-control is also approaching self-frustration. All systems or organizations operate—at different levels—in *samsara* mode. A high level of *samsara* may translate to low levels of employee engagement, higher levels of burnout and employee absenteeism and more resistance to change. The desire for perfect control, of the environment and of the organization, is founded on a profound mistrust of the controller.

Against this backdrop, the Tao represents a powerful systems principle for organizations, leaders and entrepreneurs that aim at adopting a more natural and trustful approach to learning and adaptation, a key feature of the new business paradigm. The power of the Tao is found in the words of the Taoist philospher Huai Nan Tzu:

> He who conforms to the course of the Tao, following the natural processes of Heaven and Earth, finds it easy to manage the whole world.[7]

The power of Tao rests on sensing, understanding and applying its fundamental principles of oneness, emptiness, and impermanence in the management of, and escape from, *samsara*.

Oneness

The universal original force, or ultimate reality, mother of all things, is not only the central feature of the Tao, but is also one of the most important revelations of modern physics.[8] This original force is based on the direct non-intellectual, mystical experience of the fundamental oneness as the underlying structure of any natural phenomena. Experiencing oneness is about sensing the whole. It is to be aware of the unity and the interdependent relations of all things and events that unfold as manifestations of that oneness.

The universe, as any system, is not an independent collection of isolated physical entities but, rather, a complex network of relations between the various parts of a unified whole. In the words of Heisenberg, "the world thus appears as a complicated tissue of events, in which connections of different kinds alternate or overlap or combine and thereby determine the texture of the whole".[9]

It is this determination of the whole that is critical for understanding life. Organismic biologists have already pointed out that the behaviour of a living organism as an integrated whole cannot be understood from the study of its parts alone (Capra & Luisi 2014). The interdependent nature of everything that underlies the principle of oneness has, therefore, been the missing ingredient in the study of life from a scientific standpoint. This insight has profound implications in organizational management. The performance of organizations as living organisms is a direct function of the patterns of relationships that explain its organizational behaviour.

Hence, the realization of oneness changes the worldview of the organization. The organization-as-a-machine is structured in silo-based hierarchies of command and control in which departments or business units seem islands separated from each other. Organizational performance cannot be assessed against the aggregated results based on the performance of each department, which is mostly the case. Instead, the organization as a living organism focuses on managing the quality of patterns, relationships, processes and networks that define the harmony or healthiness of the organization as a whole.

The application of oneness as an organizational principle starts with a thorough revision of the role the organization plays in relation to the planet. Why do I exist? What is the purpose of my organization? To start this process of enquiry the organization needs to connect with the planetary consciousness inherent to the Tao. The Tao represents the contextual principle that defines how the organization creates value for the planet, including its peoples, communities and the environment. Managing organizations systemically implies putting them into this context, and, thereby, establishing the nature of their relationships. This is the very foundation for adopting a stakeholder approach that is embodied in the processes of value creation that characterizes the business activities and operations of the organization in the new business paradigm.

Genuine sustainability-orientated organizations usually start with entre-preneurs whose idea comes from their experience with oneness. Oneness helps them become deeply ecologically aware of the planetary conscious-ness of the Tao. Then they react with an entrepreneurial approach to nur-ture nature through sustainable market-based solutions. As an example, Yvon Chouinard, a rock climber, kayaker and Zen follower, founded the outdoor gear equipment and clothing brand, Patagonia, as a way to allow adventurers to enjoy nature on the basis of environmental care, protection and activism.[10]

Experiencing oneness implies a spiritual awareness that is grounded in a process of enquiry driven by eco-centric values.[11] This process is condu-cive to perceiving the reality in the context of the whole. It is triggered by the fundamental values of compassion and loving-kindness, two inti-mately related values central to Buddhist thought and practice. Compassion springs from feeling the profound desire of happiness and well-being that one has for other human and sentient beings, including oneself. This is also the same as wishing oneself and other beings to be free from suffer-ing or life dissatisfaction. Oneness is the seed that grows altruistic love, or compassion in action, as the Zen master Thich Nhat Hahn calls it. Altruistic love is related to Agape, the highest form of love, according to the Ancient Greeks.

The practice of compassion, from a neuroscientific point of view, is related to increased levels of happiness and well-being,[12] with improved social connections, decreased depression, stress relief, and increased crea-tivity, among others. The study of compassion fits well with the interests of positive psychology, which "is founded on the belief that people want to lead meaningful and fulfilling lives, to cultivate what is best within them-selves, and to enhance their experiences of love, work, and play".[13]

The philosopher Nissargadatta vividly described the relationship between compassion and altruistic love: "When I look inside and see that I am nothing, that is wisdom. When I look out and see that I am everything, that is love. Between both my life goes by". The intertwined binomial of compassion and love provides the foundation for the practice of universal values such as altruism, solidarity, social justice, peace or environmental protection.

The sustainability-driven new business paradigm manifests in the way organizations connect, define and operate from a higher purpose and uni-versal values that ultimately yield a positive impact. In other words, pur-pose-orientated and values-driven organizations are spiritual organizations. Purpose and values are the gateway whereby spirituality and love enter organizations. These are words that are still taboos in the management lexi-con used in business education and practice.

Organizations cannot get rid of control. Even if they want to let go of it, the desire to do so automatically triggers an unconscious need for more control, and, thus, the need to prevent the achievement of that desire. However, oneness and compassion may help the organization operate from an altruistic ego, or eco, which facilitates the organization to eco-systemically serve the higher purpose. Thereby, when the corporate culture rides the Tao, the organization flows and operates at a higher frequency. This frequency emits the energetic vibe that resonates with, and meets the demands of, its actual and potential stakeholders—employees, clients, impact investors, suppliers, etc.—in the collaborative quest to achieve the new business paradigm.

Emptiness

Emptiness is the process that allows to fusion oneself with the Tao and, therefore, to experience oneness.[14] It is the vehicular mechanism that allows the mystical experience to emerge: a necessary condition. This principle is difficult to grasp for two reasons. First, because humans are skilled with the power of abstraction. Abstract thinking is the basis of creativity and innovation; it is what characterizes and defines modern humans and progress. Abstraction is homo sapiens' main way of knowing: we are able to figure out abstract ideas in our minds that result in the development of human systems, science and technologies that construct our societies, our cultures, our institutions, and ourselves. Without abstraction, you and I would not be communicating right now. But, paradoxically, the same abstract thinking that has facilitated the rise of modern civilization and globalization has reduced human experience to a mostly intellectual experience that has divorced us from ourselves, limiting and distorting our perception of reality.[15]

The second reason that makes the emptiness principle difficult to grasp is related to the accumulated experiential background that frames our learning skills and, therefore, our value systems. Our perception of the world and ourselves is a product of how we emotionally feel about the social, relational, leisure, educational and economic experiences we have. Feelings provide us with feedback about what is good or bad for ourselves, for our well-being.[16] Feelings provide the basis of our judgement, the capacity for decision-making that takes place in our mind, in the frontal lobe of our brain. The accumulation of learned feelings as memories associated to past experiences in our minds provides the information from which we make our decisions. This general behavioural pattern is mostly intellectual, rational-based, and it narrows down exponentially our capacity to sense and feel new things, new experiences out of the scope of our embedded mental models or value systems. This rational pattern shrinks our capacity to learn.

The inherent rationalization of experience—owing to the power of abstraction and the intellectual focus of our experience—has inflated our egocentric view of our self and our world. It is in this light that emptiness is most useful. Emptiness does not mean absence of feeling, but of judgement. This process involves the temporary suspension of judgement, which is to leave the evaluative-based duality of what is good or bad on standby, in a way that this duality does not interfere with our sensory experience.

The practice of emptiness does not take place in the conscious thinking process, not in the ego. This is a particular feature of Eastern psychology. While the West explores the mind from the mind, the East enquires into the mind from the no-mind. Therefore, emptiness is a process of ego alienation. It is like silencing the intellect in order to let the full body and mind enter a state of calmness, of void, of complete alienation that is critical for expanding the boundaries of our perception and, as a result, for expanding the horizons of our knowledge. This mindset is what the Zen master Shunryu Suzuki calls the beginner's mind, an original state of mind that powers creativity; as he recalls, "if your mind is empty, it is always ready for anything, it is open to everything. In the beginner's mind there are many possibilities, but in the expert's there are few".[17]

The beginner's empty mind is a precondition for (un)learning. This state of mind has long been central to Zen enquiry and practice, as illustrated by the following story. Nan-in, a Japanese master during the Meiji era, received a university professor who came to enquire about Zen. Nan-in served tea. He poured his visitor's cup full, and then kept on pouring. The professor watched the overflow until he no longer could restrain himself. "It's over-full. No more will go in!" "Like this cup," Nan-in said, "you are full of your own opinions and speculations. How can I show you Zen unless you first empty your cup?"[18]

The unlearning process involved in the application of emptiness is a relevant competency for organizational learning,[19] but less explored in individuals and organizations than the learning derived from the accumulation of knowledge. Unlearning is critical for questioning and abandoning underlying structures and patterns of behaviour conditioned by our mental models.[20] It is then when the mind is ready to reprogramme the mental models that will potentially drive the transformation of systems based on new behaviours. Unlearning, then, is not only a key factor for successful organizational change and adaptation,[21] but it is also critical in understanding how learning occurs, a prerequisite to enabling organizations to learn how to learn. This type of learning is called triple-loop learning, a critical skill for change and transformation.[22]

But besides unlearning as a precondition for learning, the interesting thing about approaching unlearning through emptiness is how the process of learning unfolds. It is when the mindset is non-dual and empty that the no-mind feels the whole, the fundamental oneness whereby the individual directly experiences the unity of all things, the interconnections of all processes and events. The alienation of the ego gives way to the unification of the eco.

Leading from the eco-system implies leading in relation to others, which is the same as caring for others. The practice of emptiness activates humility, a fundamental value in Taoism and Buddhism. Emptying the mind implies an internal will to let your ego go, to recognize that what you know may not be useful any more. But you are only willing to let go of your mental models when you have a growth mindset, which is connected to the inner belief that what is coming up next is a better version of yourself, a reborn altruistic ego at the service of the eco.

Humility as a value has also had a repercussion in terms of leadership in high performing organizations. This type of leadership is called humble, or servant, leadership.[23] It is consistent with the transformational type of leadership required for the sustainable transformation of the new business paradigm. These leaders have the humility to serve others—including the environment—as they trust others' creative potential. Their role focuses on helping them grow and develop, providing tangible and emotional support on their journey. As a result, employees and other partners exercise a higher degree of ownership, autonomy and responsibility, critical competences for organizations that aim at adapting to internal and external changes with agility.[24]

Impermanence

One of the most profound Taoist insights is that transformation and change are essential features of nature and that change is a constant in life. This insight was not the result of a severe crisis that altered the status quo in the lives of many—as Covid-19 has done—but the outcome of a thorough interactive observation of nature. The impermanent nature of life emerges in phases or cycles, like the four astronomical seasons or the biological cycle of birth, growth, decline and death of living systems and organisms. These cycles dynamically unfold as processes of transformation and metamorphosis, which imply changes in form from one stage to the next in the life of the organism, like the caterpillar that transforms to the pupa and from the pupa to the adult butterfly.

The problem arises when we develop a culture that lives at odds with this principle. The dominant human systems value permanence instead. People have been educated to study, work hard, apply for a stable and well-paid job, get married, build a family, buy a house, and entertain if time allows. Except in times of crisis and turbulence, where unexpected changes force them to adapt. Humans have built their identity based on the idea of permanence or stability, and, therefore, people's decisions are based on the basis of safeguarding stability.

The capitalist system, built on the cycle of production and consumption, is based on the permanent assumption that economic growth is infinite. This assumption is at odds with the Tao principle of impermanence. Within this context, modern life has propelled a materialistic culture where stability in having is more important than being. People orientate toward the actions that allow them to purse a stable life.

The challenge comes when expectations do not match reality. When people do not achieve their expected results they feel disappointed and frustrated. Expectations are formed on the basis of our judgement. We think we know what we want based on what we assume is good or bad for us. We set our goals on that basis, and when we achieve them and evaluate the experience as positive, we stick to them. Why do we have to change if things are good for us? We do not want to lose what we have gained and we become attached. Attachment arises from fear of loss. And the face of this attachment is control. We want to control all that is in our hands—and our minds. We want to control what we have, and we want to control what we want but we don't have.

The application of impermanence, therefore, requires a process of detachment. Attachment, according to Buddhism, is a natural by-product of ignorance. It arises when we think of ourselves as permanent entities separate from the rest. Attachment reinforces the illusion of a permanent ego. Therefore, to get rid of attachment, or to attain non-attachment, we need to feel the impermanent nature of life. Thich Nhat Hanh recommends "nourishing our insight into impermanence every day. If we do, we will live more deeply, suffer less, and enjoy life much more".[25]

The process of detachment is a way to frugally reframe and balance our ego. It does not mean that we can no longer enjoy the pleasures of life. On the contrary, we can develop a sharper appreciation of the present pleasures as acts of profound and volatile enjoyment. As Alan Watts points out, "we can be detached and still be fully participative".[26] Thus, the practice of impermanence requires acceptance and detachment. When you integrate and accept impermanence as a life principle, you become aware of the present moment. You become mindful.

Impermanence is inherently embedded in the value of frugality or minimalism, which is focusing the attention and action on what is essential. Marginal and economization are frugal characteristics that contribute to managing impermanence, that is, in adapting to the constant flow of change. A responsive agency to impermanence results in increased resilience. According to David Denyer, from the University of Cranfield,[27] "Organizational resilience is the ability of an organization to anticipate, prepare for, respond and adapt to incremental change and sudden disruption in order to survive and prosper".

For years I have been curious about knowing how organizations develop this ability. For that reason, I started my own research with a fundamental question: what can we learn from the oldest companies in the world that have been able to adapt to ongoing shortcomings of all sorts? In search for answers, I went to Japan, home to the *Shinise*—a term used to describe longevity companies older than 100 years. I discovered the surprising fact that this Eastern country is home to 55% of the world's most long-lived companies. There are more than 20,000 companies that are over 100 years old. Around 1,200 companies are over 200 years old; 600 are 300 years old; 30 companies have existed for more than 500 years and five companies have even survived for over 1,000 years. Most of the *Shinise* are located in the area of Kyoto, a place known for the harmonious coexistence between aesthetic simplicity and modern life complexities.

For these companies, longevity is a proof of resilience, an inherent capacity to adapt to all sorts of changes. One of their key defining features is precisely the embodiment of impermanence in their capacity to integrate frugality in their business mindsets and operations. Impermanence is a quality that they apply to optimizing processes with a special skill for the detachment and elimination of superfluous processes, while strengthening key value-generating decisions and activities. Frugality provides them with a certain degree of prudence in economizing resources; these are companies that are not burdened by the weight of maximizing economic results in the short term. Instead, their obsession resides in attaining the maximum level of excellence in each value-enhancing process in order to maximize the service to their stakeholders.

Frugality requires developing the skills of internal listening, external observation and humility in order to capture and apply learning to changes in technology, management and processes. Frugality also allows organizations to refocus their business activities to new markets and sectors while remaining loyal to their purpose. Their recipe is being loyal to the purpose—the "why" they do what they do—and, at the same time, being very flexible to changing their business activities—the "how"—for adaptation. These qualities allow *Shinise* companies to better adapt and anticipate with agility, lightness and less resistance to change. They learn to go with the flow.

Wuwei and the art of real-time decision-making

Going with the flow is not only accepting change, but also an act of making sense of change. As Alan Watts puts it, "the only way to make sense out of change is to plunge into it, move with it, and join the dance."[28] The natural flow, or natural growth, captures the essence of putting Tao into practice. In fact, the practice of the Tao requires mastering the subtle art of *wuwei*, or the art of intuitive and spontaneous decision-making. The term literally translates from Chinese as "non-action", which leads too often to a misinterpretation of the concept. *Wuwei* does not mean doing nothing, but doing nothing against the natural flow. It is about acting according to the laws of nature as natural events spontaneously emerge.

The practice of *wuwei* involves the cultivation of a mindset in which our actions align with the flow of life, without forcing them too much, and without hesitating about them too much. It is an empirical method the learning of which spontaneously emerges from direct experience and interaction with natural phenomena. This notwithstanding, its practice requires a precondition: the activation of the principles of oneness, emptiness and impermanence that open the gates of the Tao, where the self merges with the ecosystem and enters the realm of universal or absolute knowledge (see Figure 2.1). This grasp of direct experiences with the Tao empowers our inner capacity to see and trust our intuition,[29] which is the ability to know something instinctively, without the need for conscious reasoning. Intuition is our fundamental inner source of knowledge.

When we operate in turbulent contexts, characterized by the frequent emergence of unpredictable events, the reliability of our decisions depends on our ability to feel and sense the new situation. This 'feel and sense' is a key feature of the practice of *wuwei*, which is grounded on the ability to listen to our intuition. In such VUCA contexts, evidence, or data, is, most often, scarce, unreliable, insufficient or just not available. Strategic planning becomes irrelevant but the need to make a real-time decision remains urgent. Asking and trusting our intuitive knowledge is most often the only available source of information on which to make decisions.

This situation was apparent in the management of the Covid-19 crisis. When the data on people infected were not accurate—basically because

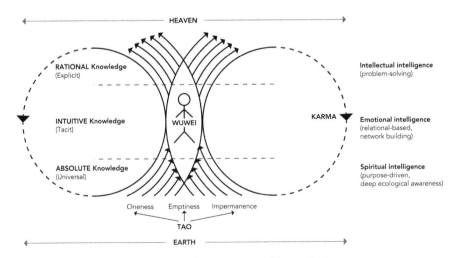

Figure 2.1 The Tao tree of knowledge

of the unfeasibility of testing the whole population—leaders had to make decisions despite not having reliable data. Most of them based their decisions on experts' views, which was a way to shift the burden, as experts did not have the data either. Leaders trusted their own ideology-driven values, prioritizing the economy, as in the US or the UK, or prioritizing population health, as South Korea and Portugal did. The latter focused on prevention, a decision that comes from the insight that, whatever the behaviour of the new virus was, it was perceived as a dangerous threat with potentially serious implications for the global systems, at all levels.

Turbulent times make visible the need for agile decision-making methods. But managing complexity and uncertainty does not only require agility *per se*. It needs an agility connected to the natural source. The point is not about taking quick action. You can make a quick decision but still be ineffective or counterproductive to nature. The critical issue is mastering a sustainable decision-making process that is based on the universal values, or laws of nature, in a given context. However, mastering this skill requires a different approximation to the way we recognize and transfer knowledge.

A scientific approximation to the idea of intuitive knowledge is the concept of tacit knowledge.[30] It can be defined as "skills, ideas and experiences that people have but are not codified and may not necessarily be easily expressed" (Chugh 2015). That means that individuals are often not aware of the tacit knowledge they possess and, therefore, they do not know how valuable it can be to themselves and to others. Michael Polanyi emphasized the importance of tacit knowledge, not only stating that it is a type of knowledge that cannot be fully articulated by verbal means, but by affirming that all knowledge is rooted in tacit knowledge.

For organizations, capturing and making use of intuitive or tacit knowledge is a critical skill for learning and adaptation. This process requires three sequence-related enablers. It requires, first, the creation of spaces for regular interactions and dialogue that, second, facilitate trust building and the generation of psychological safety that, third, enhance the flow of information between empowered social networks. When people operate within this safe environment and mindset, tacit knowledge emerges. It is then easier for the organization to capture, learn from it and use it to continuously adapt to changing conditions, in times of real-time decision-making.

On adaptability, agility and the missing element

Wuwei as the natural practice to make real-time decisions from intuitive—or tacit—knowledge is an adaptive behaviour. *Wuwei* is that natural know-how that spontaneously emerges from experience. You do not consciously think about all the decisions you make when you ride a bike without falling, you just naturally ride it and adapt to the emerging context, like the level of traffic, road conditions and so on.

When organizations face complex decisions, *wuwei* and intuitive knowledge rather complement the existing codified or explicit knowledge accumulated in the organization. Adaptability is, therefore, a function of the ability that organizations have to combine and embed intuitive and rational knowledge as a systematized pattern of behaviour in their own decision-making processes.

However, organizations—especially for-profit enterprises—approach adaptability through the agile concept of management,[31] whose main goal is to, despite exponential change, stay relevant by providing continuous speed-to-market value to customers. Agility is a concept associated with speed and, therefore, it provides iterative development methodologies to receive feedback from the market quickly. This process is aimed at increasingly providing customer value by adapting to their fast-changing needs and wants.

This organizational competency is associated to the development of an agile mindset. Steve Denning, author of *Age of Agile*, characterizes this mindset when practitioners deliver on three pillars:

> they are preoccupied—and sometimes obsessed—with innovating and delivering steadily more *customer* value, with getting work done in small self-organizing *teams*, and with collaborating together in an interactive *network*. Such organizations have been shown to have the capacity to adapt rapidly to a quickly shifting marketplace.

In for-profit organizations, therefore, adaptability is understood as market adaptability.

Public, or not-for-profit organizations, especially development cooperation agencies, are shifting their traditional results-based management to adaptive management as their main strategic approach to manage for results amid uncertain and volatile changes in context.[32] Adaptive management is a concept implicitly built on the idea of change.[33] Nonetheless, the issue is not about changing goals during implementation, it is about changing the path being used to achieve the expected results in response to unpredictable changes. Adaptability, here, is understood as context adaptability.

However, neither market- nor context-based adaptability addresses the fundamental issue, which is the sustainable transformation of the system, which is the missing element in the praxis of adaptive and/or agile management. Market adaptability serves the purpose of profitability, or sustained corporate growth, while context adaptability serves the purpose of achieving expected results that were defined beforehand. In both cases there is an attachment to the same purpose. But what if the purpose is no longer valid as new priorities emerge? Or, rather, what if the purpose does not serve the sustainability of the system?

The practice of the Tao is a behavioural tool that facilitates a natural systems decision-making process that connects the three fundamental levels of knowledge (Figure 2.1). The application of the Tao in organizations connects the rationalization of the process of agency with the intuitive and absolute knowledge that ensures decisions are made following the natural laws of the universe. The operationalization of the Tao principles—oneness, emptiness and impermanence—allows the organization to develop a deep sense of ecological awareness which translates to the embodiment of the values of compassion, humility and frugality—known as the Taoist three treasures. Absolute knowledge is purpose- and values-driven, it is the mechanism that enables consciousness to emerge.

Leaders' behaviour is, therefore, underpinned by these universal values and channelled across the organization through the practice of *wuwei*, which represents the organizational embodiment of intuitive knowledge. This type of knowledge is experiential and experimental, relationally driven, and it expands through social networks. It requires trust to spread and expand—trust in the organization as a living system and among the members of the organization alike.

Then the organization can root, connect and systematize its rational knowledge—the intellectual capacity to gather and organize information based on data and evidence—with its intuitive knowledge in an interactive and synergetic fashion. The organization can use this whole system of knowledge to solve problems, to adapt to changes in context and markets, and, foremost, to articulate its business agency—purpose, strategies, actions and impact—to sustainably and naturally transform systems.

Notes

1 Watts, A. (2019). *Out of Your Mind*. Souvenir Press.
2 Capra, F. (1975). *The Tao of Physics*. Shambala, p. 104.
3 Ibid. p. 141.
4 Midgley, G. (2000). *Systemic Intervention: Philosophy, methodology and practice*. Springer.
5 Heisenberg, W. (1958). *Physics and Philosophy*. New York: Harper Torchbooks, p. 58.
6 External forces can come from global political, economic and sectoral market dynamics, exponential technologies, environmental factors, and social and cultural trends. Internal pressures can arise from changes in leadership, changes in management structures and processes, talent turnover, or financial pressures, among others.
7 Quoted in Capra, F. (1975). *The Tao of Physics*. Shambala p. 105.
8 Capra, F. (1975). *The Tao of Physics*. Shambala.
9 Quoted in Capra & Luisi (2014), p. 72.

10 Chouinard, Y. (2006). *Let My People Go Surfing: The education of a reluctant businessman.* Pearson.

11 According to Arnae Ness, "the essence of deep ecology is to ask deeper questions". Capra & Luigi (2014) add that "deep ecology asks profound questions about the very foundations of our modern, scientific, industrial, growth-oriented, materialistic worldview and view of life".

12 Ricard, M. (2016). *Altruism: The power of compassion to change yourself and the world.* Back Bay Books.

13 International Positive Psychology Association in Donaldson, Dollwet, & Rao (2014), p. 2.

14 Buddhist philosopher Nagarjuna emphasized that emptiness does not mean "non-existence" but, rather, the lack of "independent existence", which is to say that existence is interdependent (*Nagarjuna's Seventy Stanzas: A Buddhist psychology of emptiness,* Snow Lion 1999).

15 Damasio, A. (2005). *Descartes' Error: Emotion, reason and the human brain.* Penguin Books.

16 Damasio, A. (2018). *The Strange Order of Things: Life, feeling and the making of cultures.* Pantheon.

17 Suzuki, S. (2009). *Zen Mind, Beginner's Mind.* Weatherhill.

18 Reps, P. & Senzaki, N. (1985). *Zen Flesh, Zen Bones: A collection of Zen and pre-Zen writings.* Tuttle.

19 Argyris, C. & Schön, D. (1996). *Organizational Learning II: Theory, method, and practice.* Reading, MA: Addison-Wesley.

20 According to systems thinker Peter Senge (1990), mental models are deeply held internal images of how the world works, images that limit us to familiar ways of thinking and acting. They are lenses through which we perceive reality. In this way, the model, for us is reality.

21 Hislop, D. et al. (2014). The process of individual unlearning: a neglected topic in an under-researched field. *Management Learning,* 45(5), 540–560.

22 Fahrenbach, F. & Kragulj, F. (2019). The ever-changing personality: revisiting the concept of triple-loop learning, *The Learning Organization,* ahead-of-print.

23 Humble and servant leadership are often used indistinctly.

24 Cable, D.M. (2018). *Alive at Work.* Ingram.

25 The Heart of the Buddha's Teaching (Parallax Press 1998), p. 124.

26 Watts, A. (2019). *Out of Your Mind.* Souvenir Press.

27 Denyer, D. (2017). Organizational resilience: A summary of academic evidence, business insights and new thinking. BSI and Cranfield School of Management.

28 Watts, A. (2011). *The Wisdom of Insecurity: A message for an age of anxiety.* Vintage.

29 Etymologically, intuition comes from the Latin *intuitio,* which means "insight, direct or immediate cognition, spiritual perception" (online etymology dictionary).

30 The concept of tacit knowledge is attributed to Michael Polanyi (*Personal Knowledge: Towards a post-critical philosophy,* University of Chicago Press, 1962).

31 Born with software development in early 2000, agile management is spreading rapidly to all parts and kinds of organizations.

32 USAID, a pioneering agency in implementing adaptive management defines it as "an intentional approach to making decisions and adjustments in response to new information and changes in context".

33 Adaptive is defined as "having an ability to change to suit different conditions", according to the *Cambridge English Dictionary.*

References

Argyris, C. & Schön, D. (1996). *Organizational Learning II: Theory, method, and practice.* Reading, MA: Addison-Wesley.

Cable, D.M. (2018). *Alive at Work.* Ingram.

Capra, F. (1975). *The Tao of Physics.* Shambala.

Capra, F. & Luisi, P.L. (2014). *The Systems View of Life: A unifying vision.* Cambridge University Press.

Chouinard, Y. (2006). *Let My People Go Surfing: The education of a reluctant businessman.* Pearson.

Chugh, R. et al. (2015). Managing the transfer of tacit knowledge in Australian universities. *Journal of Organizational Knowledge Management,* 2015(2015), Article ID 297669, DOI: 10.5171/2015.297669.

Damasio, A. (2005). *Descartes' Error: Emotion, reason and the human brain.* Penguin.

Damasio, A. (2018). *The Strange Order of Things: Life, feeling and the making of cultures.* Pantheon.

Denning, S. (2018). *The Age of Agile: How smart companies are transforming the way work gets done.* Amacom.

Heisenberg, W. (1958). *Physics and Philosophy.* New York: Harper Torchbooks.

Hislop, D. et al. (2014). The process of individual unlearning: A neglected topic in an under-researched field. *Management Learning,* 45(5), 540–560.

Komito, D.R. & Rinchen, G.S. (1999). *Nagarjuna's Seventy Stanzas: A Buddhist psychology of emptiness.* Snow Lion.

Midgley, G. (2000). *Systemic Intervention: Philosophy, methodology and practice.* Springer.

Polanyi, M. (1962). *Personal Knowledge: Towards a post-critical philosophy.* University of Chicago Press.

Ricard, M. (2016). *Altruism: The power of compassion to change yourself and the world.* Back Bay.

Suzuki, S. (2009). *Zen Mind, Beginner's Mind.* Weatherhill.

Thich Nhat Hanh (1998). *The Heart of the Buddha's Teaching.* Parallax Press.

Watts, A. (2011). *The Wisdom of Insecurity: A message for an age of anxiety.* Vintage.

Watts, A. (2019). *Out of Your Mind.* Souvenir Press.

Chapter 3

The quest for balance and harmony

The Yin–Yang and the Five Elements

According to Taoism, harmony is the purposeful state of life, of universal nature. It is a state that is experienced directly through the oneness of the Tao, the ultimate reality and the unity of all things. Harmony is also a fundamental idea in Buddhism: to realize the world of non-distinction, of non-thought, that transcends all dualities. The one who attains this state is the enlightened, the one who fusions herself with the Tao and embodies through experience her own Buddha-nature.

For seekers (Figure 3.1), this is an aspirational state of mind. Most seekers have had sporadic encounters with harmony, in direct experiences of deep ecological awareness. As such, these experiences spark the desire to know and learn more about them, and to cultivate the mechanisms that lead to a whole and recurrent experience of harmony. Seekers differentiate from sceptics in the sense that they have sensed, and flowed with, the Tao at some point. Seekers have an intuitive awareness of the systems view of life that they aim to embody at the physical, mental and spiritual level. However, in an anthropogenic context characterized by the human–nature disconnect, the same concept of harmony implicitly carries its opposite, disharmony. Disharmony is the feeling of discomfort associated with the failed attempt to balance all areas that are important in our lives. Disharmony is the main experiential state of affairs that frames our thinking and agency in this ultra-complex world. It is related to *samsara* and acts as a departure point.

Individuals struggle to balance all interrelated areas of life—career, education, love, family, health, social relationships, leisure time and money—and finally find—implicitly or explicitly—harmony. Originally, harmony is the resulting scenario of an internal–external balance in which the individual feels at ease with herself, with others, and with the environment. This state of being is dynamic, different from the idea of happiness in the West, which is socially understood as a "static" destination point.

The quest for balance and harmony happens in a constant interaction of interdependent phenomena that operate at the metaphysical and physical

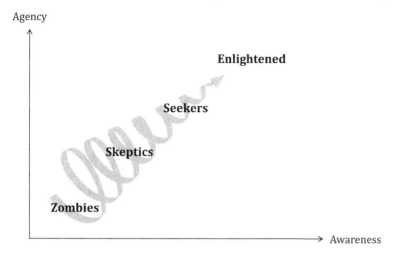

Figure 3.1 The four awareness profiles

domains (i.e., the interwoven influences between mind and body; the telluric energies of an environment that influence human health). Harmony is rather a felt knowing than an intellectualized understanding. It is a dynamic experience felt in the present moment.

The Taoist—through the School of Naturalists—conceptualized the first ever systems thinking theories—the Yin–Yang and the Five Elements—in terms of harmony. These theories build on the fundamental laws of nature, resembling the Tao principles discussed in the previous chapter. These open transformation-focused theories are still relevant today, perhaps more than ever, as their relevance and utility grow exponentially in correlation with the exponential growth in the complexity and uncertainty of the present times. In sum, the Ying–Yang and the Five Elements are two "simplexity" theories. "Simplexity" means that these theories shed clarity and provide guidance on understanding complex systems grounded in universal laws.

The Yin–Yang theory

The Yin–Yang theory is the tip of the iceberg that reflects the Taoist worldview in the most holistic sense of the word. The concepts that explain the Yin–Yang were already explicitly described in the book *I Ching* in the second millennium BC, but its ideological authorship is associated with the Taoist academic Zou Yan during the fourth and third centuries BC. Zou Yan was the first to systematize the conceptual teachings of Taoism through two interrelated theories: the Yin–Yang and the Five Elements.

Huang Di, the Yellow Emperor, had already devised the need for healing amid disharmony. He said, the law of yin and yang is the natural order of the universe, the foundation of all things, mother of all changes, the root of life and death. In healing, one must grasp the root of the disharmony, which is always subject to the law of yin and yang.

He set the foundations of Chinese medicine based on an in-depth observation of human–nature interactions and interdependencies. In his words, "from ancient times it has been recognized that there is an intimate relationship between the activity and life of human beings and their natural environment".[1]

In this context, Yin–Yang is inherently conceived as a dynamic cognitive process by which Taoists enquire about the fundamental principle of universal life. Taoist researchers observed that the answer lies in the dynamic interaction of the Yin–Yang forces, which, in turn, are balanced in emerging patterns of constant motion called *bian*—变—or change. According to Taoism, any empirical phenomenon can be explained by the coexistence of Yin–Yang, two opposite but complementary and interdependent energies. Lao Tzu vividly expressed this coexistence in the *Tao Te Ching*: "all things carry Yin yet embrace Yang. Their blended influences bring harmony".

The Yin–Yang is graphically represented by the *Taijitu*, the circular diagram that symbolizes Taoism and that in many cases is used today as one of the graphic icons most associated with Eastern philosophies. The *Taijitu* is a circle divided into two equal parts by a curved line, as can be seen in Figure 3.2. This line separates two parts: the white colour representing Yang and the black colour representing Yin. Yin and Yang symbolize the integration of two cosmic energy patterns that balance each other seeking harmony through the curved line that expresses the constant movement and dynamism of the universe and life itself.

Figure 3.2 The *Taijitu*

Yang energy is associated with sun, fire, day, strength, light, hardness, rigidity and masculinity. In contrast, Yin energy represents the moon, water, night, fragility, darkness, softness, flexibility and femininity. Both energies form a single energy (the circle as a unit)—*qi*—which constantly flows in search for balance. The Taoist anticipated before quantum physicists that *qi*, or vital energy, is the tractor principle that explains change and transformation as a universal constant. As the sinologist and intellectual Anne Cheng describes it, "the Yin/Yang binary rhythm is the fundamental rhythm of the vital principle or energy: the *qi* that moves, opens and extends is Yang; when it returns to stillness and withdraws, it is Yin."[2] Although, in the eyes of a Westerner, it may seem that Yang is more powerful than Yin, neither Yin nor Yang is, in fact, more powerful than the other. They are interdependent and are part of a whole.

In fact, the Yin and Yang interactive patterns explain the behaviour of the whole as a self-regulating system. When Yang reaches its peak, the system self-regulates; Yin starts to emerge as Yang backs off. This self-regulatory dynamic parallels with autopoiesis, the self-organization of living systems, a concept that Maturana and Varela observed in studying the biological nature of life.[3] For a better understanding of the Yin–Yang, it is necessary to delve into the meaning of three interlocking principles: duality, paradox and interdependence.

Duality

The Yin–Yang couple is the prototype of all dualities and paradigm of all couples. Duality in Taoism is treated as two apparently opposite parts of the same unitary subject. Light exists because there is darkness, they are dual states of light as phenomenon. Cold exists because there is heat, as complementary parts to the phenomenon of temperature. Quick and slow coexist in the unity of movement, and thus we could continue at length to explain any empirical subject or phenomenon. As Cheng explains,[4]

> Despite their opposite natures, Yin and Yang are both supportive and complementary; one cannot work without the other, and the decline of one implies the simultaneous development of the other. In this, the duality of Yin and Yang is the quintessential feature of Chinese thought, which often views opposites as complementary, and not as mutually exclusive.

The complementary nature of phenomena was another conclusion reached by modern science. Quantum physicist Niels Bohr coined the principle of complementarity when observing the atom's wave–particle duality of behaviour. He had already identified the correlation with the Yin and Yang, as is apparent in his coat of arms, which includes the *taijitu*. The nuclear physicist Edward Teller wrote of him,

> Bohr was the incarnation of complementarity, the insistence that every important issue has an opposite side that appears as mutually exclusive with the other. The understanding of the question becomes possible only if the existence of both sides is recognized.

The complementary relationship and influence of Yin with Yang also crosses the border of indivisibility. Yin is part of Yang and vice versa. Their energies are mixed, although in each of them one force predominates over the other when the whole is not balanced. This is reflected in Figure 3.2 by the black point (Yin) within the white part (Yang) and by the white point (Yang) within the black part (Yin). This taxonomy explains the unitary character of duality. Actually, there is light in the dark, heat in the cold and slow in the fast; it depends on the phase of time and the balance of one force with the other.

The natural nature of Taoism is reflected in the systemic, complementary and dynamic vision of Yin–Yang. In fact, when we are born, grow and begin to communicate through speech, we learn by following a Taoist-based logical pattern. We internalize in a natural way the meaning of the subjects in pairs. Thus, we know what is "low" when we learn what is "high", and the same thing happens with "heat" and "cold", "day" and "night" and "sadness" and "joy". We know what sadness is because we know what joy is. That is why it is said that there is sadness in joy and light in darkness.

As a Westerner raised in Europe, I grew and adapted to the Western-biased educational system, which systematically forgets the nature of our thinking—in line with the Yin–Yang—and adopts the Aristotelian logical–rational thinking characteristic of the Western tradition. Although, at first glance there is a certain parallelism between the principle of Taoist duality and Western dialectical thought, the Yin–Yang duality differs conceptually from Western rationality–logicality in how it deals with the inclusivity or exclusivity of opposing concepts. In this sense, the concept of paradox differs according to whether it is approached from the East or the West.

Paradox

Suddenly, thinking that there is light in the dark can seem stupid to a person who has not had any contact with Taoist thought. Nor is it strictly necessary to adopt a Yin–Yang logic to experience such a paradox, since the tasks of life itself can lead us to experience such a principle in our own lives. Western popular phrases such as "there is light at the end of the tunnel" are an approximation to the Yin–Yang duality, but fail to combine two apparently contrary concepts that complement each other as part of a whole.

The paradox between pairs is a concept deeply rooted in Yin–Yang-ism, which precisely defines the coexistence of duality as part of a whole. In the Yin–Yang, the paradox is opened out and integrated systemically in a dynamic process of balance—space and time—between the couple of the unitary phenomenon. It is like the entanglement principle, a quantum mechanical phenomenon in which the quantum states of two or more objects have to be described with reference to each other. In this dynamic process of duality, both concepts of the phenomenon are mutually inclusive. By contrast, Aristotelian rational logic adopts a linear thinking process that is mutually exclusive between contrary concepts. This process has a rather static and rigid character, and gives rise to a dichotomy between opposing concepts—either this, or the other, as Professor Peter Ping Li of the Copenhagen Business School explains.[5]

Let's look at it through an example. Rich and poor are two opposite and dual concepts that coexist in the unitary phenomenon of wealth. They are complementary because one needs the other to have a meaning (there would be no poverty without richness, and vice versa). According to the prism of Yin–Yang, the rich coexists with the poor. If we apply it to an individual, it means that being rich at a certain moment in life contains the possibility that such a person may be poor at another moment in her life. A person can be rich and poor in different time phases (it is a process of change that moves along the curved line of the *taijitu*).

From the viewpoint of the Aristotelian rational logic typical of Western civilization, a person who is rich is rich and is thought to maintain this status throughout her life. She becomes attached to that status. The word "poor" is treated as an opposite to "rich", and, as such, should be avoided, as it is an exclusive concept to "rich". This reductionist vision, more typical of a mentality cradled by Western thought, perceives the opposite concepts as independent and contradictory, and classifies them as "problems or conflicts".

In practice, this system of thought can cause problems for adaptation to the environment. Since the Covid-19 crisis erupted, it has been common to see millions of people lose assets, income, work or wealth in general, which has brought great frustration and fear to many people who thought they were immune to poverty. The prism of a circular and dynamic system like the Yin–Yang, which intrinsically conceives change and opposites as two sides of the same coin, can be of great help in anticipating and managing changes better, accepting events and learning from them to evolve and improve our lives.

It is precisely the cyclical transition of the duality of opposites that contains change and transformation. Day turns into night, the rich into the poor, the fast into the slow, the youth into the elder, health into disease, and vice versa. We are continually transitioning, and, as a Taoist proverb says, change is the only constant. The meaning of the word "crisis" and its relation to change illustrates the principle of the paradox and its divergent interpretation, depending on whether it is approached from the Eastern Yin–Yang or the Western rational logic. In Mandarin, the word "crisis" is made up of two characters (wei ji)—危机. The first character (wei) means "danger" and the second (ji) means "incipient moment or a crucial point in a cycle". The union of the two characters anticipates a change.

Specifically, "crisis" in the Far East means the coexistence of a phase of "danger" that leads to a different phase or crucial point; that is, they are two complementary forces that belong to the subject "crisis". Thus, crisis is not without danger, pain, misfortune and imbalance at the beginning, but, at the same time, the crucial point also represents an opportunity to learn, grow and transform towards an opposing force, such as fortune, balance and harmony in a future time. In the West, on the other hand, the word crisis has another meaning that is reduced to the slope of danger that the same phenomenon entails. According to the *Oxford English Dictionary*, the word "crisis" is defined as "a time of intense difficulty or danger", a definition that closes the door to the possibility of future change and transformation.

In short, it is not a matter of judging both systems of thought in order to choose one or the other meaning. The purpose here is to use the best features of both thought systems simultaneously and complementarily. The rational logic allows us to analyse different hypotheses in depth, discarding and classifying results based on what we are looking for; and Yin–Yangism allows us to systemically analyse phenomena and synthesize the whole by studying the interrelationships that are generated between objects and their subjects, since reality is relative and, therefore, a matter of perception.

Interdependence

The principle of interdependence places special emphasis on the relationship between the two opposite concepts of Yin–Yang that, in turn, form the observed phenomenon or unity. Specifically, the relationship established between the two concepts is one of mutual dependence, or interdependence. That is, the meaning of one depends on the state of the other and vice versa. The following metaphor illustrates the principle of interdependence in the following way; the two sides of the same coin represent the duality of the Yin–Yang; both concepts are related and interact as if they were communicating vessels. When the coin is tossed in the air, it can come out heads or tails. If "heads" repeatedly appears, there will be more and more possibilities of "tails", and vice versa. As the French sinologist and expert in Taoism, Isabelle Robinet, describes,[6]

Yin and Yang represent the principle of difference that creates attraction, as well as the becoming and the multiplicity that they produce through their combinations; but also, due to the close correlation that unites them, they are proof of the underlying unity that underlies the world.

Eastern thought, instead of observing succession of phenomena, registers alternations of patterns of the same phenomenon. The theory of Yin–Yang suggests, as Professor Tony Fang of the Stockholm Business School explains, that

> human beings, organizations, and cultures, like all universal phenomena, intrinsically long for variation and harmony for their mere existence and healthy development. We are 'both/and' instead of 'this or the other'. We are both Yin and Yang, feminine and masculine, long-term and short-term, individualistic and collectivist ... depending on the situations, context and time.[7]

This difference is essential to understanding the interdependent nature of opposite concepts in contrast to the mutual negation proper to Western rational logic. If we do a comparative analysis between both taxonomies of knowledge, the Yin–Yang offers a broader paradigm for reflection and study, an analytical meta-framework. The Yin–Yang not only aspires to compare and value the coexistence of a concept compared to its opposite, but also provides a systemic framework that allows the integration of the Aristotelian rational–logical system. This framework goes beyond ruling whether something that is "rich" cannot be "poor," or if something that is "clear" cannot be "dark."

The duality of apparently contradictory phenomena is related in a model of thought that has important implications at personal and organizational level. These complementary paradoxes often emerge as tensions, which hamper the development of individuals and organizations, and, therefore, play a critical role in resisting change and transformation. These same tensions, systemically framed and understood in the context of Yin–Yang, have the potential to turn frustration and entropy—the degree of internal disorganization of a system—into the liberation of syntropy—the level of internal organization—as a creative energy that facilitates an organizational process of change and transformation.

Yin–Yang creative tensions

Yin–Yang creative tensions is a conceptual method and enquiry-driven tool to facilitate an organizational process of diagnosis, learning and sustainable transformation. I grounded this conceptual method on the association and application of Yin–Yang to creative tensions, a concept developed by Robert Fritz in his book *The Path of Least Resistance* (1984) and popularized by Peter Senge in his book *The Fifth Discipline* (1990). A creative tension emerges when there is a clear articulation between the vision—a desired goal or objective, the way it should be—and the current reality—the unsatisfactory current state of reality, the way it is—and the gap between the two becomes apparent. This gap creates an emotional and energetic tension that automatically seeks to be resolved.[8]

The creative tension becomes Yin–Yang—a Yin–Yang creative tension—when the vision and the current reality are articulated as Yin–Yang polarities or opposites of the same phenomenon or component. This happens in paradigm shifts.[9] The transition between old to new paradigms is articulated by contrasting complementary, interdependent and undesirable old ways of doing—current situation—with apparently opposing, desirable emerging new ways of doing—goal/objective. This is the case of the transition to the new business paradigm, which emerges in dualistic but complementary patterns of aspirational behaviour—principles—that point out how the key business management components are changing from the old extractive paradigm to the new sustainable one (see Table 1.1 in Chapter 1). Figure 3.3 illustrates the dynamics of the Yin–Yang creative tensions.

An organization can apply the conceptual method of Yin–Yang creative tensions through collective dialogues that explore the tension through the Yin–Yang polarities. Let's examine it through an example. One of the main Yin–Yang creative tensions when transitioning to the new business paradigm is whether the organization can introduce a purpose-driven management system towards sustainability while remaining profitable (Figure 3.4). In a collective dialogue in an organization, some executives affirmed that

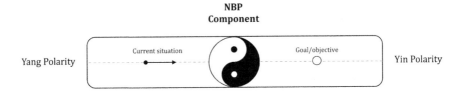

Figure 3.3 The Yin–Yang creative tensions: the concept

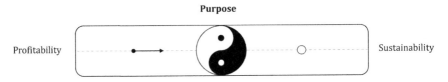

Figure 3.4 Yin–Yang creative tension on purpose

this transition is doable when the company is highly profitable and financially strong. Others claimed that it is precisely the shift towards sustainability that makes the company more profitable. The mere identification of sustainability as the Yin polarity of profitability opens the door to a sustainable transition as profitability engenders sustainability and vice versa (as in any Yin–Yang relationship). The discussion about these two polarities of purpose facilitates an open, creative and balancing collective process of enquiry on how to transition to the sustainable business paradigm.

Furthermore, the initiation of this process may induce the organization to identify emerging interrelated Yin–Yang creative tensions that enrich the quality of the systems thinking dynamics. For example, the discussion around the Yin–Yang creative tension on purpose brought to the table the Yin–Yang creative tensions on beneficiaries and organizational typology. Some people in the organization argued that the focus of the company should shift towards providing value to all stakeholders equally, while others remained loyal to prioritizing shareholders as its main beneficiaries. The discussion on beneficiaries led to the Yin–Yang creative tension on leadership. The point was that, if the organization took a stakeholder approach, it should shift towards a more transformational type of leadership.

When discussing the differences and implications between transformational and transactional leadership, the discussion moved on to what kind of organization people wanted (Yin–Yang creative tension on organization). They discussed whether to stick to a mechanistic type as it was more typical, or whether they wanted to move toward a living, human-centred organization. This discussion provided the ground for the Yin–Yang creative tension on structure to emerge. The enquiry here was what type of organization would be more adaptable to a VUCA context, and they related a mechanistic organization (hierarchical-based) less prone to adapt than a living organization (network-based). The discussion on the structure of the organization led to the Yin–Yang creative tension on power, as people associated that changing the structure implied a change in the power dynamics of the organization (moving from centralized to a more distributed power).

The Yin–Yang creative tensions collective dialogue ended here as the people involved in the discussions decided that they had the elements to redefine the purpose of the organization. The discussion on purpose drew a feedback loop of six interrelated, mutually reinforcing Yin–Yang creative tensions, as illustrated in Figure 3.5. Yin–Yang creative tensions trigger an emerging self-regulating process of organizational development based on collective dialogues.

The conceptualization and application of Yin–Yang creative tensions in the organization is based on the implementation of a five-step awareness-driven process through collective dialogues. These dialogues initiate a collective creative process in the organization by focusing the creativity

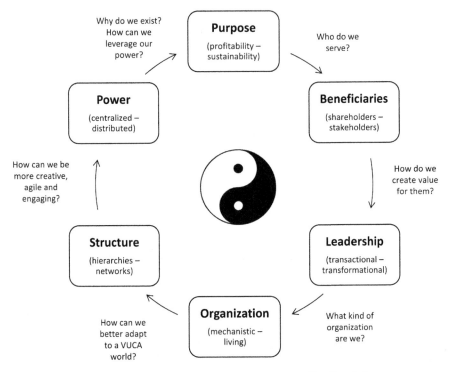

Figure 3.5 Yin–Yang creative tensions: a feedback loop

on what is being developed, by empowering values of inspiration, trust, imagination and an explicit commitment to transitioning towards the aspirational polarity.

This approach transcends the single focus on problem-solving: the key focusing question here is *what are we trying to create in order to transition?* instead of *what problem are we trying to solve?* Peter Senge recalls this approach "systems thinking and the gap between aspirations and performance", advocating that, for organizational development, the power of aspiration is much greater than the power of desperation. This power is the basis for generating syntropy, which—as opposed to entropy—is the structured utilization of the organizational energy to attract, evolve and bring together new forms and new solutions for the sustainable transformation of the organization.

Yin–Yang creative tensions collective dialogues facilitate an unfolding pattern that emerges from the acceptance and exploration of paradoxical and simultaneous multiple realities. The Yin–Yang creative tensions that emerged in the example illustrated in Figure 3.5 are ways to illuminate and understand problems systemically. This deep and interconnected level of understanding helps the organization create new ideas and solutions to manage and solve the tensions. These five steps are as follows.

1. *Context awareness: putting the organization in relationship to meta-trends and global events and dynamics, identifying the interdependent polarities and making sense of the situational information from a dynamic systems perspective—balance and imbalance. This exercise, facilitated through a collective dialogue, allows synthesizing the current situation through a Yin–Yang diagnosis of the same.*

In a business perspective, the current economic system of capitalism is Yang-driven. The mechanistic worldview of an extractive economy designed and dominated by the patriarchy and based on the short-term profit maximization for shareholders in an ultra-competitive market approach to value generation are Yang features of the system. Through the Yin–Yang, we can diagnose that the system is, overall, imbalanced by an excess of Yang. When this happens, the same system self-regulates—by means of internal and/or external drivers of change—towards the adoption of Yin-like patterns of behaviour and action. Events such as the global recession and the Covid-19 crises are change signals evidencing the human–nature disconnect. They enter new information—in terms of principles—into the economic system, captured by its agents or sub-systems—individuals, communities, organizations and institutions—that can potentially change the behaviour of the system.

In this context, the features of the new paradigm are Yin-driven, overall. Well-being or happiness at work and work–life balance; cultural, gender, race and age diversity; employee empowerment and intrinsic motivation; values-driven leadership; non-violent communication; regenerative design and innovation; sustainable business modelling; impact or ESG investing; holacratic structures; organizational learning; and impact evaluation are examples of Yin-based corporate practices that counterbalance the dominant Yang paradigm.

2. *Tension awareness: identifying and mapping the tensions that the organization is currently experiencing. These tensions are mostly issues, gaps, or bottlenecks that prevent the organization from transitioning to the new paradigm. They can be recurrent problems or challenges and/or emerging issues or trends that have—or will have—a profound impact on the organization and that create uncertainty and resistance to change. The persistence of unresolved tensions creates entropy.*

An organization may tacitly know that there are issues in certain areas, such as having a disengaged workforce, high degree of absenteeism, experiencing constant difficulties in adapting to market changes, lacking a results culture, or resisting digitalization. There is a risk in internalizing these issues and assuming they are normal unless there is a critical reflection and a genuine will to explicitly identify them, relate them to tensions and recognize they are problems that are undermining organizational performance.

3.   *Polarity awareness: identifying and assessing the complementary patterns of behaviour and associating the tension(s) with their interdependent opposite or polarity. This is a scoping exercise that allows the organization to identify and connect with desired scenarios. They are within the realm of possibility, as one polarity already includes the other one. The organization enquires about these new possibilities, collecting evidence and drawing the linkage between the current and desired realities.*

The awareness of the envisioned polarities allows the articulation of a clear vision within the organization. This step motivates the organization to act with a sense of urgency and renewed hope that elevates the engagement of all stakeholders involved. If the envisioned polarities are not recognized, the risk is that organizations may relieve the tension by implementing quick fixes or by narrowing their vision so that they reduce the gap between their desired and current reality.

4.   *Co-creation awareness: facilitating an organizational multi-stakeholder dialogue by fostering a critical enquiry into the problems and their root causes and, at the same time, creatively envisioning ways of resolving the tension by identifying and reflecting on the complementary polarity as the desired vision or goal.*

This step requires identifying the stakeholders involved in the tensions and engaging them in a collective dialogue where people openly discuss the component, its Yin–Yang polarities, its transitioning dynamics and its implications for the development of the organization. Participants in the dialogue freely express their position at points along the line between the poles, which triggers further discussion while creating group empathy. It is a pause-and-reflect type of intervention[10] focused on collective learning that liberates lateral and futures thinking.

5.   *Transition awareness: anchoring the results of the collective dialogue— or dialogues—in strategy workshops aimed at identifying leverage points and activating the transition with clear and concise actions. The main outputs of these workshops are (i) to identify, design and pilot the transitioning interventions and (ii) to shape the multidisciplinary task force teams that will be implementing, monitoring and evaluating them.*

In this last phase of the Yin–Yang creative tensions collective dialogues the organization leverages the creative energy that has been collectively unleashed in order to design the actions and assign the roles and responsibilities to the people in the organization that will lead the expected transformation. In this phase, the organization is fully aware of the transition, and the role it is playing in that transition.

The Five Elements theory

Together with the Yin–Yang, the Five Elements[11] is the systems thinking theory that reflects the universal dynamics of the Tao. The academic Zou Yan—the promoter of the Yin and Yang School—was also a pioneer in systematizing a theory that explained the evolutionary dynamics between the five transformational energies observed in nature: Wood, Fire, Earth, Metal and Water.

These Five Elements represent five energetic phases that are framed in the complementary dynamics of Yin–Yang. Specifically, the Five Elements phases evolve following the Yin–Yang cycle; Wood and Fire are considered Yang energies (they are represented in the white part of the *Taijitu*, as illustrated in Figure 3.6, while Metal and Water represent Yin energies (represented in the black part of the diagram); Earth is a balancing energy that is present in the transitions from one element to another, therefore it is placed in the centre of the *Taijitu*, as can be seen in Figure 3.6.

The Yin–Yang and the Five Elements form the backbone of Taoist or Chinese Metaphysics. In all its disciplines—astrology, Feng Shui, medicine and the martial arts—understanding the Five Elements is essential in order to apply the comprehension of the system into practical analogies.

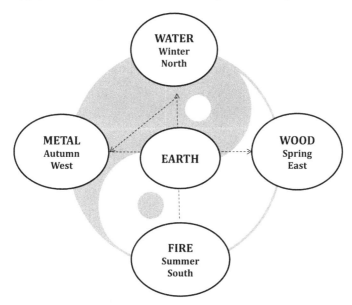

Figure 3.6 The Yin–Yang and the Five Elements

The transfer of the cosmological vision of the universe to specific fields of nature–human knowledge and behaviour is what renders these systemic theories useful. Like Yin–Yang, the Five Elements are the result of thousands of years of empirical research through direct observation of the human–nature interaction in relation to its universal nature.

The natural behaviour of the Five Elements

The Five Elements represent the five phases through which *qi* circulates in a natural cyclical process. Wood, Fire, Earth, Metal and Water are transitory energetic states whereby energy adopts a distinctive behaviour characteristic of each elemental phase. As a result of the study of nature and its behaviour, the Taoist sages managed to classify and systematize the types of universal energy in these Five Elements. Each element has a behaviour that characterizes it and gives it a specific personality; it is related to the natural symbol that it represents (Wood, Fire, Earth, Metal and Water), the temporal and spatial relationship that it embodies and the characteristics associated with its behaviour.

In this context, the five transitory phases are not only integrated into the Yin–Yang cycle, as illustrated in Figure 3.6, but each of them also embodies the Yin and Yang character at the same time. The elements are time-related to the four seasons, as a symbol of transition and cyclical transformation. Everything is in constant motion, nothing is static or permanent. Reality is relative. These dynamics parallel with Einstein's theory of relativity. Movement in time has an anchor in space, in place; this is manifested in the temporal–spatial character of change. A change is a moment of transition that occurs in a specific time and in a specific place. The behaviour of the Five Elements—natural Yin–Yang symbol, temporal and spatial relationship, characteristics—is manifested as follows (Figure 3.7).

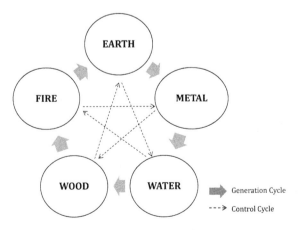

Figure 3.7 The Five Elements

Wood is the youngest energy of the five. Its Yin symbol is a flower, a bush or a bamboo, while its Yang symbol is a tree. Both represent growth, expansion and provide direction to achieve goals. It has the ability to transform ideas into matter. Wood is an internal creative energy that grows thanks to Water. It is associated with honesty and benevolence. The season that is identified with Wood is Spring, when nature grows, flourishes and expands. According to the lunar calendar, Spring is the first season of the year, the youngest. On a spatial level, Wood is related to the east, where the sun rises every day.

Fire is generated from Wood. Both are considered Yang energies—active, expanding, blooming—so they are found in the white part of the *taijitu*, as can be seen in Figure 3.6. The Yang symbol of Fire is the sun or flames, while its Yin counterpart is symbolized by the moon or candlelight. Fire is an expansive energy from the inside out, dynamic, passionate, charismatic and adventurous. Fire illuminates, scorches and produces a feeling of comfort, but in excess it can burn and destroy. It is powerful. It is associated with courtesy, good manners and elegance. Fire corresponds to the Summer season, the warmest and brightest. Its spatial direction is south.

Earth is generated from Fire. It is the most complex and subtle energy, playing a pivotal role in the Five Elements. Earth is not seasonally classified as a Yin or Yang energy, as it switches between them. It is the transitional element that regulates the change of seasons. That is why it is positioned as the energy of passage between seasons and visually placed at the centre of the spatial model, as can be seen in Figure 3.6. The Yin symbol of Earth is a fertile field, while Yang is represented by a mountain. Earth is patient, prudent, diligent, disciplined, ambitious, and energetic. It is associated with trust and integrity, and is governed to provide a service to others, as Earth nourishes growth and transformation.

Metal originates from Earth. Its Yang symbol is illustrated by a great rock, a powerful energy that contrasts with the Yin symbolism of a more subtle, shaped jewel. It is a conductive energy that shapes, solidifies and consolidates processes and objects. Metal has the property of becoming a precious product of great value, such as gold or a diamond, and also a dangerous material, such as a knife or a sword. It is associated with the power of decision, justice and honesty. Autumn is the season of Metal, also represented by the direction in which the sun sets, the west.

Water flows from Metal. It is the element that best embodies the philosophy of the Tao. Its quintessential Yin symbol is the river, which always flows downwards from its source and adapts to any vessel and topography. It is a source of life, it incubates energy and nourishes Wood, the energy that purposefully grows and expands with direction. Its Yang counterpart is illustrated by an ocean or a large lake. Water is cohesive, emotional, intuitive and flexible. It is soft, and transparent, but in excess it also has the ability to explode and destroy any barrier that tries to contain it, as with a river overflowing or a tsunami. It is associated with intelligence and sagacity. It is represented by Winter, the last season that concludes the cycle but also engenders the beginning of the new lunar year and the prelude to Spring. Water, along with Metal, flows through the Yin cycle of *qi* (as can be seen in Figure 3.6), the two Yin energies—passive, contracting, declining—that complement and counterbalance its Yang opposites.

To understand the patterns of behaviour and relationship between the Five Elements, it is necessary to combine a natural understanding of the universe and a pictographic abstraction that illustrates the dynamic movement of the five energies between them and their behaviour in natural phenomena. The Five Elements have the virtue not only of synthetizing the attributes of each energy, respectively, but also of analysing the dynamic relationship between them, as we can see below.

The dynamic cycles of the Five Elements

The *Taijitu* is presented as a diagram that lacks straight lines. Its circular outer shape denotes the cyclical movement through which the Five Elements flow (sometimes in the Yin, sometimes in the Yang). Furthermore, its curved line running through the interior represents the transition and change between the opposing forces of Yin and Yang. This dynamism inherent in any phenomenon of nature is also reflected in the type of mutant relationships that are generated between the elements or the five energetic phases. These relationships are classified into two cyclical processes of change: a generation cycle that circulates along the outer line of the model from one element to another (its substitute), and a control cycle that flows through the interior of the circle, in which an element interacts with its bi-substitute. The two cycles,[12] operating according to different but complementary natural laws (creation/order and destruction/chaos), act in a complementary way as a system of weights and counterweights that has as its purpose the self-regulatory attainment of harmony.

Generation cycle

Generation is the cycle that sequentially circulates through the exterior of the model from one element to another, as can be seen by the circular lines that illustrate such a circuit in Figure 3.7. This cycle forms a circle whose function is to generate each element from the energy that precedes it. Each element or energy phase has the potential to nurture the next element. Their relationship can be graphically illustrated from the natural nourishment between the elements. In this way, Wood feeds Fire, just as when we want to make a Fire, we first use sticks to generate it. In turn, Fire creates Earth from the ashes. The Earth contains, generates and solidifies Metal, which is often represented in the form of rocks and stones. Metal purifies and enriches the Water that flows from its spring. And finally, closing the cycle, Water nourishes Wood, as when rainfall sustains fields and flowers and waters the trees and plants to bear fruit.

In its proper measure, that is, in a balanced presence and proportion of each element, the generation cycle Wood ⟶ Fire ⟶ Earth ⟶ Metal ⟶ Water ⟶ Wood becomes a harmonious cycle where each energy flows, nurturing in sequential virtuosity. However, direct observation teaches us that the elements are not always present in nature in a balanced way. In the desert, for example, Earth (sands) and Fire (scorching sun) abound but it lacks Water, Wood and Metal. Or in the jungle, excess of water (rain and tropical storms) can flood the ecosystem, in the same way that a summer sun can cause dryness and fires in the forest. The elements, when present in excess or by default, have the potential to introduce imbalances to the system, which will need the control cycle to counteract it.

Control cycle

Therefore, the nature of the control cycle is precisely to rebalance the system following an excess of energy from the bi-substitute element of the Five Elements model. The purpose of this control cycle is to guarantee and ensure the flow of transforming energy between the five phases, thus avoiding collapse, which would lead to a profound imbalance in the system. In this way the cycle works to preserve the balance between the dynamic interactions of the Five Elements for the harmony of their whole.

Control is the opposite force to generation. The control cycle is sometimes called the destruction cycle, illustrating the opposite meaning to generative or creative (creation and destruction are two opposite and complementary Yin–Yang concepts). An element restricts and restrains its opposite, so its function is to control the opposite element. Against this backdrop, the control cycle between the elements is illustrated in the following pictographic metaphor. Wood can penetrate Earth, like the roots of a large tree that anchor it in the ground and crack the Earth. Earth can block Water, like a large dam that controls river water and contains it in a lake. Water can control and extinguish Fire, like the effect of rain putting out a conflagration. Fire melts Metal, can shape it and even melt it. Metal cuts Wood, like an axe cutting down a tree or scissors cutting a flower stem.

Therefore, the control cycle restricts and drains the energy of the element, when it manifests itself excessively, in a relational logic between opposite elements following the pattern Wood ⟶ Earth ⟶ Water ⟶

Fire $\longrightarrow$ Metal $\longrightarrow$ Wood, as represented by the internal star shape in Figure 3.7. The two cycles of generation and control operate simultaneously in a complementary dynamic. If an element manifests in excess, the system will need the control of its opposite element to moderate it; if an element manifests itself as lacking, the system will need the generation of its predecessor element to incentivize it. An efficient performance of both cycles is what drives the system to balance and harmonize as a whole.

Complementary cycles in the Five Elements

The generation and control cycles are the main balance mechanisms of the Five Elements. For a complete understanding of possible imbalances and rebalances, however, there are also two complementary cycles of (a) reverse restriction and (b) subjugation. Although their influence is less than that of the main generation and control cycles, they also play a harmonizing role in the interactions between the Five Elements.

The inverse restriction explains the over-generative phenomenon that the excess of an element can cause in its predecessor. That means that an excess of an element can drown the energy of its predecessor. For this reason, this relationship circulates in the opposite direction to the generation cycle. For example, too much Wood can end up drowning the Fire and extinguishing it; too much Water can excessively moisten and render the Wood useless; too much Metal can promote an extra-mineralization of the Water; too much Earth can block Metal formation; and too much Fire can overact in the formation of Earth.

Subjugation circulates in the opposite direction of the control cycle, and also affects the excess of an element over its previous opposite. For example, an excess of Wood can numb the Metal, as when an axe tries to cut a huge log of Wood without success; an excess of Metal can become a shield against Fire; an excess of Fire can evaporate the Water; an excess of Water can wash away and penetrate Earth; and an excess of Earth can break the Wood.

Balance and harmony in the Five Elements

In sum, the main cycles of generation and control, together with the secondary cycles of reverse restriction and subjugation represent the four natural laws of balance and imbalance in the Five Elements theory. Together with the Five Elements, or energetic phases, they make up the constant transformation process that is the basis for the self-regulation of the system. The balance of the system and, therefore, its harmony, will depend on the presence and qualities of the Five Elements and their relationship and interaction.

A system, such an organization, is considered healthy or prosperous when energy is dynamically flowing from element to element managed by the two generation and control cycles. Furthermore, the strength of the system is also proved when it has the ability to apply its own contingency effect by overcoming and correcting any possible imbalances—either by reverse restriction or subjugation. Consequently, the ultimate goal of the Five Elements is to comprehend the evolutionary change dynamics of a system—an individual, an organization, or an ecosystem.

Overall, the Five Elements provide a systemic compass that allows the system to be aware of its relationships, processes and patterns of behaviour, as well as of its change and self-regulation dynamics. In disciplines such as medicine, the Five Elements are used as a means to integrally diagnose the imbalances of the system (in this case the human body), to prevent potential illnesses and to heal current ones.

In an organization, the application of the Five Elements theory introduces a different logical approach to solving problems compared with Western logic, as also happens with the Yin–Yang theory. The classic way to look at problems in the West is to focus on the problem itself. For example, when there is a low level of team engagement and low group cohesion, the organization usually reacts by analysing the problem in the scope of team engagement and focusing the intervention on the same area of team dynamics.

This, nonetheless, the application of the Five Elements theory focuses on identifying how problems are generated, through the interrelational dynamics of the generation and control cycles. Thus, by applying this systemic logic, if there is a team engagement and cohesion problem (this problem is related to the Earth element), the organization looks at what is generating this problem: there could be a lack of leadership that is creating entropy in the team (related to the Fire element, as Fire generates Earth) or a type of culture that blocks the group flow (related to the Wood element, as Wood controls Earth).

Chapter 5 explores how the Five Elements theory is applied to organizational management, through the Zen Business model. This is a model for guiding organizations to transition to the new sustainability-driven paradigm. But before diving into the Zen Business model, I will explore the Buddhist and Taoist systems thinking approach to cognition in the next chapter.

Notes

1   Excerpts from *The Yellow Emperor's Classic of Medicine* (Maoshing Ni; Shambala 1995).
2   Cheng, A. (2002). *Historia del Pensamiento Chino*, Ediciones Bellaterra.
3   Capra & Luisi (2014), p. 129.

4 Cheng, A. (2002). *Historia del Pensamiento Chino*, Ediciones Bellaterra.
5 Li, P.P. (2011). Toward research-practice balancing in management. The Yin-Yang method for open-ended and open-minded research. West meets East: Building theoretical bridges research methodology, *Strategy and Management*, 8, 91–141.
6 Isabelle Robinet (1991). Histoire du taoïsme, p. 17, en *Historia del pensamiento chino* de Anne Cheng.
7 Fang, T. (2003). A critique of Hofstede's fifth national culture dimension. *International Journal of Cross Cultural Management*, 3(3), 347–368.
8 This constructivist approach was already observed by Martin Luther King Jr. who, in one of his letters from prison, stated, "I am not afraid of the word *tension*. I have earnestly opposed violent tension, but there is a type of constructive, nonviolent tension which is necessary for growth" (Letter from a Birmingham jail, 1963).
9 Capra and Luisi explain in detail how paradigm shifts in science and society evolve as pendulum swings between different ways to think about mechanism and holism (*The Systems View of Life*, 2014, pp. 5–15).
10 IDEO and the Sundance Institute use a similar approach called "Creative tensions: conversations that move".
11 The original name of the theory in Mandarin is *wu-xing*, which means the five energy phases, the five agents, or the five processes, as it is commonly called. This theory is not related to Empedocles "four elements" or originally "four roots", which refer to the four elements that make all the structures in the world.
12 These two cycles are indistinctively also called creation–generation and destruction–control cycles.

References

Capra, F. & Luisi, P.L. (2014). *The Systems View of Life: A unifying vision*. Cambridge University Press.
Cheng, A. (2002). *Historia del Pensamiento Chino*. Ediciones Bellaterra.
Fang, T. (2003). A critique of Hofstede's fifth national culture dimension. *International Journal of Cross Cultural Management*, 3(3), 347–368.
Fritz, R. (1984). *The Path of Least Resistance*. Fawcett.
Huang, A. (1998). *The Complete I Ching*. Inner traditions.
Lao Tzu & Hamill, S. (2005). *Tao Te Ching: A new translation*. Shambala.
Li, P.P. (2011). Toward research-practice balancing in management. The Yin–Yang method for open-ended and open-minded research. West meets East: Building theoretical bridges research methodology. *Strategy and Management*, 8, 91–141.
Ni, M. (1995). *The Yellow Emperor's Classic of Medicine*. Shambala.
Patton, M.Q. (2019). *Blue Marble Evaluation: Premises and principles*. Guilford Press.
Senge, P. (1990). *The Fifth Discipline*. Doubleday.

Chapter 4

T-Qualia, a bio-logic of learning for transformation

The Eastern systems approach to the process of knowing

For a long time, humans have believed, and still do, that social and cultural behaviour and its resulting political, scientific and economic systems and institutions are a product of the human intellect.[1] The expansion of human intelligence and language, coupled with an exceptional degree of human sociality, certainly contributed on the making of cultures. But the importance of human intelligence is overrated. This is mainly because the progress made by intelligence does not take into account feelings, the principal motivator of human agency. Feelings are the missing element in the design and construction of cognitive models for human systems' decision-making, agency, learning and transformation.[2]

Feelings, as the renowned neuroscientist Antonio Damasio explains in his book *The Strange Order of Things*, are not an independent fabrication of the brain. They are, rather, the product of the direct non-intellectual experience that is captured—and perceived—through our body. As Damasio points out "they are the result of a cooperative partnership of body and brain".[3] This notion is consistent with the concept of the "embodied mind" introduced by biologist Francisco Varela, which states that the very structure of reason arises from the human experience sensed through our bodies and brains in an intricate process. This association is inherent in Buddhist psychology. In fact, Varela et al. (1991) in their influential book, *The Embodied Mind*, blend insights from cognitive science and Buddhist theory of mind in order to shed clarity on the meaning of consciousness and the process of cognition.

Therefore, feelings perceived by the embodied mind act as a powerful motivator for the making of human systems and cultures. Specifically, they contribute to shape systems in three ways: as motives for intellectual creation, as monitors of the success or failure of human systems, and as participants in the negotiation and formulation of adjustments required by the systems to adapt.[4]

The neglect of feelings as the subjective experience that triggers cognition is a root cause that explains the current Anthropogenic crisis of perception, the consciousness gap and, therefore, the disconnect between humans and nature. Changing this pattern of behaviour entails a renewed understanding of nature and its interplay with humanity. Therefore, transforming the current human systems requires a profound revision and change of mental models, starting at the subjective experience level. If science does not have the answers yet, where should we look then?

Buddhism and Taoism have long enquired about the subjective experience of nature and how this experience triggers learning and transformation, as we have seen in the theories of Yin–Yang and the Five Elements. The experience of nature—that awakens deep ecological awareness—is a precondition for transforming the way humans and organizations perceive, feel, understand, learn and behave. This chapter argues how sustainability is directly related to the experience of nature as the seed that triggers the process of transformation. In doing so, the chapter unfolds a five-phase nature-based empirical model of cognition and learning, which I named 'T-Qualia'. This model is for people and organizations that aim to transition to the new business paradigm. It is elaborated from the experiential biologic of learning and transformation that is the basis of the Buddhist and Taoist process of cognition (Figure 4.1). Not surprisingly, this bio-logic is

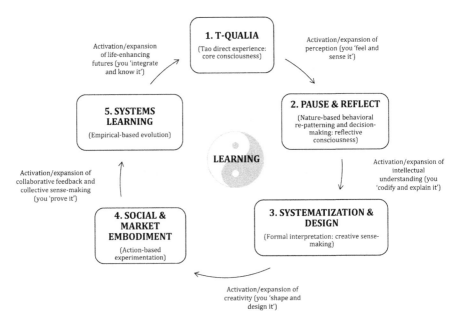

Figure 4.1 T-Qualia model

validated by the latest developments of modern science, particularly in the fields of quantum physics and neuroscience.

Phase 1: T-Qualia (and core consciousness)

Systems thinking requires the ability to feel the nature of life in order to set the interdependencies between its elements. The backbone of Taoism and Buddhism is the mystical experience of natural life and how this experience shapes the felt knowing of the ultimate reality, the realm of wholeness and non-duality: that which quantum physicist David Bohm defined as "an uninterrupted whole in fluid motion".[5] There is, however, a subtle distinction between Taoism and Buddhism. Whereas the Tao-type of experience is based on the direct observation of external nature, in relation to the individual; the Buddha-type of experience focuses on the direct observation of the internal nature of the individual, in relation to external nature. In both cases, the internal and external dimensions of nature synergistically influence each other.

It is fascinating how the spiritual experiences of Taoist and Buddhist mystics developed, millennia ago, such an advanced knowledge of human nature and the universe based on conscious experience. Spirituality, understood as a way of being that flows from a profound non-intellectual experience of reality independent of cultural and historical context,[6] hinges upon the direct perception of the Tao. Consciousness is, in this light, the insightful awareness of this fundamental nature, where the ego surrenders to the Tao and the eco. Our consciousness of the whole enlightens our compassionate Buddha-nature.

Spirituality has been more effective than science in comprehending the nature of consciousness. The reason for this is methodological. The access to mystical experience requires the practice of life experiences based on the principles of oneness, emptiness and impermanence. In Capra and Luisi's words, this practice develops a "profound sense of connectedness, of belonging to the cosmos as a whole—incapable of being adequately expressed in words—often accompanied by a deep sense of awe and wonder together with a feeling of great humility".[7]

These words could vividly describe the feeling of systems thinkers when discovering new connections between the elements of a system. I can think of the unclassifiable Leonardo Da Vinci, a pioneering systems thinker, when he was writing his famous words, "Learn how to see. Recognize that everything connects to everything else". Or Albert Einstein, in his praise of intuition as the source of great scientific achievements.[8] In the study of consciousness, science's greatest difficulty is to precisely capture something that cannot be grasped by the linear pattern of language and, therefore, cannot be measured. Lao Tzu poetically wrote in the *Tao Te Ching*, "The Tao that can be told is not the eternal Tao. The name that can be named is not the eternal name".[9]

The modern scientific study of consciousness, despite the difficulties, is arriving at similar elucidations. The first is the recognition that consciousness is a way of knowing, that is, a cognitive process. The second is the distinction of two types of consciousness: core consciousness, which is the awareness that arises through perceptual, sensory and emotional experience in the present moment, and reflective consciousness, which involves the concept of self-awareness held by a thinking and reflecting subject.[10]

The spiritual experience, as a qualitative, subjective and internal experience, is related to core consciousness. The different instances of this experience are called "qualia", a concept developed by cognitive scientists, "because each state is characterized by a special 'qualitative feel'".[11] I named the nature-based empirical model of decision-making T-Qualia (Tao Qualia) to emphasize that the origin of the process of knowing starts with the Tao-like qualities of our conscious experiences. As sentient beings, the qualities of our experiences determine our intuitions and worldviews, triggering intentionality and action.

The practice of T-Qualia facilitates the non-judgemental conscious experiences of the Tao. This practice activates and expands the practitioner level of perception in two ways. First, it is the motivator that triggers the emergence of a deep ecological awareness and awakens the desire for human–nature reconciliation. This reconciliation happens internally when the individual feels part of nature, or just nature, as a sentient being. The interest in sustainability is a product of this desire.[12] When we feel the interdependent unity of all things, we develop a profound sense of love for nature, which translates to a deep sense of compassion, humility and frugality that conditions our inter-being.

As humans, we recognize our fragility. This process is like an initiation, a sort of eco-spiritual literacy that contains the seed of change. Change is an inside-out job. T-Qualia unleashes the energetic capital that determines the frequency and vibration of the individual. This vibration determines the energetic field that sustains the rest of the nature-based cognitive process (see Figure 4.1). The natural law of vibration determines our perception and, thereby, our state of consciousness.

The second way in which the practice of T-Qualia activates and expands the practitioner level of perception builds upon the first: the practice of T-Qualia breeds a strong desire to make a positive impact in the world. It unleashes the willpower to be of service in the construction of a happier and more sustainable world. His Holiness the Dalai Lama advocates in his book, *Ethics for the New Millennium*, the qualities of spiritual practice—detached from any particular religion—centred on compassion and a sense of responsibility, which brings happiness to both the self and others. Change and transformation require energy, and T-Qualia liberates a set of feelings and emotions—energy in motion—that kick starts the motivation to act.

T-Qualia unleashes a level of potential that fuels a world of possibility that can emerge by design, as a result of our creative potential. This energetic field sustains the design of emerging futures, where the power of anticipation overrides the anxiety of coping with constant adaptation to unpredictable changes. Max Planck, one of the fathers of quantum physics, related the conscious experience as the energetic motivator that shapes matter. In one of his lectures he stated, "all matter originates and exists only by virtue of a force. ... We must assume behind this force the existence of a conscious and intelligent mind. This mind is the matrix of all matter".[13]

It is actually in the design of emerging futures[14] where T-Qualia becomes especially relevant in the context of the Fourth Industrial Revolution. This revolution is seeing unprecedented levels of technological disruptions that are reformulating the meaning of humans and life. The physical, virtual and biological convergence due to new developments in artificial intelligence, quantum computing, nanotechnology or synthetic biology, among others, carry transcendental ethical implications in the increasingly technified human being. To what extent can humans use technological implants to increase their capacities? Can humans become immortal? How can humans use bio and nanotechnology to modify genetics for preventing illnesses? Who will decide this? Who will have access to all these disruptive technologies?

These implications require the development of an advanced state of consciousness that takes a systemic perspective on the analysis of the problem and a compassionate perspective in the design and development of solutions. It is precisely in this area where T-Qualia becomes particularly relevant. Closing the consciousness gap is critical at this stage. Klaus Schwab, the founder of the World Economic Forum, recognizes the risks and the opportunities of the development of these technologies, and launches a global call to develop a moral consciousness that allows the positioning of new technologies in ways that will best serve humanity.[15]

However, I wonder to what extent an extractive economic system dominated by the *homo egonomicus* can develop such a moral compass without a profound shift in consciousness. What is known as the Fourth Industrial Revolution or Industry 4.0 requires a spiritual revolution that reassesses the human–nature disconnect. Morality should stem from a process of deep ecological awareness, anchored in nature-based principles and criteria for the design and application of new technologies at the service of the regeneration and sustainable transformation of our socioeconomic systems.

The Fourth Industrial Revolution can be an extraordinary opportunity if its agents operate from the eco-system in the transition to the new business paradigm. This nonetheless, economics and business education, as well as business organizations, do not yet integrate the T-Qualia dimension in their competency frameworks for educating and training current and future leaders. These organizations have traditionally approached socially responsible decision-making through the satellite intellectual study of business ethics in the frame of the ego-system. This does not mean that there are not responsible leaders, but their education is usually shaped by their life experiences outside the economic system.

The Anthropogenic Covid-19 and the Fourth Industrial Revolution are two contextual variables that signal the urgency for the human species to find its natural place in the planet. T-Qualia, as a nature-based empirical model of decision-making in turbulent times, starts by experiencing the extraordinary interdependence of the whole: a model to redirect the ego at the service of the eco, and not the other way around. Buddhism and Taoism have long enquired about the practice of consciousness. The practice of the following perennial methods,[16] presented in the boxes below, is a doorway to experiencing the inspiring qualities of oneness, interdependence and impermanence with a blissful sense of awe and love for the natural world.

Box 4.1 T-Qualia methods

- **Meditation and mindfulness**: meditation is the cornerstone of Buddhist and Taoist practice. It is the whole vehicular technique used for the transformation of the self towards enlightenment through the Four Noble Truths: identifying suffering and dissatisfaction as the *samsaric* state of our mind; recognizing ignorance as the root cause of our suffering; acknowledging that suffering can be ended; and knowing that there is a way to reconcile ourselves with our true nature. This technique allows developing the compassionate mind, the empty mind that allows the ego to detach from itself as it connects with universal values and places itself in a state of service to others (referring to other human and non-human beings, including the environment). The practice of meditation leads to mindfulness, which is the purposeful non-judgemental practice of attention to the present moment.

  These practices have been largely studied by science, with reported benefits on the reduction of, and coping with, stress, anxiety, pain, and illness. In management, the practice of meditation and mindfulness is associated with increasing levels of creativity and innovation. These practices are increasingly being adopted by business organizations such as Google, General Mills, Goldman Sachs, Nike and Apple. However, most of these corporations invest in these trainings for the purpose of increasing the creativity and innovation capacities of their employees, which is directly correlated to their higher productivity and profitability. The purpose of meditation and mindfulness is to develop wisdom about, and compassion for, the natural and social worlds. Therefore, these practices should not be decoupled from their original purpose, that, applied to organizations, is developing the vision, strategies and initiatives that might guide the organization's transition to the new, sustainable business paradigm.

- **Tai Chi and Qi Gong**: Tai Chi is the embodiment of the Taoist principles through the movement of the body. The soft, curvilinear flowing motion of the body allows to feel and re-perceive oneness, the non-dualistic and impermanent nature of the universe. The practice of oneness through movement activates three levels of energy. First, the energy that inhabits the space or surrounding environment; second, the spiritual energy that motivates purpose; and third, the genetic energy inherited from our ancestors. Tai Chi is often combined with the practice of Qi Gong. Qi Gong represents a life energy cultivation of the body through a set of meditative postures, slow-flowing movements and rhythmic breathing exercises that foster a calm meditative state of mind that releases the energy levels.

- **Elemental nature dives**: Buddhism and Taoism are the result of a deep process of contemplation, observation and interaction between humans and nature. Nature contains all the guiding principles for living a harmonious life, in flowing motion with the Tao. Recurrent immersion in nature includes sitting in silence, walking or hiking. These types of immersion activities foster our connection with our essential being by feeling the beauty, complexity and mystery of life. Further, they reveal truths, principles and insights that we can analogically apply to life-inspired innovations in the fields of management, science and technology. The mindful contemplation of nature can be guided by the Five Elements: enhancing observation through deep forest walks—a popular practice called *shinrin yoku* (forest bathing) in Japan—is related to the wood element; witnessing sunrise and sunsets represents the presence of the fire element; gardening is related to earth element; working with mineral rocks is related to the metal element; and immersing oneself in the fresh waters of rivers, lakes or seas is related to the water element.

- **Geobiology and Feng Shui**: human life has always developed under the influence of earth's natural energies, such as radiation that comes from natural radioactivity and magnetic fields. These environmental energies influence the health and well-being of individuals that inhabit a particular environment. Taoists, based upon the observation of nature, developed Feng Shui, a complex geobiological system that determines the positive influence of spaces on the people that inhabit them. Nowadays, it has become a popular practice all over the world, applied to both houses and organizations' facilities—offices and factories.

- **Learning journeys**: consist of full immersion of individuals into different economic, cultural and organizational contexts. The most life-changing format is travelling to culturally distant countries—the motives for which may be personal leadership development, leisure, studying or work, but in all instances the outcome is a powerful transformation of the individual based on immersive learning. This learning unfolds in five ways: it facilitates the practice of detachment; it challenges your mental models and preconceived worldviews; it allows appreciation of the world's diversity and complexity; it fosters the interaction and adaptation to new cultural and social behaviours; and it tests one's adaptability to unpredictable events. Ancient Taoists and Buddhists called these experiences pilgrimages, and they were aimed at the spiritual awakening of the seeker.

- **Artistic expression**: the development of artistic expression is a Yin-based effective practice to reconnect and cultivate our inherent creativity and intuitive knowledge at the service of the manifestation of our true nature. The practice of Zen has long considered the arts as an essential dimension for human–nature reconciliation to emerge. However, the extractive economy is sustained by an educational system primarily aimed at training individuals to produce and consume and not for artistic disciplines. Humans are often considered a resource, or commodity, among many. In this context, the system has valued linguistic and mathematical competencies over the development of the arts. And the arts are a remarkable way of knowing, complementary to science and spirituality.

Phase 2: Pause and reflect (and reflective consciousness)

Experience alone is a necessary but insufficient element of cognition. To continue with the process of knowing, the second phase requires pausing and reflecting on the quality of the direct experience itself. In this process, individuals and organizations observe their own experience. They do so by identifying and reflecting upon the feelings and emotions that emerged from the experience, and how they are connected to current and emerging value systems and behavioural patterns.

Overall, this is a sense-making exercise that focuses on the intuitive knowledge gained through the experience—the felt knowing—in relation to the context. What does this experience mean and imply to me/us/the organization? What can I/we learn from the experience? How can I/we use the experience for leveraging sustainable change and transformation? This reflective enquiry process allows us to (i) understand the larger system, its elements, interconnections, purpose and behaviours, to develop an intellectual understanding of complex problems and challenges, thus capturing tacit knowledge; (ii) identify cognitive dissonances; (iii) see our place and role in the system; (iv) recognize that we are part of the system we seek to change; (v) generate conversations to examine underlying assumptions and mental models; and (vi) enable a learning environment based upon interaction, psychological safety, trust-building and shared responsibility.

I want to emphasize the point on cognitive dissonance because it is an issue that is widely ignored that generates a lot of frustration when transitioning to the new paradigm. Cognitive dissonance is a concept widely used in psychology in order to explain inconsistency between our beliefs and our actions. This is a tension that arises when we think in one way and act in another. The classic example is when you really believe that smoking is damaging your health but you are unable to quit. The same conflict often happens in sustainability. For example, you know that single-use plastics or fossil fuels are major problems in relation to environmental degradation, but you still consume them. Pause and reflect has a major impact in identifying and observing this process, the first step for seeking ways to resolve this tension. Buddhism has long enquired about the nature of this tension. The first steps of the Dharma Wheel[17] are precisely focused on aligning the right thinking with the right action, and, therefore, increasing consistency throughout our behavioural patterns.

The pause and reflect phase produces an activation and expansion of our reflective consciousness, which involves the cognitive abstraction that leads to the intellectualized understanding of the experience. This abstraction is self-contextualized. That means that it is conducted upon the concept of the self, in which the experience is related to the autobiographical, relational and cultural perspective of the individuals and teams. The outcome of this process is the development of a collective change narrative that connects the current situation with the desired one. The change narrative should be shaped in terms of a theory of transformation[18] that explains how the organization expects to contribute to sustainable transformation.

Box 4.2 Pause and reflect methods

- **Real-time journaling and note taking**: this is an individual exercise that is conducted right after the T-Qualia practice with the main objective being to write down the feelings and emotions that have just emerged as a result of the practice. This exercise of codification facilitates the integration of feelings into an organized thought process that will be the basis for aligning the creative process with the Tao principles of the experience.

- **Retreats**: these are a collective method aimed at working on the core and reflective consciousness of individuals and teams alike. They can include a wide variety of activities, such as T-Qualia methods, team-building initiatives, systems visualization workshops, scenario foresight and future-thinking workshops. Retreats are normally conducted in beautiful natural settings that foster disconnection and mindful presence of both individuals and teams, far from the distractions of the inherent busyness of daily life.

- **Communities of practice**: organic and self-organizing groups of people that are informally bound together by a shared motivation and expertise around a common objective or enterprise.[19] These communities aim at sharing the T-Qualia experiences and reflecting upon them in free-flowing creative ways that foster new approaches to incorporate the natural laws into the process of knowing. Although this concept is relatively new in management, communities of practice have long existed. It is, for instance, one of the three jewels of the Buddhist learning process: *Sangha* or community, *Buddha*—the ultimate reality or *Buddhahood*—and *Dharma*, or the teachings of the Buddha.

Phase 3: Systematization and design

Phases 1 and 2 aim at raising the awareness—core and reflective consciousness—of individuals and teams of the need to regenerate and sustainably transform the economy. The underlying assumption of a nature-based theory of transformation that I postulate in this book is that if you feel and see the world as if you are part of it, you treat it better. Transformative storytelling, *per se*, does not change reality, but it does change our embodied mind's perception of reality, and by changing this perception we change ourselves, which somehow changes reality.

But this "somehow" needs further elaboration. How will our theory of transformation allow us to learn and change the system, as well as ourselves? This exploration depends on the ability of individuals and teams to systematize the theory into the organization and its ecosystem. This phase activates and expands the process of co-creation among the different stakeholders involved in finding sustainable solutions and innovations. Systematization and design is the intermediate phase where the *yin*-based previous phases—working within the abstract realm of the invisible and intangible—give way to the *yang*-orientated phases of making the intangible tangible.

This process requires three sequential steps. First, it requires a purposeful formal interpretation of the narrative that persuades and engages the rest of stakeholders. Second, it needs the embedding of the theory of transformation into the strategies, processes and operations of the organization. And third, it requires the adoption of nature-based design frameworks, mostly focused on principles, that help shape new products, services, activities, projects, programmes, policies or any other nature-based solutions aimed at regenerating and transforming the system. Box 4.3 briefly describes some of the methods used in systematization and design.

Box 4.3 Systematization and design methods

- **Regenerative design**: this is a multi-disciplinary whole systems approach to design aimed at restoring and revitalizing equitable systems that support the co-evolution of human and natural systems in a partnered relationship. Biologist Daniel C. Wahl offers a grand synthesis in his book, *Designing Regenerative Cultures* (2016), pivoting around four interrelated dimensions: living systems thinking, biologically inspired design, health and resilience and transformative innovation.

- **Permaculture**: this is a set of design principles centred on whole systems thinking that simulates or imitates the patterns and resilient features observed in natural ecosystems. David Holmgren first described the twelve principles of permaculture most commonly referred to in his book, *Permaculture: Principles and Pathways*

Beyond Sustainability (2002). These principles include observing and interacting; catching and storing energy; obtaining a yield; applying self-regulation and accepting feedback; using and valuing renewable resources and services; producing no waste; designing from patterns to details; integrating rather than segregating; using small and slow solutions; using and valuing diversity; using edges and valuing the marginal; and creatively using and responding to change.

- **Biomimicry**: according to the Biomimicry Institute, this can be defined as an approach to innovation that seeks sustainable solutions to human challenges by emulating nature's time-tested patterns and strategies. Janine Benyus, author of *Biomimicry: Innovation Inspired by Nature*, defines her approach as "a new discipline that studies nature's best ideas and then imitates these designs and processes to solve human problems". The goal is to create products, processes, and policies—new ways of living—that are well adapted to life on earth over the long haul. Biomimicry is a multi-disciplinary design approach that benchmarks nature as a model, a measure and a mentor, following life's principles of adapting to changing conditions; being locally attuned and responsive; using life friendly chemistry; being resource efficient; integrating development with growth; and evolving to survive.

- **Circular economy**: according to the Ellen MacArthur Foundation, is a framework for building an economy that is restorative and regenerative by design. It is based on three core principles: design out waste and pollution; keep products and materials in use; and regenerate natural systems. The concept is aimed at eliminating waste and the continual use of resources, building blocks of the current degenerative and extractive economic system. Circular systems employ the closed loop of recycling, making, using, reusing, and remaking, thus minimizing the use of resource inputs and the creation of waste, pollution and carbon emissions.

Phase 4: Social and market embodiment

The final output of Phase 3 is to turn ideas into tangible nature-based solutions. As this process is embedded in VUCA contexts (volatile, uncertain, complex and ambiguous), the million-dollar question for most organizations is: how can we deliver continuous life-sustaining value to our customers in shorter time-to-market spans? Traditionally, companies have assumed that resource-consuming analytical market research was the key to reducing the risk from building wrong things. Thereby, it was the prevailing cost-efficient approach in research and development processes—often referred to as the waterfall approach.

However, this approach may not fit the urgency inherent in creating and delivering nature-based solutions to the market. The design of nature-based solutions is developed with the expectation that there will be a demand for that solution out there—be it a product, a service, a project, a programme or a policy—and a sense of urgency that comes with Anthropogenic rush. The emerging environmentally conscious consumer is driving major trends in the design and development of life-sustaining solutions, such as renewable energies, reduction of single-use plastics, organic foods, sustainable fashion, positive construction or green cities. The social and market embodiment (the acceptance of the market) depends on the following question: to what extent are nature-based solutions acceptable, accessible, available and scalable?

The answer largely lies in the practice of experimentation, a fundamental idea that is inherent to the empirical nature of Buddhism and Taoism. Both thought systems ground learning on experience, by means of observation and also experimentation. One of the main principles of Eastern mysticism is "try it out and see whether it works for you"; an empowering statement detached from any dogma or outer truth. You implement it and prove whether it works or it doesn't. Experimentation in complex, uncertain and unpredictable environments requires *wuwei*, the natural real-time decision-making based on the interplay between the absolute, intuitive and explicit knowledge available. The reason is because, in such contexts where data is limited or unreliable, individuals and organizations can only ground their decision-making on intuition, rooted in the connections that are given in experience.

The solution is validated by the market through experimentation as a feedback mechanism rooted in the interaction between the solution, the target users and the structures that sustain that relationship and the system(s). In this market-based context, this phase fosters the activation and expansion of collaborative feedback and collective sense-making. The solution is tested by means of the launch of iterative rounds—called sprints—of small-scale pilots that accelerate the feedback loop of definition, design, release and provision of feedback from the market. This approach is the basis of adaptability and agility, as organizations today struggle with quickly reacting to, and anticipating, rapidly changing consumer demands by replacing planning with experimentation. Box 4.4 illustrates some of the most used experimentation approaches.

Box 4.4 Market embodiment methods

- **Agile**: agile development, or agility in general started with an Agile Manifesto[20] in 2001 as an approach to fast-paced software development and an alternative to the waterfall model, but it is also used in any business-related context. It is based on iterative development, where requirements and solutions evolve through collaboration between self-organizing cross-functional teams. Scrum—a framework for helping teams and organizations generate value through adaptive solutions of complex problems—is one of the most used agile methods—along with Kanban—a scheduling system to improve manufacturing efficiency—and Lean—a management approach that supports continuous improvement. Agile methodologies allow focusing on delivering customer value in the shortest time by iterating fast feedback loops of market iterations, assessing and reviewing on the basis of what worked well, what could be improved and what the team commits to in the next iteration.

- **Growth hacking**: a process of rapid experimentation across marketing channels and product development to identify the most efficient ways to grow a business. It is especially used by startups as a way to creatively test strategies to deliver stakeholder value through cost-efficient experimentation.

- **Rapid prototyping**: mainly applied to industrial product development, is a set of techniques used to quickly manufacture a scale model of a physical part or assembly using 3D printing or additive layer manufacturing, in which 3D parts are built up in successive layers of material under computer control.

Phase 5: Systems learning and transformative adaptation

Systems learning is a type of organizational learning that emerges in complex contexts by studying the interrelationships between the elements of the system and between the systems that are interconnected. When the organization transitions to the new business paradigm of sustainable transformation, it needs to learn how, and to what extent, it is contributing to that transformation.

At this stage of learning for transformation, a systems thinker is becoming a *Boddhisattva*, that is, a person who is on the path towards *Buddhahood*. This is, in other words, a 21st-century hero or change-maker who is motivated by the compassionate wish to help others (in Buddhism, this is reflected in the term *bodhicitta*). As a participator, the performance of the change maker happens in a context of mutual causality with other stakeholders—the community and society at large—in the organization, and in the larger systems the organization operates with (social and eco-logic). Causality, according to Buddhist scholar Joanna Macy, is

> usually defined as the interrelation of cause and effect, is about how things happen, how change occurs, how events relate. The Buddhist term Dharma carries the same meaning. It also refers to the Buddha's teachings as a whole ... for the ways that life is understood and lived are rooted in causal assumptions.[21]

Proaction and reaction to the feedback received through the relation of mutual causality dynamically emerge as phases of the T-Qualia learning model unfold. This happens in a *samsaric* context characterized by the willpower of the change-maker to relieve Anthropogenic tensions and transform the system. To do so, the change-maker needs to master the skills of wisdom and compassion, skills that are central to the *Boddhisattva*.

The *Boddhisattva* appears in the Shambala[22] teachings in the figure of the Shambala warrior. The Buddhist scholar, Chogyam Trungpa, claims the relevance of these teachings today, as they are founded on the premise that there is basic human wisdom to solve the world's problems. Warriorship, in this Tibetan context, means bravery and fearlessness. The change-maker, as a participator in the *samsaric* system, does need courage and bravery in his duty to serve, in order to deal with entropic forces like the feeling of suffering, managing uncertainty, resistance to change and frustration with unmet expectations.

In the context of the Anthropocene, the human–nature reconnection in times of planetary degradation requires great courage. The capacity of the Shambala warrior to perform and learn is built upon two critical skills. Buddhist scholar and systems thinker Joanna Macy, who brought the Shambala prophecy into life, calls them weapons. "One weapon is compassion; the other weapon is wisdom, or insight into the radical interdependence of all phenomena [...] . One is fearless experience of pain in the world. The other is insight into the radical connectivity of all life".[23]

The embodied compassionate and insightful mind of the Boddhisattva is, thus, critical for successfully managing the transformation. Transformation in a *samsaric* context is subject to the "*karma* trap". *Karma*, or conditioned action, is the active principle of *samsara*. It is an action arising from a motive that is implicitly seeking a result, the consequence of the action, which always requires the necessity for further action. Humans are involved in *karma* when they interfere with the world in such a way that they are compelled to go on interfering, inspired by the will to solve problems. When the goal is to transform a system, *karma* automatically brings the need to control the system.

This need to control the system raises questions such as: to what extent are we getting the expected results? To what extent have our actions worked? Why? As long as we have permanent expectations we will have a need for control, and, therefore, we cannot get rid of *samsara*. *Karma* is, in this way, as Alan Watts vividly describes, the fate of everyone who "tries to be God. Man lays a trap for the world in which he himself gets caught".[24] The first loop of learning takes place in the *karma* trap. There is learning in knowing whether our actions have worked, how and why. It is a single-loop type of learning (see Figure 4.2), which focuses on correcting errors without questioning existing structures or underlying assumptions.

But, taking the participator as a living system, that is, a person or an organization, that operates in impermanent and interdependent contexts, the question that arises after the intervention is: what did we learn so far? Have our actions changed behaviour? The participator's insight is constantly emerging as long as she or he is interacting with the system; this insight is being compounded throughout all phases in mutual causality between the participator and the system observed and intervened in. In any of the phases, learning happens when there is a modification of behaviour on the basis of previous experience.[25] This type of learning, called double-loop learning (see Figure 4.2), questions the validity of previous underlying structures and mental models, and assesses profound changes in the system correlated to previous transformative actions. This approach renders a more adaptive effect of learning to contextual changes. It is the fit-for-purpose approach when the overall goal of organizations is adaptation.

Nevertheless, the complexity and acceleration of change, along with the emergence of new systemic properties and insight, can make us question the relevance and worthiness of what we have been doing in applying our theory of transformation. Deep enquiry takes place, with questions such as: are we doing the right thing? How do we know what is right? What does the system need in this moment? This type of learning, which involves a higher level of abstraction, is called triple-loop learning (Figure 4.2). It was first conceptualized as "deutero learning" by the anthropologist Gregory Bateson,[26] which is about developing the "learn-how", the organizational ability of learning how to learn.

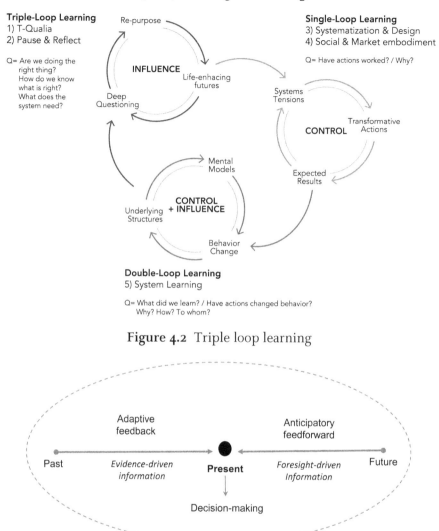

Figure 4.2 Triple loop learning

Figure 4.3 Transformative adaptation: an adaptation of Hodgson's "anticipatory present moment" (Source: Hodgson, 2020)

Systems learning encompasses the three learning loops in the context of mutual causality and the *karma* trap. In Phase 5, the process of deep enquiry focuses on the meta-learning that is captured in the present moment (Figure 4.3), nurtured by evidence-driven information from the past (adaptive feedback) and foresight-driven information from the future (anticipatory feedforward) alike. This view is consistent with Anthony Hodgson's conceptualization of the "anticipatory present moment", in which the system is responsive to influences from the future as well as adaptive to responses from the past.[27]

In this context, the systems thinker integrates both types of incoming information and expands his or her ability to perceive and envision the future in relation with the past. It is not an isolated act of imagination or wishful thinking. Rather, it is the outcome of the past and future knowledge that resides in the participator's embodied mind during the mindful experience of the present moment. This phase of learning is a precondition for the transformative adaptation of the system. The system not only reacts to changes in the context-reality but it proactively transforms reality. Transformative adaptation is a process that expands the capacity to redefine the purpose of the system and to design life-enhancing futures that are incubated in the mind-like realm of possibility and opportunity. It is the process that triggers systems transformation by design.

Knowing that you are learning, learning how to learn, is a syntropic force for the systems thinker. The thinker (the change agent or *Boddhisattva*) needs to be at peace and at rest with the system, and with herself. That means that she needs to find ease and comfort in *samsara*, feeling the suffering and the joy within all nested systems. Only within this compassionate mindset can she do work that reconnects.[28] She no longer becomes obsessed with controlling the system, and instead she focuses her energy in optimizing her influence on the system, thereby honouring her role as participator. The power of the *Boddhisattva*, or the Shambala warrior, unfolds when she is detached from control and thrown to the natural flow and creative power of the *wuwei*, the freedom of interdependent action that influences the system in a transformative way. She has learned how to identify the leverage points and how to influence the system to transform it. With joy.

Notes

1 The sociologist Talcott Parsons affirms this idea by stating that the brain was "the primary organ for controlling complex operations, notably manual skills, and coordinating visual and auditory information ... and above all was the organic basis of the capacity to learn and manipulate symbols". In "Evolutionary Universals in Society", *American Sociological Review*, 29(3) (1964), 339–357; and "Social Systems and the Evolution of Action Theory", *Ethics*, 90(4) (1980), 608–611. Quoted from Damasio, A. (2018). *The Strange Order of Things*. Pantheon Books: New York.

2 Classic, Cartesian-based science has long dismissed feelings in the study of objectifiable phenomena. Classical science, eminently shaped during the Enlightenment, traditionally emphasized the rationalization of the intellectual thinking process as the basis of knowledge and decision-making.

3 Damasio, A. (2018). *The Strange Order of Things*. Pantheon Books: New York, p. 12.

4 Ibid.

5 Bohm, D. (1987). *Unfolding Meaning: A weekend of dialogue with David Bohm*. Ark: London.

6 Capra, F. & Luisi, P.L. (2014) p. 278.

7 Ibid.

8 In *Conversations with Einstein* by Alexander Moszkowski (1970).

9   Capra affirms "the use of complexity theory and the systematic analysis of first-person conscious experience will be crucial in formulating a proper science of consciousness".

10 Capra, F. & Luisi, P.L. (2014) pp. 268–270.

11 Capra, F. & Luisi, P.L. (2014) p. 260.

12 I have personally observed the relationship between T-Qualia and the interest on sustainability in personal interviews with my students of the Master in Sustainable Business & Innovation at EADA Business School, where I assessed their motivation on the topic.

13 From a speech given by Max Planck in Florence, Italy, in 1944, entitled "Das Wesen der Matterie". Quoted in Gregg Baden's book *The Divine Matrix* (Carlsbad: Hay House, 2007) p. 211.

14 The design of emergent futures includes the disciplines of futures thinking or foresight thinking, but it goes one step further as it also entails experimentation.

15 Schwab, K. (2017). *The Fourth Industrial Revolution*. Random House.

16 This box just includes a brief description of some of the most recognized T-Qualia practices related to Eastern mysticism; it does not aim to include all of them.

17 It is also called "The Noble Eightfold Path", an early summary of the path of Buddhist practices leading to liberation from *samsara* (*The Heart of Buddha's Teaching*, Thich Nhat Hanh).

18 Michael Patton, in his book *Blue Marble Evaluation* (Guilford Press, 2019), explains the theory of transformation as follows,

> A theory of change specifies how a project or program attains desired outcomes. Transformation is not a project. It is multi-dimensional, multi-faceted, and multilevel, cutting across national borders and intervention silos, across sectors and specialized interests, connecting local and global, and sustaining across time. A theory of transformation incorporates and integrates multiple theories of change operating at many levels that, knitted together, explain how major systems transformation occurs.

19 Wenger, E.C. & Snyder, W.M. (200). Communities of practice: the organizational frontier. *Harvard Business Review* (January–February).

20 See agilemanifesto.org.

21 Macy, J. (1991). *Mutual Causality in Buddhism and General Systems Theory: The Dharma of natural systems*. State University of New York Press.

22 Shambala is portrayed in Tibetan Buddhism as a legendary kingdom that was a source of learning and culture, governed through the two fundamental principles of compassion and wisdom (*Shambala: The sacred path of the warrior*, Chogyam Trungpa).

23 See Macy, J. & Brown, M. (2014). *Coming Back to Life*. New Society, pp. 69–71.

24 Watts, A. (1989). *The Way of Zen*. Vintage Books.

25 Capra, F. & Luisi, P.L. (2014), p. 255.

26 Visser, Max (2003). Gregory Bateson on deutero-learning and double bind: A brief conceptual history. *Journal of the History of the Behavioral Sciences*, 39, 269–278. 10.1002/jhbs.10112.

27 According to Hodgson, "anticipation implies deciding what to do now in terms of what is perceived to be the consequence of that action at some later time than the immediate now and in radically changed circumstances", in *Systems Thinking for a Turbulent World* (Routledge, 2020).

28 The "work that reconnects" is an approach to grow courage, resilience and solidarity for the healing of our world, developed by Joanna Macy.

References

Benyus, J. (2002). *Biomimicry: Innovation inspired by nature*. William Morrow.

Bohm, D. (1987). *Unfolding Meaning: A weekend of dialogue with David Bohm*. Ark: London.

Capra, F. & Luisi, P.L. (2014). *The Systems View of Life: A unifying vision*. Cambridge University Press.

Dalai Lama (2001). *Ethics for the New Millennium*. Riverhead.

Damasio, A. (2018). *The Strange Order of Things*. Pantheon Books: New York.

Hodgson, A. (2020). *Systems Thinking for a Turbulent World*. Routledge.

Holmgren, D. (2002). *Permaculture: Principles and pathways beyond sustainability*. Holmgren Design Services.

Macy, J. (1991). *Mutual Causality in Buddhism and General Systems Theory: The Dharma of natural systems*. State University of New York Press.

Macy, J. & Brown, M. (2014). *Coming Back to Life*. New Society.

Moszkowski, A. (1970). *Conversations with Einstein*. Horizon Press.

Schwab, K. (2017). *The Fourth Industrial Revolution*. Random House.

Thich Nhat Hanh (1998). *The Heart of the Buddha's Teaching*. Parallax Press.

Trungpa, C. (2007). *Shambala: The sacred path of the warrior*. Shambala.

Varela, F., Thompson, E., & Rosch, E. (1991). *The Embodied Mind*. Cambridge, MA: MIT Press.

Visser, M. (2003). Gregory Bateson on deutero-learning and double bind: A brief conceptual history. *Journal of the History of the Behavioral Sciences*, 39, 269–278.

Watts, A. (1989). *The Way of Zen*. Vintage Books.

Chapter 5

The Zen Business model

From metaphysics to sustainable management

For centuries, Taoist metaphysics have been applied to a wide array of disciplines, such as medicine, martial arts, self-development and geobiology. All these disciplines share a fundamental idea: the salutogenic application of the universal principles of the Tao into the methodological domains of human health and well-being in dynamic interaction with nature. This approach is holistic and integrative. It explores the human–nature interactions in mutual causality.

For example, traditional Chinese medicine explores health in constant balance and imbalance with nature's energy flows through the human body. Martial arts apply Tao principles through a set of techniques that seek body energy optimization through movement. Self-development applies the natural behaviour of cosmic energies, from Chinese astrology, to personal behaviour and self-awareness across time, in a discipline called the Studies of Life. And geobiology explores the interactions between humans, physical spaces and the surrounding environmental energies of the biosphere.

The application of Tao metaphysics into organizational behaviour and development is, however, a road much less explored. Its application has been approached through the implications that some principles and concepts—such as the Yin–Yang—have in management, especially in leadership and well-being at work. But the systemic application of Taoism to sustainable management and transformation is unchartered territory, with extraordinary potential for the human-nature reconnection.

By systemic application I mean the direct application of the Yin–Yang and the Five Elements, Tao's overarching systems theories, to the process of holistic value creation in organizations. The result of such systemic application is the Zen Business model.[1] I define the Zen Business as a biomimetic systems model of sustainable business management and transformation for entrepreneurs and organizations that aim at creating and delivering social, environmental and economic value.

This chapter explores the rationale of the model, its functioning through the five corporate stars and its dynamics as an adaptive process-based methodology. In this chapter, I also present the five organizational archetypes as a tool to diagnose dominant patterns of behaviour, and the Zen Business wheel as the tool to guide the organizational process of transformation.

Biomimetic analogy: the rationale behind the model

The Zen Business model is designed under three premises. The first premise is based on the assumption that organizations are living systems,[2] a key feature of the new business paradigm. As such, an organization is a human system, which is hierarchically nested within other systems, such as communities, society and the environment. The defining component of the organization-as-a-system is people—individuals and teams—whose behavioural patterns, relationships and processes factor in the whole self-regulatory performance of the system.

The second premise assumes that universal natural laws can be embedded in organizational development and transformation by design.[3] The underlying assumption here is that organizations that integrate nature-based developmental processes are organically adaptive, resilient and anticipatory to internal and external drivers of change. This applies to "biomimetic analogy", the method I used to design the model, which is based on applying the biological patterns observed in natural laws to the Zen Business model. Taoists developed a branch of metaphysics that is precisely related to the analogical observation of human–nature interaction, called the Studies of Life, applied to personal development.

In the Zen Business model, the analogical behavioural patterns observed in the individuals are systematically associated with the energy-based behavioural patterns of the Five Elements. Humans are considered a small universe—the Taoist way of referring to a living system—that is mutually influenced by the metaphysical heavenly energies and the physical earthly energies alike. By nested extrapolation, organizational development biomimetically behaves following the same elemental-based patterns that explain personal development and self-knowledge (Figure 5.1).

The field within the Studies of Life that enquires into the nature, factors and dynamics of an individual's harmony and well-being is called *Bazi* (八字) or *Saju* (사주) (in Mandarin and Korean, respectively), often translated into English as the four pillars. *Bazi*, or *Saju*, is a systemic method aimed at decoding and interpreting the human being's cosmic energies

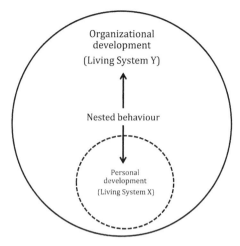

Figure 5.1 Analogical interpretation

displayed at birth that explain his behaviour in life based on the theory of the Yin–Yang and the Five Elements. Human behaviour is, thus, explained by the relationship between the elements, or dynamic energies, observed in nature—Wood, Fire, Earth, Metal and Water. The Five Elements are analogically correlated with the five areas that qualify for harmonization in the life of the individual, called the five stars: career and social recognition, knowledge, social (or interpersonal) relations, expression and money, respectively. Nature's Five Elements—or dynamic energies—also exist in the individual from a behavioural point of view.[4]

As a *Saju* scholar and practitioner, I am fascinated by the scope and depth of application of this method to behavioural science. Particularly, *Saju* contributes to gaining a thorough understanding of the dynamic natural energies that influence a person's personality, motivations and life experiences. As a tool of self-awareness and cognition, *Saju* provides a detailed framework for the practice of *wuwei*, or natural decision-making. *Wuwei*-based decisions are aligned with the natural cycles and flow of life, which optimize the individual *qi* energy levels as a syntropic force that unleashes the creative agency in individuals, teams and organizations.

The third premise of the Zen Business is that value means, for organizations, what *qi*, or vital energy, means for individuals. The health of a business organization in the new business paradigm depends on its capacity to identify, create, deliver, sustain and recognize the value it generates for its stakeholders. Value is the vital energy that makes a company healthy, flourishing and prosperous. The Zen Business is a value optimization process based upon the dynamic and interdependent relations between and among the five corporate stars, as is explained in detail in the section titled "Model dynamics", below.

The five corporate stars

Analogical correlation between the five individual stars and the five corporate stars

The Zen Business correlates the Five Elements associated with the five stars from the individual level with the corporate level, as we can see in Table 5.1 These stars correspond to different interrelated areas of value and the proper functioning of the system depends on the balance and harmony between these areas. The knowledge star (Fire) is associated with the corporate star of Human Leadership; the social relations star (Earth) corresponds to the corporate star of Stakeholders; the expression star (Metal) corresponds to the corporate star of Marketing and Innovation; the money star (Water) corresponds to the corporate star of Full Profit, and the career star (Wood) corresponds to the corporate star Brand Impact Recognition. In line with the logic of how the Five Elements work, the balanced relationship between these five corporate stars is fundamental to the performance and harmony of the organization.

Elemental-based behaviour of the five corporate stars

The analogical interpretation of the model biomimics the natural patterns of behaviour of the Five Elements into the behaviour of the five corporate

Table 5.1 Elements-based behaviour of the five corporate stars

Five stars	Five Elements	Elements' behaviour	Five corporate stars
Knowledge	Fire	Light. Exploding outward. Diffusion, prosperity	Human Leadership
Social relations	Earth	Balance, decline, transition, transformation	Stakeholders
Expression	Metal	Cutting, reforming, construction, reconstruction, execution. Creativity	Marketing and Innovation
Money	Water	Vitality, pregnancy, life	Full Profit
Career	Wood	Sprout, growth. Expansion	Brand Impact Recognition

stars. Fire is the energy that represents the knowledge star. It symbolizes light; its behaviour is of diffusion, exploding outwards. It warms up and inspires all around, a precious resource. It is associated with knowledge, understood in its wide meaning: the integration of absolute knowledge with tacit and explicit knowledge that facilitates self-awareness. In the Zen Business, the integration of these three levels of knowledge is embedded as the *Human Leadership star*, which reflects the purpose and values of the organization, the strategic compass that starts with why the organization exists, and what the organization stands for.

Earth is the balancing energy, the transitioning energy between polarities, between growth and decline. It symbolizes transformation and it nurtures all sentient beings. It is associated with social relations, so it's grounded on people. In the Feng Shui compass (*luo pan* in Mandarin), which features the diagram of the Five Elements, Earth is the central element that connects all other elements. It is represented by the *Stakeholders' star*, as stakeholders include all the different actors that, with different roles, participate in the co-creation of value in the organization with the goal of achieving the higher purpose.

Metal is the energy that shapes, playing a transformational role in the making and formatting of products and technologies. Metal cuts, reforms, builds and rebuilds. Metal embeds the power of action, execution and communication. It is associated with expression in all its forms, including creativity as the energy that fuels any form of expression. Metal is represented by the *Marketing and Inovation star*, the frontline value generating functions of any organization that play a decisive role in the satisfaction of customers' needs and problems through tailored solutions.

Water represents life, vitality, health. Taoists have always symbolized the Tao as a river that constantly flows down, embracing all its living creatures while adapting its course to the topography it encounters. The *Full Profit star* reflects the vitality of the organization, that is, how the organization contributes to its own sustainability and of the society and the planet. It plays a supportive role, as the energy incubator that allows the organization to operate, grow and flourish.

Wood is the element of sprouting, growth and expansion. It represents the vegetable realm, which constantly seeks expansion in the direction of light. Wood reflects the growth principle embedded in both human and nature. It is associated with the Brand Impact Recognition star, in which the organization becomes aware of how it is growing. Growth is understood as impact on society and the environment. This star realises its value as it develops the capacity to evaluate and communicate the results of its actions and business activities. When this know-how is internalized and externalized, the corporate brand is recognized by the impact it generates, which serves as the foundation for learning and adaptation that nourishes Fire, the Human Leadership star.

The five corporate stars: definition, function, and value

Human Leadership: Fire

Human Leadership is the enabling and empowering influence that change agents exert on their teams and collaborators for the identification and fulfilment of a higher purpose. This higher purpose energizes the organization and its ecosystem by providing meaning, values-driven identity, clarity and a focused strategy for operational decision-making and action. It is the Fire that keeps the organization burning, intrinsically motivated and hungry to make a positive impact.

The term "human" encompasses the virtuous qualities of the self-aware human being: wisdom, compassion and humility. Wisdom is related to the systemic realization of interdependence, belonging and the overarching role of the organization in the community, society and the planet. Compassion refers to placing people's well-being and concerns at the centre of organizational decision-making. It entails a profound appreciation of connection, which is reflected in the genuine practice of gratefulness and the attitudinal development of service to others. Humility is grounded in the beginner's mind. It requires the confidence to recognize one's weaknesses and strengths, courage to trust oneself and others, curiosity to constantly nurture a learning mindset and a disciplined respect for others, regardless of titles or job positions.

Human Leadership in the model is consistent with related human systems approaches to leadership, such as systems leadership,[5] values-driven leadership,[6] servant leadership[7] and humble leadership.[8]

The operational function of this corporate star is to set and define four interrelated processes that provide meaning, structure organizational behaviour and frame the mental models of that behaviour (Figure 5.2).

- **Higher purpose**: this is the fundamental reason why the organization exists, its transcendental nature. The *raison d'etre.* Higher purpose is the answer to questions such as: why does the organization exist? What for? What do we want to offer to the world? It's *higher* because it transcends profit maximization, by including a sustainability related purpose of contribution towards society and/or the environment. Authors such as Raj Sisodia,[9] Simon Sinek,[10] Daniel Pink[11] and Richard Barrett,[12] among others, define purpose as a powerful intrinsic motivator that correlates with higher levels of organizational performance.

- **Mission**: this is the strategy and goals set for achieving the higher purpose. How do you expect to achieve the higher purpose? What is your strategy? And your goals? Strategizing the higher purpose facilitates integrating sustainability at the core of business activity, beyond often satellite functions such as corporate social responsibility or philanthropic initiatives. The mission elucidates the theory of change—how the organization expects to generate positive change—and it guides sustainable business decision-making.

- **Vision**: this is the mid- or long-term desired scenario that mentally positions the organization at the place it wants to be. What do you want to become? Where do you see the organization in ten years from now? Vision paints a visual landscape that motivationally reminds employees and stakeholders that they are putting their energy into creating an impactful organization.

- **Values**: these are the principles of behaviour that illustrate and guide what is most important for the people in the organization. What do we value most to carry out our work creatively, efficiently and satisfactorily to achieve our higher purpose? What do we stand for? What values should guide our decisions? Values define the DNA of the organization; they shape the organization's personality and set the foundation for creating an impactful culture.

Human Leadership is the first phase in moving towards sustainable transformation. Through a developmental capacity to sense and perceive the world, Human Leadership identifies the value that the company aims for its stakeholders. Human leaders are able to shine, share the fire and engage others, persuading stakeholders to align with the organizational purpose and values. When this alignment happens, there is a stakeholder–organization fit. This fitness is key for attracting, keeping and nurturing the talent of the organization. This talent feels compelled by the sustainable value proposition that the organization communicates in this corporate star.

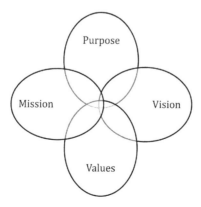

Figure 5.2 Human Leadership star tools

Stakeholders: Earth

The Stakeholders' star represents the organizational ability to successfully engage, nurture and balance the different stakeholders' interests through a shared value proposition grounded in the mutual aspiration of fulfilling the higher purpose. This star involves all actors that intervene in the value cycle and that have a direct or indirect impact on the company's operations: employees, suppliers, shareholders and impact investors, customers, communities, outside collaborators, and the environment (yes, the environment is a critical actor in the company!).

Nurturing this star requires the adoption of mutually beneficial strategies (*win–win*) bringing together the organization and its business partners or stakeholders. This process requires seeing the interconnections between stakeholders' interests with a high degree of empathy, respect and emotional intelligence, which is the basis of any successful collaboration. The main function here is to identify and assess stakeholders' relationships, define the mutual influence on the value creation process and determine the expected impact on both sides of the collaboration. This can be done by applying the following tools (Figure 5.3):

- **Stakeholders' mapping**: the identification of actors is done through the principle of mutual causality; this means that the company identifies the actors that form its ecosystem by assessing the nature and quality of their relationships. This includes internal stakeholders, such as employees and shareholders, and external ones, such as suppliers, impact investors, customers, the community, government agencies, media, unions, and the environment. This exercise can be done in combination with the current and the desired stakeholders. The criteria are set by the degree of alignment and fitness with the organization's higher purpose and values.

- **Definition of shared value propositions**: once the appropriate actors have been identified, the function of the star is to integrate and associate with those who (i) fit with the company's higher purpose, mission and core values, and that (ii) contribute to co-creating and generating social, environmental, emotional and economic value for the ecosystem. Key questions to be answered are: what is the shared value proposition for our stakeholders? How do we attract and engage them, such as employees, investors and suppliers? For this, it is important to define the expected value that the company offers and requires from each stakeholder, which can be assessed by applying contribution analysis. To this end, the higher purpose, mission and values act as a compass that sets the criteria for selection, recruitment and assessment of stakeholders, ensuring its harmonious alignment to the organization's higher purpose and values.

Figure 5.3 Stakeholders' star tools

- **Holistic impact estimation**: this is a critical strategy for ensuring the organization is consistent with its overarching goal to achieve the higher purpose through estimating the expected impact by design, from the beginning. This is an ex-ante exercise where the organization estimates the expected impact of its business activities and operations, by stakeholders and value dimensions: social, environmental, economic and emotional. This assessment internalizes all costs and benefits that derive from business operations, thereby disabling the assumed social and environmental externalities characteristic of the old business paradigm.

The Stakeholders' star is the second phase in the journey towards sustainable transformation. It is the corporate star that attracts and nurtures the talent that the organization needs in order to collaboratively create value for the customers and the rest of the targeted stakeholders. This star defines and shapes the tribe, the living system, with given names and surnames, which are critical to creating the market-based solutions that will be embodied by society and the environment in the marketing and innovation star. The Stakeholders' star reminds us that in order to be competitive in the market, we first need to think and act collaboratively in the organizational eco-system.

The function of this star is consistent with Edward Freeman's stakeholder theory[13] and Michael Porter and Mark Kramer's concept of shared value.[14]

Marketing and Innovation: Metal

Marketing and Innovation reflects the ability of the organization to wholly express its creativity for researching, designing, developing and marketing sustainable solutions. Solutions are developed in terms of products, services or any other interventions aimed at satisfying unmet needs, solving problems and/or improving customer experiences efficiently.

This star considers Marketing and Innovation as two complementary and interdependent functions of the same process of value delivery. This is due to the centrality of the primary target of any business organization: the customer.[15] This interdependency is a systemic opportunity to incentivize the collaboration between technically orientated business units such as research, design, operations and production (traditionally focused on achieving standardization) with socially orientated units such as marketing, communication and commercialization (traditionally focused on customization or personalization).

The function of Marketing and Innovation in the Zen Business model is twofold. On the one hand, it ensures that the brand value proposition is people-focused and delivered to the market in a timely fashion in contexts of high volatility, complexity and uncertainty. On the other hand, and at the same time, it ensures that solutions are purpose-driven and regenerative by design in all supply and demand phases of the value cycle. Both functions can be achieved through the synergistic combination of agile and human-centric development of solutions that are designed and produced according to principles based on nature and circularity. These tools are the following (Figure 5.4).

- **Human-centric design**: this is an approach to complex problem-solving that empowers teams to design products, services, systems and solutions that address the core needs of those people who experience the problem. It is widely used in the design of social innovations.[16]

- **Agile development**: this is an experimentation-based methodology that promotes continuous feedback loops of iteration, product and service development, testing and single-loop learning based on what worked well, what could be improved and what the team does in the next iteration. Agile development is aimed at increasing time-to-market efficiency (speed and value) in rapidly changing markets.

- **Nature-based design**: this is a bio-logical principle-focused approach to sustainable product and service development that seeks to learn from nature. Nature-based design aims at distilling the design function in products, services and processes; translating it to biology; discovering natural patterns and models; emulating nature's strategies; and evaluating the design against life principles.[17]

- **Circularity**: this is the approach that incorporates the principles of the circular economy (design out waste and pollution; keep products and materials in use; and regenerate natural systems) into the design of new products and their embedded business models and processes to make them more circular and, thereby, regenerative.[18]

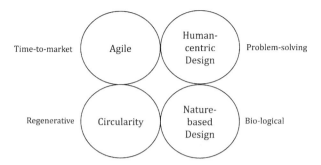

Figure 5.4 Marketing and Innovation star tools

Marketing and Innovation is the third phase on the way to sustainable transformation. This is the corporate star that channels the stakeholders-driven co-creative power to the design and market of sustainable solutions that target the customer by delivering value to her or him and to other related stakeholders simultaneously. The value delivery approach of this corporate star is, therefore, ecosystemic, holistic, and makes tangible the value process that was identified and envisioned in the Human Leadership star.

This approach is consistent with Philip Kotler's Marketing 3.0 framework.[19] The brand value proposition adds the dimension of the spirit in gaining customers minds—1.0—and hearts—2.0—thus achieving market differentiation by making a difference in the provision of sustainability—3.0.

Full Profit: Water

The Full Profit star represents the company's ability to capture the value delivered to the market by means of optimizing the revenue streams generated by its offerings and the full cost of doing business. Full profit is generated by the marketing and innovation star, so it is a direct result of the social and market embodiment of the organization's products and services.

Profit is the means that allows the company to reach the financial, social and environmental abundance—the triple bottom line[20]—needed to implement its sustainable business operations that drive the achievement of the higher purpose. Placing profit as a "means to an end" is thereby crucial for the behavioural repatterning proper of the transition to the new business paradigm. Money itself provides the energy that the company needs to operate. Like water, we need it for living but we do not live for drinking it.

Besides the optimal financial management of business activities, the function of profit is to financially nurture stakeholders. Profit has an enabling effect for generating socioeconomic well-being for employees, shareholders, suppliers, communities, the government as tax administrator and ecological well-being if it is directed to regenerate the environment. Profit also acts as a catalyst of new purpose-driven, impactful investments. When consciously channelled, profit is a key dynamic of prosperity in the current economic system, revealing its power as a social technology invented by our ancestors centuries ago.

Implementing this star implies working on the following tools (Figure 5.5).

- **Abundance mindset**: sustainable financial management requires approaching money with a mind that is open towards abundance, by internalizing social and environmental benefits and costs in the concept of Full Profit (the triple bottom line). Therefore, an abundance mindset refers to holistically approaching business and life as a potential source of economic, ecologic, emotional and social wealth. This work entails removing entrenched mental barriers that may prevent financial wealth: a single focus on financial cost, victimization in regard to resource scarcity, recurring fixation on competition, and primary interest in receiving and taking, for example. Rather, this work requires prioritizing a mental state of abundance based on an authentic focus on giving and delivering, an appreciation of present circumstances and context, an attitude crafted around resourcefulness, opportunity and investment, and an assumed behaviour built upon responsibility and trust.[21] The implications of managing abundance are further explored in Chapter 8.

- **Revenue modelling**: this is the method that frames how the organization sources its financial income. It identifies revenue streams for each market segment, which illustrates the cash the company generates from customers. Essentially, it reflects the point of equilibrium between the brand value proposition and the customers' willingness to pay for that value. Revenue streams may be transactional—revenues resulting from one-time customer payment—or recurring—revenues coming from ongoing payments to either deliver offerings to customers or provide post-purchase customer support. It is a key building block of any business model. According to Alex Osterwalder and Yves Pigneur, different revenue streams include asset sales; usage fees; subscription fees; lending, renting and leasing; licensing; brokerage fees; and advertising, among others.[22]

- **Full cost structure**: this defines the fixed and variable expenses—costs—that the organization incurs in operating its business activities across the financial, social and environmental dimensions. Fixed costs are costs that remain unchanged regardless of the amount of output the organization produces, while variable costs change along with production volume. Cost structures differ depending on the sector of the business; for example, a manufacturer or a service provider. They can be identified, accounted and monitored by business activities and

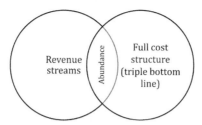

Figure 5.5 Full Profit star tools

aggregated into the organizational triple bottom line statement alike. Cost optimization can either be produced by economies of scale–marginal cost decreases by increasing the quantity of the same outputs produced—or economies of scope—total average cost decreases by increasing variety of outputs produced.

The Full Profit star is the fourth phase on the path towards sustainable transformation. It is the corporate star in charge of sustaining the value that has been delivered by the Marketing and Innovation star. This star reflects the financial and non-financial health of the organization, a necessary condition to achieve the higher purpose, in the framework of the triple bottom line. Full Profit captures, therefore, the sustainability contribution of the company from an economic point of view. It transcends the classic profit maximization paradigm, and, rather, it focuses on sharing the value captured for generating holistic impact, a concept explored in the next corporate star.

Brand Impact Recognition: Wood

This star reflects the company's capacity to build a corporate brand recognized by the impact it generates upon society, the environment and the economy (the holistic impact). This is only possible when the organization is mindfully aware of the consequences of its business activities and is able to communicate the impact to its stakeholders and society at large. That is, of how it contributes to societal change and transformation. Evaluating and communicating impact requires the development of an organizational culture focused on impact. Such a culture is assessed against the company's ability to achieve its higher purpose. This process starts by enquiring about to what extent we have walked the talk. Success is an element of that enquiry; it depends on the quality of impacts generated compared to the expected value created by and for stakeholders. In this light, the status and social recognition of the company as a force for good defines the role it plays in society, the economy and the environment.

Building such an impact brand implies working on four important interwoven areas. First, it requires evaluating the impact by setting up an internal process of evidence-based reflection. This process of evaluation allows the organization to reflect and become aware of its effects by capturing both its positive and negative aspects, and intended and non-intended impacts on its stakeholders, by measuring these (ecological, social, emotional and economic). Second, it requires the organization to be able to genuinely communicate the impact generated to its stakeholders and society at large. The social recognition of an impact brand stems from an honest and effective communication of its impact. Third, it requires developing a culture focused on evaluating and communicating the impact generated: a culture of an impact that sustains, facilitates and nurtures the company's sustainable business model.

And fourth, it requires systematizing organizational learning, the process of capturing, transferring, sharing and integrating knowledge—tacit and explicit—within and across the organization and its ecosystem. This process facilitates learning, adaptation and transformation of its members and the organization as a whole, becoming what Senge called a learning organization.[23] These areas are workable processes that can be implemented in the organization with the following features (Figure 5.6).

- **Evaluation of impact**: this approach, introduced in the development cooperation field, aims to demonstrate how an intervention leads to expected outcomes, whether these changes are intended, unintended, positive, negative, direct or indirect. Evaluating impact is an internal approach that implies setting up an evidence-based critical enquiry as to whether the impact has been generated, why, how and for whom and in what circumstances. However, the corporate world, which is involved in the inception of assessing and evaluating impact, approaches this idea through measurement. It normally focuses on the definition of a set of observable dimensions of impact—mostly economic, social, environmental and governance—and it sets a number of measurable criteria and targets that quantify the corporate's non-financial impact. Measurement, although it is part of an evaluation, does not allow the organization to capture the entire process of why and how impact is generated.

- **Communication of impact**: a major challenge for organizations is not only to evaluate the impact, but also to genuinely and transparently communicate the impact generated to stakeholders and society. Communicating impact is an external process of organizational awareness. Most often, organizations focus on measuring and communicating the intended positive impacts of its business activities, which is only a part of any evaluation of impact (impacts can also be unintended and negative). When this is the case, it can foster reluctance in stakeholders and even create a feeling of brand green-washing. Stakeholders increasingly demand more impact-based information and transparency. For organizations, effective communication is an asset in engaging stakeholders and achieving the social recognition desired by accomplishing its purpose.

* **Culture of impact**: evaluating and communicating impact requires having a workforce whose mindsets and behaviours are geared towards capturing impact. Having executives and managers with an evaluative mindset implies, on the one hand, having people in the organization with the ability to generate enquiries, skilled in collecting and analysing data, and focused on learning. On the other hand, it requires having the time, space and resources to pause and reflect on results. Often, such a culture needs a governance system that empowers employees to develop such an evaluative mindset, as, for example, having evaluative processes and tools in place, and developing decentralized management structures through empowered networks of self-managing teams that can evaluate and make decisions based on results.

The Brand Impact Recognition star is the fifth phase to be negotiated towards sustainable transformation. It recognizes the value it delivers to the ecosystem and it reinforces its commitment as a socioeconomic and ecologic agent. Becoming an organization with a highly recognized impact brand is like attaining enlightenment for a Buddhist monk. It is a state where the organization is evidently guided by its higher purpose and led and managed by servicing its stakeholders, in a transformative act of systems rebellion.

This notwithstanding, the journey across the five corporate stars does not stop here. Indeed, it follows an evolutionary dynamic cycle where the Brand Impact Recognition star constantly nourishes the Human Leadership

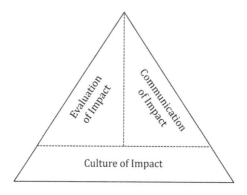

Figure 5.6 Brand Impact Recognition star tools

star (Wood generates Fire), in a developmental process of organizational learning and adaptation to internal and external changes. The next chapter discusses the Zen Business model dynamics in detail.

Zen Business model dynamics

The functioning dynamics of the Zen Business model replicates the same generation and control cycles that are featured in the Five Elements theory (see Chapter 3). The five corporate stars continuously interact in a dynamic interplay featuring a feedback loop that is both reinforcing and balancing. The value generation and control cycles interdependently influence each other at the same time, seeking the balance and harmony of the system as a purposeful self-regulating mechanism (Figure 5.7).

In the context of organizational development, a systemic intervention in any of the five corporate stars triggers a change in the other stars. This change happens through activation of the value generation and control cycles, as is discussed below, purposefully seeking the harmonization of the living system in constant interdependence among the stars. Therefore, a targeted intervention in the corporate stars is what allows and facilitates the transformation of the system.

Value generation cycle

Each star's interdependence is manifested by a relationship of mutual influence. In the generation cycle, each corporate star has a value nourishing or reinforcing effect—also called creation—on the following star. This means

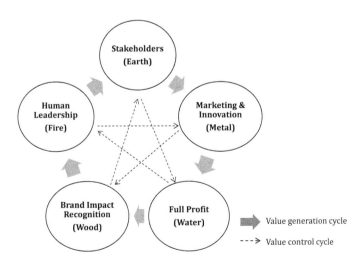

Figure 5.7 Zen Business model dynamics

that a healthy star has a value creation effect on the next star. For instance, an organization that works on the Human Leadership star, with a clear higher purpose consistent with its mission, vision and values, attracts the right stakeholders (Human Leadership ⟶ Stakeholders). Different stakeholders feel compelled and energized to balance their interests in accordance with the Human Leadership, thereby aligning and bringing their creative energy and resources into the design and development of sustainable solutions (Stakeholders ⟶ Marketing and Innovation). The successful market embodiment of these solutions results in higher profits for the organization, which sees a reward in its capacity to sustain the value delivered in the previous star (Marketing and Innovation ⟶ Full Profit). The triple bottom line of profits confer on the company the credibility, social recognition and reputation needed from the market, a necessary condition that shapes the recognition of the corporate brand and a culture of impact that any company needs in order to become a reference point as an example of an organization transitioning to the sustainable paradigm (Full Profit ⟶ Brand Impact Recognition). The loop continues as the evaluation of impact and reflection on the learning acquired allows the organization to adapt according to evolutionary changes in culture, markets and context, which can result in changes to the purpose and values of the organization (Brand Impact Recognition ⟶ Human Leadership). And the cycle goes on and on (Figure 5.8).

In a perfectly balanced scenario by means of this generation cycle, each corporate star would be a syntropic force contributing to the organization's systemic energy—the company's *qi*. Value would flow freely from one star to the other with a creative and nourishing effect in a virtuous generation cycle (Human Leadership ⟶ Stakeholders ⟶ Marketing and

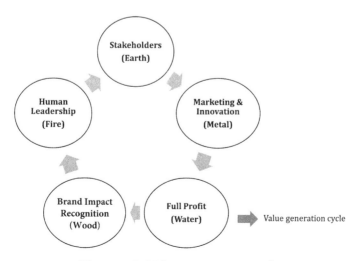

Figure 5.8 Value generation cycle

Innovation $\longrightarrow$ Full Profit $\longrightarrow$ Brand Impact Recognition $\longrightarrow$ Human Leadership). However, organizations very seldom find themselves in such a permanent state of affairs. Indeed, they may find that they are excelling in one star but failing in others, a situation that could result in the disequilibrium of the system and the generation of entropy. When this is the case, the system itself seeks to balance the situation.

Value control cycle

Alterations in the system caused by either excess or lack of value in one or more corporate stars can be regulated by the value control cycle. This cycle— also called the balancing cycle—can correct the organizational imbalances and reset the circulation of the *qi* energy. The controlling effect is active between the starts juxtaposed to each other. Let's explore this. An excess of the Human Leadership star could melt the Marketing and Innovation star (as too much Fire melts Metal); an excess of Marketing and Innovation could destroy the Brand Impact Recognition star (as Metal cuts Wood); an excess of Brand Impact Recognition could restrain the Stakeholders star (as Wood digs into Earth); and an excess of Stakeholders could block the Full Profit star (as Earth blocks Water), whereas an excess of Full Profit could jeopardize the Human Leadership star (as Water extinguishes Fire), thus closing the feedback loop of the value control cycle (Human Leadership × Marketing and Innovation × Brand Impact Recognition × Stakeholders × Full Profit × Human Leadership) (Figure 5.9).

Systems disequilibrium can be caused by the disproportionate strength of one of the corporate stars, or a lack of control between stars. For example,

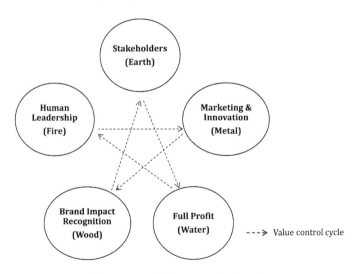

Figure 5.9 Value control cycle

an obsession with improving financial performance at all costs (Full Profit) could have a negative effect on the achievement of the company's higher purpose (Human Leadership). Water extinguishes Fire. This is precisely one of the main imbalances of current corporate dynamics, where the majority of companies concentrate on maximizing economic shareholder value in the short term. This corporate behaviour—globally unveiled during the Great Recession—is at odds with implementing a purpose- and values-driven strategy that is intended to generate holistic impact.

An excess of Human Leadership can over-control the Marketing and Innovation star (too much Fire melts Metal), thus limiting an organization's ability to develop the Full Profit star (Metal, which generates Water, is too limited). This is a common drawback of non-profit organizations and social entrepreneurs, very much focused on accomplishing great higher purposes with far-reaching social and environmental impact, yet most of them lack the financial sustainability needed to carry out their operations. The Great Recession led to drastic cuts in most state budgets allocated to aid development programmes and projects. This affected many organizations that were highly dependent on public funding and private donations in order to survive.

The Human Leadership star can also control an excess of Marketing and Innovation. This is the case with companies that have a tendency to flood the market with brands, most often experiencing cannibalization. To correct this imbalance, the brand portfolio rationalization is guided by the criteria defined in the purpose and values of the organization. When Unilever and Danone embraced a higher purpose-driven strategy, they rationalized and reframed their product portfolio based on the "fit-for-purpose" criterion.

The excess of Marketing and Innovation can cause strong diseconomies of scale, which translate into a more bureaucratic and rigid culture, making it less adaptable to change. This was the case of the e-commerce firm Zappos. Rapid growth translated into new product and services developments that required the systematization of processes. The company decided to implement a reformulation of its purpose- and values-driven strategy (Human Leadership) coupled with a decentralized governance system, holacracy, in order to correct the imbalance (Brand Impact Recognition).

An excess of Brand Impact Recognition can overcontrol stakeholders. This happens when companies become obsessed with imposing a type of culture that is not co-created by all stakeholders, especially when employees do not drive it. Zappos, for instance, suffered from change resistance when it introduced holacracy (with the aim of achieving its purpose and becoming recognized as a "delivering happiness" organization). As a result, a reported 18% of its employees decided to leave their jobs as they found it inconsistent with their values.

At the same time, excesses in the Stakeholders' star can be regulated by the Brand Impact Recognition star. Brand Impact Recognition provides, with the embodied organizational beliefs, values and behaviours that continuously drive stakeholders' engagement, adaptability and co-creation capabilities. These are indispensable elements for unleashing the capacity of the organization to deliver economic, social and environmental value alike. Japan-based Kyocera's culture leveraged on Amoeba management, a decentralized management system with small self-managing business units that were key in fostering collaboration and empowering employees decision-making; which, in turn, resulted in greater dynamism, agility and adaptability to changing market conditions and a great degree of brand recognition internationally.

The Stakeholders' star, in parallel, can correct excess in the Full Profit star. This star takes on a balancing role by safeguarding an inclusive distribution of profit across the organization. This may entail ensuring fair pay for employees, giving them company shares or raising their salaries. Dan Price, CEO of Gravity Payments, decided to compensate workers by reducing 90% of his salary and establishing a minimum wage of $70,000 per employee. Another corporate policy in this vein is to periodically reinvest a percentage of profits in stakeholders, by means of training and learning, life–work balance, team-building, and environmental regeneration initiatives.

The Zen Business model provides a systemic methodology grounded in internalizing impermanence as a value generator. Change, interdependence and self-regulation are the foundation of the organization's dynamics and performance, and constitute the pillars for learning, adaptation, anticipation and organizational development overall. The objective of this model is to develop an adaptive corporate culture devoted to accepting and seeing change as an opportunity for generating and developing the company's higher purpose.

The five archetypes

In systems thinking, archetypes are "classic stories" that describe common patterns of behaviour and structures that occur repeatedly in different settings.[24] In the Zen Business model, archetypes describe the five elemental patterns that drive the dominant behaviour of the organization. Although the dominant archetype stresses a predominant behaviour, the five archetypes actually coexist and interplay at different levels and at different moments in time.

Overall, archetypes have a double utility. First, they can be used as a diagnostic tool that provides a synthetic insight into the underlying structures and mental models from which behaviour and discrete events emerge over time. Second, as prospective tools, archetypes alert managers of future unintended imbalances if the dominant patterns of behaviour keep repeating over time. These imbalances help the organization to identify the leverage points and to design interventions, as is explained in Chapters 6 and 7.

- **The Fire archetype**: this describes a transcendental organization, which dreams easily and comes up with highly engaging and motivating purposes and ideas to make a difference. This organization has a strong capacity to envision the future, to inspire to change the world, to energize and mobilize teams through purpose-based storytelling. However, it may have difficulties in grounding its ambitions in marketable customer-orientated innovations. It is typical of non-profit organizations, NGOs, social businesses and the like.

- **The Earth archetype**: this one describes a family kind of organization, which operates in line with shared defining values and interactive networks of influence based on members' recommendations and outreach. It believes that happy employees make customers happy. Decision-making places a lot of emphasis on caring about the "tribe", with special emphasis on respecting personal processes, employee well-being, team cohesion and work–life balance. It is characteristic of family businesses, peer-based companies such as tech startups and small enterprises.

- **The Metal archetype**: describes a customer-obsessed organization that considers the customer as king. Decision-making revolves around the customer, and the organization asks employees to go the extra mile to constantly deliver more customer value in quicker time spans, which results in extra stress for the teams. This organization places agile processes at the centre of its operational strategy. It may create confusion in its impact culture, as it justifies its corporate decisions on satisfying customers' needs. This archetype is characteristic of software-based companies, consulting firms the retail industry and business schools.

- **The Water archetype**: this describes a profit-focused organization, obsessed with corporate growth. People are understood as a resource for achieving profit, and cost efficiency and maximizing revenue streams drive strategic decision-making. This archetype believes corporations are economic agents solely and that social value should be channelled through philanthropic initiatives via foundations or corporate social responsibility departments. It is typical of the banking industry, multinational enterprises and large business conglomerates.

- **The Wood archetype**: describes a culture-driven organization, above all concerned with its corporate brand reputation. It invests in building an attractive employer brand value proposition based on a compelling governance system and incentive packages, including professional growth plans. This archetype constantly seeks to set and standardize processes, procedures and methodologies and is fixated on measuring impact and organizational performance. In excess, such an obsession may lead to increased bureaucracy, rigidity and diseconomies of scale. This archetype is typical of longevity companies, fast-growth organizations and international development agencies.

The Zen Business wheel

The Zen Business wheel, illustrated in Figure 5.10, is the guiding tool aimed at facilitating sustainable business model design and transformation by implementing the organizational development process through the Zen

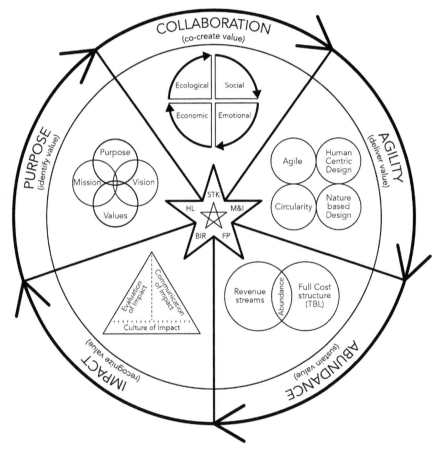

Figure 5.10   The Zen Business wheel. Key: HL = Human Leadership; STK = Stakeholders; M&I = Marketing and Innovation; FP = Full Profit; BIR = Brand Impact Recognition

Business model. It provides a visual synthesis of, first, the operating principles and its value phase associated to each of the five corporate stars; and second, it visualizes and frames the applicable tools that guide the implementation of the model.

Notes

1 I developed the Zen Business model through a personal and organizational enquiry process during my research and consulting work in South Korea and Japan between 2012 and 2014. The conceptualization of the model was sponsored by the Maastricht School of Management, where I published the model in a working paper presented at a research seminar in February 2014. The whole model and background philosophy was published in the book *Zen Business: los beneficios de aplicar la armonía en la empresa* (Profit editorial) in 2015. Since then, the model has been applied in organizations and by entrepreneurs as a tool for guiding sustainable design and/or transformation.
2 By definition, living systems are open, self-organizing systems that have the special characteristics of life and interact with their environment. This takes place by means of information and material–energy exchanges. www.isss.org/primer/asem14ep.html.
3 Design by analogy to biology is often called biomimicry, which is a process of "innovation through the emulation of biological forms, processes, patterns, and systems", in Emily Barbara Kennedy (2017) Biomimicry: Design by analogy to biology. *Research-Technology Management*, 60(6), 51–56.
4 The analogical interpretation of the five elements also applies to medicine, with the five elements associated with the five organs of the human body.
5 Macdonald, I. et al. (2018). *Systems Leadership: Creating positive organizations*. Routledge.
6 Barrett, R. (2013). *The Values-driven Organization: Unleashing human potential for performance and profit*. Routledge.
7 Greenleaf, R. (2002). *Servant Leadership: A journey into the nature of legitimate power and greatness*. Paulist PR.
8 Schein, E. (2018). *Humble Leadership: The power of relationships, openness and trust*. Berrett-Koehler.
9 Sisodia et al. (2002). *Firms of endearment: How world-class companies profit from passion and purpose*. FT Press.
10 Simon, S. (2011). *Start With Why: How great leaders inspire everyone to take action*. Portfolio.
11 Pink. D. (2009). *Drive: The surprising truth about what motivates us*. Penguin US.
12 Barrett, R. (2013). *The Values-driven Organization: Unleashing human potential for performance and profit*. Routledge.
13 Freeman, E. (1984). *Strategic Management: A stakeholder approach*. Boston: Pitman.
14 Porter, M. & Kramer, M. (2011). *Creating Shared Value*. Harvard Business Review.
15 Peter Drucker vividly emphasized the relevance of this connection: "business has only two functions, marketing and innovation".
16 The Human-Centered Design Toolkit, IDEO (2009).
17 These are the five stages of the Biomimicry design spiral, developed by Biomimicry Guild (2007).
18 The Ellen MacArthur Foundation and Granta Design developed the Circularity Indicators methodology as a decision-making tool for designers, among other utilities.

19 Kotler, P. et al. (2010). *Marketing 3.0: From products to customers to the human spirit.* Wiley & Sons.
20 The triple bottom line, coined by John Elkington in 1994, "aims to measure the financial, social and environmental performance of the corporation over a period of time. Only a company that produces a TBL is taking account of the full cost involved in doing business", in "25 years ago I coined the phrase 'triple bottom line.' Here's why it's time to rethink it" by Elkington (Harvard Business Review, June 2018).
21 As a concept, "abundance mindset" is consistent with Suzuki's "beginner's mind" and Covey's idea of "abundance mentality".
22 Osterwalder, A. & Pigneur, Y. (2010). *Business Model Generation.* Wiley & Sons.
23 Senge, P. (1990). *The Fifth Discipline: The art and practice of the learning organization.* Doubleday.
24 Stroh, D. (2015). *Systems Thinking for Social Change.* Chelsea Green Publishing.

References

Barrett, R. (2013). *The Values-driven Organization: Unleashing human potential for performance and profit.* Routledge.
Coll, J.M. (2015). *Zen Business: los beneficios de aplicar la armonía en la empresa.* Profit Editorial.
Drucker, P. (1954). *The Practice of Management.* Harper & Row.
Elkington, J. (2018). 25 years ago I coined the phrase "triple bottom line." Here's why It's time to rethink it. Harvard Business Review, June.
Freeman, E. (1984). *Strategic Management: A stakeholder approach.* Boston: Pitman.
Greenleaf, R. (2002). *Servant Leadership: A journey into the nature of legitimate power and greatness.* Paulist PR.
Kennedy, E.B. (2017). Biomimicry: Design by analogy to biology. *Research-Technology Management*, 60(6), 51–56.
Kotler, P. et al. (2010). *Marketing 3.0: From products to customers to the human spirit.* Wiley & Sons.
Macdonald, I. et al. (2018). *Systems Leadership: Creating positive organizations.* Routledge.
Osterwalder, A. & Pigneur, Y. (2010). *Business Model Generation.* Wiley & Sons.
Pink. D. (2009). *Drive: The surprising truth about what motivates us.* Penguin US.
Porter, M. & Kramer, M. (2011). Creating shared value. *Harvard Business Review.*
Schein, E. (2018). *Humble Leadership: The power of relationships, openness and trust.* Berrett-Koehler.
Senge, P. (1990). *The Fifth Discipline.* Doubleday.
Stroh, D. (2015). *Systems Thinking for Social Change: A practical guide to solving complex problems, avoiding unintended consequences and achieving lasting results.* Chelsea Green.
Sinek, S. (2011). *Start with Why: How great leaders inspire everyone to take action.* Portfolio.
Sisodia et al. (2002). *Firms of endearment: How world-class companies profit from passion and purpose.* FT Press.

Chapter 6

Building the Gaia organization

Principles and practices

Why Gaia?

The Gaia organization is a living system that aspires to build the new business paradigm. This organization plays the role of a transformation agent that seeks to channel the creative power of business organizations and entrepreneurs into the regeneration of the economy and its natural ecosystems. It is named after Gaia for two reasons.

First, Gaia is the name of the mythological Greek goddess who symbolizes the personification of the Earth and mother of all life. This metaphor captures a common feature in perennial philosophies and indigenous wisdom, the fact that planet Earth is a living entity, a home for humans, a dynamic place where life unfolds, with all its beauty, suffering and mystery. Gaia is associated to the feminine, the Yin energy of creation, the one that gives life and takes care of it.

Second, it is the name of the Gaia theory, a relatively new—and revolutionary—scientific stance developed by James Lovelock that proposes Earth as a living organism that is constantly interacting and synergistically evolving as a self-regulating, complex system that helps perpetuate the conditions for life on the planet. This hypothesis radically challenges the previous scientific prevailing proposition that held the Earth to be a purposeless inanimate conglomeration of matter that wanders the galaxy for no particular reason.

The Gaia organization has "skin in the game". It is shaped by seekers (you are probably one of them if you are reading this book), bold people that challenge themselves and undertake the risky enterprise of changing the rules of the game, or just simply creating a new one. This chapter introduces the Gaia organization's overarching principles of lifefulness, awareness and bio-logic, as well as the operating principles that guide the practices of Gaia-type organizations when transitioning to the new business paradigm (Figure 6.1).

Figure 6.1 Artistic representation of Gaia. Source: the artist and art consultant Daniel Berdala, who took on the challenge to portray the Gaia organization as it is described in this chapter. I met Daniel in a Zen Business workshop I facilitated, and since then we have had a series of dialogues on ways to bridge arts and business as a way to unleash purpose and creativity in organizations

The Gaia organization is driven by principles

Principles are the basis of a powerful yet quite unexplored strategy to inform and guide choices and behaviour in complex sustainability-based initiatives. Using principles is an effective approach to apply values-driven leadership in organizations by design. Michael Quinn Patton[1] makes a strong case for the usefulness of applying principles for navigating complex environments. He states,

> an effectiveness principle provides guidance about how to think or behave toward some desired result (either explicit or implicit) based on norms, values, beliefs, experience, and knowledge. A high-quality principle provides guidance about what to do, is useful for inspiring decisions and actions, provides inspiration as an expression of values, is relevant to diverse contexts and situations, and can be evaluated.

The Gaia organization is principles-focused because it is aimed at helping principles-driven people engaged in principles-based sustainable transformation. In living systems operating in rapid changing and complex contexts, principles provide guidance but do not specify concrete action-based procedures, fixed methods or standard solutions because such details are dependent on the context. The Gaia organization is adaptive by nature and principles are its navigation tool, a tool that facilitates developmental transformation.

The Gaia organization is guided by three overarching principles and five operating principles, as illustrated in Figure 6.2. The distinction between overarching and operating principles, according to Patton (2017), "is like the distinction between goals and objectives. Overarching principles provide big-picture, general guidance and operating principles provide more specific guidance". The Gaia organization's principles can guide the nature-based process of sustainable transformation in organizations, from a leadership, managerial and operational point of view, while embedding a changed management perspective in all the actions taken from strategizing to design, implementation and monitoring and evaluation. It is important to clarify that the Gaia organization is both an approach to sustainable transformation and a way of thinking systemically across all levels, value phases and stakeholders in organizations.

Overarching principles

Lifefulness

Lifefulness principle articulated:

Nurture life in any form, interdependently and (w)holistically.

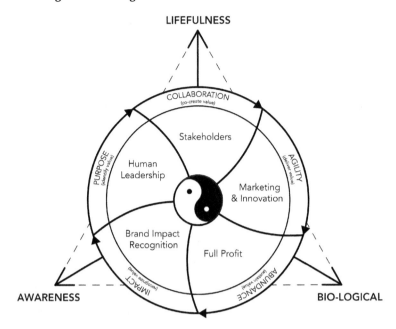

Figure 6.2 Principles of the Gaia organization

In the context of the Anthropocene, where humans are causing the deterioration of the Earth in unprecedented ways through an extractive economy, human systems need to counterbalance this effect through a regenerative approach to doing business and transforming the economic system. Classic silo-based sustainability approaches based on doing less harm, such as corporate social responsibility, environmental compliance, ESG (environment, society and governance) investing, triple bottom line accounting, have helped. But they have not decisively contributed to changing the systems' rules of the game, still governed by shareholder profit maximization.

Approaching sustainability systemically requires thinking beyond sustainability. This further thinking reflects the necessary paradigm shift to transcending the classical boundaries that limit sustainable practices within the realm of business. Regenerative economies require vibrant business organizations, life-creating and life-caring business practices at all levels and scopes, aligning nested subsystems and integrating the different value-generating dimensions—social, economic, emotional and environmental—of any business innovation process.

The principle of lifefulness conveys the message of the Gaia theory: the organization is a Gaian subsystem that is constantly interacting and synergistically evolving as a self-regulating, complex system that helps perpetuate the conditions for life on the planet. This principle builds on the premise that organizations that are designed to create and take care of life have a positive impact on the planet as a whole, help to regenerate it and nourish new, emerging and vibrant forms of life that anticipate, and adapt to, the future.

Awareness

Awareness principle articulated:

Be aware of the human potential and its boundaries; and act with virtue, accordingly.

In line with an ecosystemic understanding of the world and the planet, the principle of awareness advocates a conscious enquiry into the human condition, the quest for meaning and knowledge (absolute, intuitive and explicit). Organizations have traditionally assumed their purpose to be financial profitability, considering themselves as action-orientated. Management science did not alter this assumption and business practitioners did not question the foundational pillars of the system in which they operated. As the idiom goes, it's like fish that do not question why they are wet because they are always in water.

But organizations are a social construct, a human system nested in natural systems, in constant interaction. As a social construct, they need to constantly enquire about their nature, their meaningfulness and relevance to stakeholders and the environment, and the way they create a culture of results, of service and value to others and to society, with all its consequences.

Awareness of the human condition in organizations implies, on the one hand, exerting self-reflective T-Qualia practices that are grounded on the universal principles of the Tao. And, on the other hand, it entails recognizing the inherent humility of that human condition. Despite human power, in all its destructive and creative forms, humans are part of the Earth system and, as such, they are fragile, as they operate within nature's boundaries.

Lynn Margulis, the microbiologist who contributed to developing the Gaia theory with James Lovelock, vividly expresses this meaning. In her book, *A Symbiotic Planet*. She writes,

> Life is a planetary level phenomenon and the Earth has been alive for at least 3000 million years. To me the human move to take responsibility for the living Earth is laughable – the rhethoric of the powerless. The planet takes care of us, not we of it. Our self-inflated moral imperative to guide a wayward Earth or heal a sick planet is evidence of our immense capacity for self-delusion.

Between the ambition to achieve a higher purpose and the humility to make a contribution along with many others, Gaia organizations need to balance these two forces. The combination of ambition and humility is the conscious approach to create unique corporate cultures that are recognized for the way they nurture life, the previous principle. The principle of awareness builds on the premise that consciousness starts with a process of self-enquiry on the meaning—the intended result—and impact of organizations—the consequence of that result; it is precisely this consciousness that is the seed that allows the organization to transform itself by becoming a positive agent of regeneration and lifefulness in the planet.

Bio-logic

Bio-logic principle articulated:

Inform, design and evaluate strategies, decision-making and business operations in synergistic harmonization between human and natural interests and behaviors.

Organization-driven systemic transformation should be contextually sensitive and grounded on the interaction between human and natural systems. In the current business paradigm, economists, business practitioners and organizational scientists have mostly focused on the inherent human interactions required to do business. Environmental consequences—called externalities by economists—have mainly been the concern of ecologists or environmentalists who have traditionally focused on "pristine environments in which humans are external and rarely dominant agents".[2]

Achieving sustainability depends on new bridging approaches that facilitate radical changes in human and organizational attitudes, intentions and, most importantly, behaviours. The coupled human and natural systems framework (CHANS)[3] is a relatively new research area that advocates the integration of both systems, as sustainable transformation occurs in the nexus where human (social and economic) and natural (environmental) systems meet.

In this light, organizations need to integrate a bio-logic approach, narrative and design principle into business decision-making and action in order to guide their sustainable behaviour. The principle of bio-logic builds on the premise that any business decision at all levels of the results cycle—strategy, design, development, implementation, monitoring and evaluation—made in harmonization with human and natural interests and behaviours is conducive to sustainable transformation. If that is not the case, there is a high risk that organizations will keep on externalizing the ecological costs of doing business.

Operating principles and practices

While the three overarching principles provide big-picture guidance to sustain the transitioning process of transformation, operating principles specifically guide and support the business practices in the organization with the objective of achieving desired results. The operating principles of Gaia organizations are the five principles guiding the Zen Business model that we saw in the previous chapter (see Figure 5.10, the Zen Business wheel). They are associated with the five stages of holistic value generation in the organization and to the five corporate stars that are subject to the systems dynamics of this sustainable value-creating process.

Purpose

Purpose principle articulated:

Be purpose driven; use purpose and values to illuminate, inform and lead organizational behavior.

Closing the purpose gap

Purpose has become mainstream in the business world, especially since the Business Roundtable[4] issued a new statement redefining the purpose of a corporation to promote "an economy that serves all Americans". This notwithstanding, genuinely working on the purpose of an organization is still quite uncharted territory. Especially when it comes to closing the gap between the definition and the application of the purpose across the organization.[5]

A company may decide to have a purpose for two main reasons. The first reason may stem from an inner calling inspired by a process of self-enquiry that brings business leaders to question the meaning of their companies, their work and, thereby, their lives. This is the case of Bob Chapman, Chairman and CEO of Barry-Wehmiller, who turned its business-as-usual management style into a purpose-driven, human-centred organization thanks to three insightful experiences—he calls them revelations—that he had during the 2000s, all outside business schools.[6]

The second reason may arise out of necessity. Companies that find it hard to engage employees and clients, to adapt to changing contexts and market pressures, and that, as a result, suffer from financial problems, may decide to use purpose as a strategy to revitalize the company's leadership and culture. FM Logistic Iberia,[7] in view of shrinking margins and increasing competition, decided to launch, in 2016, an employee engagement programme that started with a reflection on the purpose of the company conducted by and for the executive committee. This process resulted in the definition of a sustainability strategy, in 2018, based on the pillars of employee well-being, carbon footprint reduction and the development of sustainability services.

In any case, defining the organizational purpose depends on the degree of organizational awareness, which is a direct function of the awareness of its employees, whether they are executives or managers. A high level of awareness facilitates setting up an open process or intervention by involving different executives, managers and employees in general. Purpose is then the result of a collective reflection that assesses the relevance and meaning of the organization in relation to the context, to the market and, above all, to the employees. Opening up this process implies trust and communication with employees. It requires senior leadership to rely on their ownership and creativity to involve the rest of employees in an open innovation process.

This is the case of the Voxel Group. This IT company embarked, in 2016, on a journey towards building a values and purpose-driven corporate culture.[8] Inspired by the senior leadership, the journey began with the formalization of the organizational identity. The initial reflection was guided by the following questions: "why do we exist? How do we like doing things? Why keep growing? What would we do without the company?" As an outcome of this process, they started defining its values in an open co-creation exercise with the majority of its employees. The result was the definition of four overarching values that became the building blocks for guiding the company's behaviour: people freaks, "fun-tastic" team players, challenge maniacs and change lovers.

What makes the Voxel case particularly insightful is how they closed the purpose gap by applying the new values to business decision-making in two critical strategies. The first was in redesigning the company's recruitment process based on the new values as the main candidates' evaluation and selection criteria. The company set a new matching protocol to ensure that new employees align with, and are driven by, the company's set of values. This allowed the company to achieve higher levels of alignment, which drives higher employee engagement. The second strategy was the setting up of four open days a year—one per trimester—called "live the values". All employees pause and reflect on the corporate values, providing direct evidence on how they apply values to decision-making in daily business operations and co-designing a values-driven action plan. This initiative fosters strategic alignment, employee recognition and engagement and collaboration.

Working on values first led Voxel to induce the purpose of the organization, which captured its why: "creating happy business fabric". This purpose reflects the essence of the organization, which considers growth as extended joy, and the company as a means to generate wealth and community impact.

When this degree of leadership maturity is still not there (or there is certain reluctance to open the process to the rest of the company due to trust issues), but there is a true desire to work on the purpose, organizations can start the intervention by narrowing the scope of the exercise. This happens by keeping the reflection with the senior leadership in a first stage, which usually means the executive committee (CEO and business units directors or executives) and board. In a later stage, when the senior leadership is confident about the benefits and implications of having an organizational purpose, this can be shared and consulted on with the rest of employees.

That was the case of Margon, a family business that questioned the purpose and identity of the organization when the second generation of the family was taking over from the founder of the company.[9] The new generation, with the vision of building an Earth archetype, was inspired by contributing to the community by taking care of employees' well-being, which has a direct impact on their families. They were aware of the low levels of employee engagement and high cultural entropy that was manifested through regular complaints, absenteeism and low commitment to the company's goals. They were courageous enough to challenge a Water archetype, and a new purpose was defined for the first time, aimed at "making employees proud of their organization", as a strategy to transform its corporate culture.

Once there is a first articulation of the purpose, consistent with senior leadership views, the company can start designing collective consultation-focused events where they communicate, share and engage with the rest of employees, leaving some degree of openness to incorporate their feedback in order to fine tune the initial purpose. This is a critical step for leveraging employees' ownership of the purpose. In all cases, it is important that the senior leadership openly communicates why they decided to embed a new purpose, the relevance, benefits, implications and expectations from and with employees.

For companies that are not fully convinced about the impact of purpose, or that they do not feel it, or they are solely driven by the expectation of a higher financial return, it is recommended not to mess with it. Developing and applying a purpose requires financial resources, long-term orientation, perseverance, trust in people's intelligence, and a passionate belief that this is the way forward.

Collaboration

Collaboration principle articulated:

Co-create value with and for stakeholders, harmonize their different interests synergistically.

Collaboration as teenage sex

In a working session at the United Nations in New York with my colleagues Jordi del Bas, Michael Quinn Patton and Valeria Carou-Jones, I became impressed when Patton illustrated the complexity in facilitating co-creation with the following metaphor: "collaboration is like teenage sex; everyone talks about doing it; everyone thinks everyone else is doing it; those that are doing it aren't doing it very well; despite that, they all talk about how wonderful it is". The first step for conducting effective collaborations is to use purpose as an intrinsic and extrinsic motivator.

Operationalizing purpose leads to engaging with stakeholders that are driven by the same energy that emerges out of the genuine desire to solve the same problems and satisfy the same needs. This problem-solving based resonance is what makes different stakeholders with apparently different needs to buy into, be inspired and guided by, the same purpose. When the focus of the problem is a common good, framed in the generation of social and environmental value (besides economic), the scope of collaboration enlarges and includes non-business traditional stakeholders such as non-profit organizations, local communities, governmental agencies, media and the environment.

Casa Luker, a century-old company from Colombia,[10] is well aware of this principle. It sees purpose as an opportunity to connect with society, providing solutions to relevant problems. In 2016, the food company launched Chocolate Dream, an initiative aimed at facilitating long-term sustainable transformation in rural cocoa regions, historically impoverished by war and drug trafficking. The project focuses on fostering rural economic diversification, protecting regional biodiversity and preserving local indigenous cultures through education, entrepreneurship, art and cultural initiatives.

Collaboration started with the identification of the key stakeholders with a shared value proposition. The cornerstone of this proposition lay with agricultural smallholders, along with farm workers, and the extended rural communities that interact in the ecosystem. The company provides training, technical capacity building and access to finance for smallholders, while these commit to raising the quality standards of the product and bringing long-term stability to the supply chain. It is a win–win approach.

In order to deal with the various challenges that smallholders face in the regions, Luker utilized Cocohabs, a platform-based collaboration space that is physically clustered in the farms. This place catalyses innovation by creating the conditions that bring academia, the private and the public sector and citizens together to co-create socioeconomic and technical solutions to improve the living standards for the local communities. Luker's clients act as social impact investors to the initiatives that are co-created between volunteers (artists, designers, architects, chefs, etc.), research groups, local farmers, coaches and local administrations. This collaboration strategy was critical in fostering client engagement and loyalty, and engaging the different interests among all stakeholders.

Despite the benefits of collaboration, not many organizations know how to do it well. Sergio Restrepo, vice-president of Innovation at Luker, outlines five key elements that are critical in ensuring that the process of collaboration works well for co-creation: (1) making sure that everybody understands the value of collaboration, with a long-term vision embedded in the management of expectations; (2) fostering alignment, visualization and individual–collective balancing of different stakeholders' interests; (3) managing and placing the different egos at the service of the common good, which requires the balancing art of giving credit and recognition to every stakeholder in the right proportion, while replacing attribution with contribution; (4) ensuring that all voices present are heard, balancing the visibility and participation of all stakeholders equally; and (5) defining clear roles for each player, with concrete rules of the game that are shared and communicated transparently to all participants. Restrepo understands collaboration as a journey of exploration, especially in complex contexts with high uncertainty, where "experimenting with collaboration is a critical leverage to the process of innovation".

In this regard, effective collaboration is correlated to high performing teams. Team performance is a result of group flow, the peak experience that team members display out of creativity-based spontaneous collaboration. Keith Sawyer,[11] building upon the concept of flow developed by Mihaly Csikszentmihalyi,[12] establishes ideal conditions for group flow to emerge: group goals, close listening, complete concentration, being in control, blending egos, equal participation, knowing team mates, good communication, and being progress-orientated.

Agility

Agility principle articulated:

Design and timely deliver human and nature-friendly solutions with agility

Leaving a positive footprint

Applying the principle of agility in the context of sustainable transformation requires developing the capacity to find timely market solutions that are designed to provide the needs of both human and nature and/or for improving their experience. The term "timely" deserves special attention in this context of sustainable value delivery. Timely, here, refers to the ability of the company to rapidly respond to consumer needs in fast changing markets. But it also includes the capacity of the organization to anticipate and influence sustainable patterns of consumption and market behaviour (being innovative also means being able to satisfy still unrecognized but latent customer needs).

The relationship between supplier and customer is mutually reinforcing when approached through power balance. This relationship evolves in a pattern of mutual causality, in which the company influences the demand by offering satisfaction of hitherto unmet needs and the customer influences supply by revealing patterns of consumer behaviour. In the context of sustainability, agile companies should not only adapt, but also anticipate and influence markets through sustainability-driven behaviours that leave a positive footprint on society and the planet.

EMMA Safety Shoes is a Dutch company near Maastricht that manufactures and commercializes high-quality safety shoes for industrial workers.[13] The firm is driven by the purpose "let's make a positive footprint", which led the company to make the world's first recyclable safety shoes. Traditionally focused on safety and comfort, the organization added sustainability to its brand value proposition, contributing to Sustainable Development Goals 9 (industry, innovation and infrastructure), 12 (responsible consumption and production) and 8 (decent work and economic growth).

Targeted to an upscale market segment that values durability, the company developed a strategic mission based on guaranteeing safest foot protection based on socially responsible production, with control of the circular supply cycle. Closing the circularity loop presented implications not only along the supply chain, but also in the incorporation of disassembly and recyclability in product design. These implications were related to a longer production cycle and additional costs in the supply chain, which were hampering an agile delivery of the value to the customer. The challenge, therefore, was to develop a social and environmental value proposition for the customer that could also be agile.

In order to address the challenge, the company launched six operational strategies for achieving full circularity of their products: anchoring the positive footprint in the cultural DNA of the organization; developing a sustainable supply chain; greening the production process through a zero waste factory and energy neutral production; market positioning as the progressive, circular company in the safety field; designing a circular shoe collection; and developing a circular system including reverse logistics, material passports and next use applications.

As a result, the company couples sustainable innovation in product development with a strong customer orientation, which allows EMMA to respond in a timely fashion, and with agility, to customer needs. The brand places a QR code in every shoe, that, together with an app, allows interaction with users and the collection of customer data and feedback that is used to tailor solutions at the clients' company level.

The Danish brewing company, Carlsberg, is a pioneering firm in developing sustainable disruptive innovations that anticipate market needs in a timely way. In 2014, the company identified biomaterials as a socio-ecological megatrend among consumers and opinion leaders. In 2015, Flemming Besenbacher, president of the Carlsberg Foundation, presented the green fibre bottle initiative[14] at the World Economic Forum in Davos, a nature-inspired biodegradable bottle made from sustainably sourced wood fibre. This initiative was framed within the objective of reducing the carbon footprint and plastic waste, fitting Carlsberg's purpose of "brewing for a better today and tomorrow".

A major challenge for delivering nature-inspired innovations is to create the demand for them. To develop the new solutions with agility requires prototyping (which, in this case, requires having the technology), eliciting potential customers' feedback and iterating this process until there is a viable product with a projected demand.

In this context, the Davos presentation was cleverly targeted at raising the interest of, and calling on, other organizations to join the challenge. Carlsberg partnered with ecoXpac, a packaging-based startup, and the Denmark Technical University in a three-year project sponsored by the Innovation Fund Denmark. Besides communicating the challenge, this initiative had three additional objectives: kicking off the open innovation process to attract talent and resources to work on the development of the product; creating the market expectation targeting ecologically aware consumers (the early adopters), key for driving demand and reducing time to market once the prototype translates into a viable product; and sparking the purpose-driven culture at Carlsberg by engaging employees in the challenge.

The company developed two prototypes in 2019 and attracted a community of companies that shares the vision to develop sustainable packaging with the objective to increase resources for the initiative (Coca-Cola and L'Oréal, among others) so that the alliance can proceed to test and iterate the product and launch it to the market as soon as possible.

Abundance

Abundance principle articulated:

Be open and grateful to financial nourishment, reflect the full social, environmental and economic costs of doing business and ensure profit is inclusively distributed.

Walking the triple bottom line

It is becoming a common practice to talk about the importance of generating shared value, but still few companies dare to account for the full costs that the organization incurs in doing business this way. The traditional sustainability approach focuses on zooming in on the reduction of environmental harm and in highlighting the social successes in helping stakeholders. For example, estimating how much the company has reduced CO_2 emissions or fossil fuels' energy consumption. Yet, few companies transparently reflect the total amount of greenhouse gas emissions or energy consumption that they account for in running their operations. In some cases, big global corporations such as Google, Facebook, Apple, Microsoft, Netflix and Amazon do not even disclose their fiscal contributions to the communities where they operate and from which they benefit,[15] although some of them have private philanthropies that work on social and environmental issues.

The principle of abundance starts by welcoming with appreciation the financial returns that the organization accrues thanks to its capacity and ability to generate value for its stakeholders. Abundance is the principle that fuels a genuine approach to sustainable transformation, alienated from green- and brand-washing impulses. This awareness-based practice requires, first, an appreciation of the resources and their full environmental and social costs associated with operating the business, besides the economic; and second, ensuring that profit is inclusively and fairly distributed to stakeholders. This appreciation translates to openly reflecting them in the company's accounting systems and accountability frameworks.

There are several triple bottom line accounting tools on the market, but, as John Elkington affirms, the triple bottom line "was supposed to provoke deeper thinking about capitalism and its future, but many early adopters understood the concept as a balancing act, adopting a trade-off mentality".[16]

In this context of adopting the triple bottom line to drive sustainable change, Life Food is a German organic tofu producer that decided to apply the Economy of the Common Good Balance Sheet as an accounting system that led to rethinking the sustainability strategy and revising the culture of the organization.[17] The company's senior leadership resonated with Felber's ideas on how to foster environmental sustainability, solidarity and social justice, human dignity and transparency and co-determination, the four dimensions of the Common Good Matrix.[18] These dimensions are an expression of the triple bottom line, and they involve all stakeholders (making a direct link to control between the Stakeholders and Full Profit corporate stars).

The main challenge in implementing the Common Good Matrix was how to engage employees and build a shared culture connected with a reframed concept of abundance. This implied, on the one hand, changing the incentives system that models individual and organizational behaviour. This, to me, is actually one of the structural root causes that explains why the adoption of the triple bottom line has not contributed enough to systems change. Changing the culture without changing the incentives is like telling a fish to climb a tree. It is just unfair. On the other hand, changing the accounting system was an opportunity to form a multidisciplinary task force team of twenty employees that co-created the balance sheet and defined the indicators corresponding to the aforementioned matrix dimensions.

As a result of these practices, the company experienced an increase in employee engagement and participation. Among other things, these practices help employees become more aware of the abundance that the company was already implicitly generating. Furthermore, the process allowed the company to prioritize new strategies and actions aimed at improving the system based on employees' direct suggestions and recommendations.

When the company reflects the full costs of doing business and openly engages employees and stakeholders, abundance creates more abundance. Abundance, the principle that corresponds to the Full Profit star, can be a contributing factor to creating an impact brand, which reflects the generation cycle to the Brand Impact Recognition star.

Dornbirn, a savings bank founded in the nineteenth century, incorporated the Common Good Balance Sheet in its corporate strategy in 2014. This allowed the company to revitalize the foundational values based on trust, openness, determination, courage and sustainability. It proved to be an effective intervention to amplify the DNA of the company to employees and other stakeholders (illustrating the direct relation of value control between the Full Profit and the Human Leadership corporate stars).

As a consequence, employees proposed and designed a mobility management plan to foster ecological behaviour, incentivizing alternative and cost-effective means of transportation. The senior management of the bank also applied new criteria for guiding ethical financial investments based on the four dimensions of the Common Good Balance Sheet. Adopting the Common Good Balance Sheet triggered the application of the principle of abundance. This was reflected in the behaviour of the employees, who became empowered to propose environmentally friendly and ethical strategies in order to increase the positive impact of the organization.

Impact

Impact principle articulated:

Develop a corporate brand that is recognized by the impact it generates to stakeholders and society; to do so, evaluate and communicate impact

Evaluating a cultural transformation

Building an impact brand is the dream of many contemporary organizations transitioning to the new business paradigm. They want to be recognized by the impact they generate on the world, how and why they do it. It is the ultimate organizational awareness step, topping Maslow's hierarchy of needs, the greatest challenge. If impact is the result of business activities across time, an impact brand requires a culture where results are systematically evaluated on the basis of what an organization's intended social, environmental and economic aims are, why it has those aims and how it has achieved its desired outcome, or not.

There are two main purposes behind developing an impact brand, and they are not mutually exclusive. One is accountability to stakeholders. Being aware of, and duly communicating, the value and the impact the organization generates for its stakeholders is a strategy to engage them, to account for the purposes and objectives of the organization and to increase the corporate brand recognition from there.

The second purpose in developing an impact brand is learning and innovation. In both cases, the organization utilizes evaluation to gather evidence on the impact it has generated to its stakeholders. When the purpose is learning, this evidence is then used to trigger an internal discussion to inform impact-based decision-making for improving current initiatives or developing new innovations, so that the organization can adapt to constant changes in context and markets.

AMEC, the Association of Internationalized Industrial Companies in Spain, has been a pioneer in exploring the dynamics of the Brand Impact Recognition star. This association plays a pivotal role in supporting the international expansion of Spanish industry, one of the sectors that drives innovation and the creation of employment.

Amid a VUCA context characterized by rapid changes in digitalization, industry 4.0 and geopolitics, in 2017, AMEC developed a three-year strategic plan called Vision 2020. The plan put forwards a new value proposition that promised a 25% increase in the impact of AMEC on the international competitiveness of its associates. This was the first attempt of the organization to measure the impact it has on its member companies.

Against this backdrop, my partner and world-class evaluator Jordi del Bas and I helped AMEC in developing and implementing a system for evaluating and measuring impact through a process of co-creation. The first challenge we faced was to set up a system of evaluation that could measure the 25% impact increase in three years, so that AMEC's management could be accountable to stakeholders. In this context, AMEC soon realized that such a system could not only provide information on the extent of the impact but should also be able to generate information for learning and innovation. AMEC senior management also realized that, in the mid- and long-term, this had to become the primary purpose of the impact system.

In developing the system, we started with the following enquiries: what does impact mean to AMEC staff? What does impact mean to AMEC member companies? How is that impact generated? To whom and under what circumstances? This process of enquiry included the participation of an illustrative sample of AMEC's associates in a number of co-creation workshops and focus groups.

The impact system allows the identification of the areas of current value of AMEC from the user's perspective, that is, the value perceived by AMEC's user companies. The system also identifies unrealized expected value. Impact was defined as AMEC's contribution to the international competitiveness of its associate organizations. The association operates as a value-generating ecosystem by facilitating spaces for networking and inter-business collaboration, the transfer of knowledge in areas directly related to internationalization, brand influence and visibility to support the internationalization process.

The system is grounded on a tailored impact model called the Pyramid of Impact (Figure 6.3) that emerged as a result of the process of enquiry.

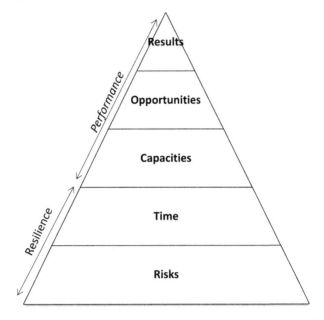

Figure 6.3 AMEC's Pyramid of Impact. Source: courtesy of AMEC

The model features five dimensions that capture how AMEC actions generate impact: reduction of risks and timings (dimensions that reinforce the resilience of the companies in the internationalization process), increased capacities, access to new opportunities and increase in positive results (dimensions that have a direct impact on the international performance of the companies).

The system collects data through in-depth semi-structured interviews with AMEC associate companies. Data is quantitatively and qualitatively analysed and used to feed into innovation and strategic planning, learning and adaptation and customer engagement. The whole process of setting up a system for evaluating impact led to a series of takeaways that are summarized as follows.

- Developing an impact system for the first time requires the vision and commitment of the senior leadership. Leaders need to clearly communicate the benefits, expectations and implications of the newly implemented system to the rest of the organization. Further, leaders need to assign resources to the development and implementation of the system.
- The implementation of the system requires a continuous effort in developing the internal capacities of the employees to collect, analyse, and reflect upon the utility of impact data.

- Since the system captures the impact in terms of value perceived by the associates, it was critical to engage associates in a continuous process of discussion and co-creation.

- The organization needs to align staff incentives to the implementation of the impact system, so that incentive measures actually foster the behaviours and capacities that are conducive to develop an impact-focused culture.

- The organization reorientated its marketing and communication strategies to incorporate an impact perspective, with a clearer focus on the real value that AMEC is delivering to its associates (as opposed to a focus on delivery, that is, activities and services provided by the organization).

Working on the development and implementation of the impact system had three direct effects that illustrate the dynamics of the Brand Impact Recognition star. The first was that evaluating the impact of AMEC led to the transformation of the culture of the organization towards a culture of impact. The transformation was driven by changes in mindsets and behaviours of the employees, who mainstreamed the impact approach and linked it to the rest of business processes in the organization. The second effect was the engagement of the associates, who welcomed AMEC's efforts and strategic vision in adopting impact as the focus and approach of its strategy. And the third effect was the recognition and appreciation that AMEC had in the community, as shown by numerous articles featuring AMEC's impact approach published in the media.

In the words of Joan Tristany, AMEC's CEO,

> the association carries out a continuous task of innovation in order to proactively offer the best services to the internationalized companies, as well as to respond with the highest efficiency to their needs. This pioneering system of impact measurement and evaluation allow us to ensure that AMEC services are the most accurate and effective to our industry in the current scenario of increasing global competitiveness.

The Brand Impact Recognition (Wood) star feeds the value generating process to the Human Leadership star (Fire). The value generating and control dynamics of the Zen Business model plays a continuous role in the balance and development of the organization. The relationship between the two stars (Brand Impact Recognition ⟶ Human Leadership) links the learning acquired in the Brand Impact Recognition star to feed a process of reflection on the revision and evaluation of the purpose of the organization that is stated in the Human Leadership star. This process is aimed at finding new strategies and innovations that allow the organization to anticipate, and adapt to, the continuous changes of a complex environment.

In this chapter we explored how seekers can use the natural principles-based power of Gaia organizations to lead and develop the transition towards the new business paradigm. But this is not the only way. Seekers who do not fit within any organization, or do not simply see the potentiality of transformation in their current organization (or who have just been fired) have the option to create their own entrepreneurial project. This is the subject of the next chapter.

Notes

1 Patton, M.Q. (2017). *Principles-focused Evaluation: The GUIDE.* Guilford Press.
2 Liu et al. (2007). Coupled human and natural systems. *AMBIO: A Journal of the Human Environment,* 36(8), 639–649.
3 The CHANS framework is defined as "systems in which human and natural components interact", which is fully applicable in business organizations. Ibid.
4 Business Roundtable is an association of chief executive officers of America's leading companies working to promote a thriving U.S. economy and expanded opportunity for all Americans through sound public policy (www.businessroundtable.org retrieved 27th August 2020).
5 The business case for purpose, *Harvard Business Review* (2015).
6 Chapman shared his insights in the interview with the Spanish newspaper *La Vanguardia,* published April 20 2020 in La Contra section.
7 This analysis is based on my own interpretation of the Zen Business workshops I facilitated in the company in 2016.
8 Voxel Group analysis is based on a webinar that CEO Àngel Garrido delivered to the Master in Sustainable Business & Innovation at EADA Business School and personal interviews we conducted in June 2020.
9 This analysis is based on my own interpretation of the organizational development process that I facilitated in the company in 2019.
10 Casa Luker analysis is based on personal interviews I had with Sergio Restrepo, vice president of Innovation, in June 2020.
11 Sawyer, K. (2015). Group flow and group genius. *The NAMTA Journal,* 40(3).
12 Csikszentmihalyi, M. (2008). *Flow: The psychology of optimal experience.* HarperCollins.
13 EMMA analysis is based on a field visit to the company in 2019 and on an interview with the head of the corporate social responsibility of the company.
14 My own analysis based on the case: "Sustainability through open innovation: Carlsberg and the Green Fiber Bottle", authored by Henry Chesbrough et al. (2018, UC Berkeley – Haas School of Business).
15 Tax avoidance has become a recurrent issue among big tech companies, as the non-profit Fair Tax Mark argues in its report *The Silicon Six and Their $100 billion Global Tax Gap,* published in 2019.
16 In: 25 years ago I coined the phrase "triple bottom line." Here's why it's time to rethink it, by Elkington (*Harvard Business Review,* June 2018).
17 Felber, C. et al. (2019). The Common Good Balance Sheet, an adequate tool to capture non-financials? *Sustainability,* 11(14), 3791.

18 The case analyses of Life Food and Dornbirn are based on the paper "Foundations and applications of the Economy of the Common Good" (published by the Institut für Gemeinwohlorientiertes Wirtschaften).

References

Csikszentmihalyi, M. (2008). *Flow: The psychology of optimal experience*. HarperCollins.
Felber, C. et al. (2019). The Common Good Balance Sheet, an adequate tool to capture non-financials? *Sustainability*, 11(14), 3791.
Liu et al. (2007). Coupled human and natural systems. *AMBIO: A Journal of the Human Environment*, 36(8), 639–649.
Lovelock, J. (2016). *Gaia: A new look at life on earth*. Oxford Landmark Science.
Margulis, L. (1998). *Symbiotic Planet: A new look at evolution*. Basic Books.
Patton, M.Q. (2017). *Principles-focused Evaluation: The GUIDE*. Guilford Press.
Sawyer, K. (2015). Group flow and group genius. *NAMTA Journal*, 40(3).

Chapter 7

Designing the Gaia startup

Practical guidelines

When I facilitate Zen Business workshops,[1] it is recurrent that some of the participants—they all fit with the seeker profile—realize that their current job positions do not fulfil them. It is a painful insight at first. While navigating the emotional ups and downs associated with this process of self-awareness, some of them start figuring out alternatives to reverse this situation.

Some of these participants end up refocusing their learning objectives during the workshop to design their own purpose-driven entrepreneurial projects. Purpose-driven entrepreneurship is a chance to realize their dream jobs outside of an established organization. This option is becoming more plausible nowadays for two reasons. First, because many established organizations are not yet people centred or purpose driven. There is a structural global pandemic of demotivation that illustrates that a large majority of companies does not know how to engage and motivate employees in their work.[2] Second, the labour market supply—demand decoupling is provoking a larger number of people to work under part-time arrangements or freelancing. This trend is known as the gig economy, which is pushing more people to work as self-employed.[3]

It seems, then, that either one option, the necessity to find a meaningful job, or the other, the need to find employment in the context of the gig economy, paves the way for the emergence of the Gaia entrepreneur. This type of entrepreneur, however, is not only moved by the idea to do business. She sees her own project or startup as an opportunity and a channel to express her creativity at the service of a higher purpose, a purpose that, in most cases is there, latent, waiting to be discovered and activated.

The journey of the Gaia entrepreneur is one of personal and professional discovery, a developmental and transformational journey. This chapter explores the premise that this journey provides not only a business-orientated experience, but also, and above all, a meaningful life experience.

Alignment to the Gaia principles

Gaia entrepreneurs (such as the ones that are featured in this chapter) are intrinsically aligned and motivated by the Gaia principles, even though quite often they do not realize this. How can you know that you are a Gaia entrepreneur? Here's a quick test.

* *Lifefulness*: are you pushed by an internal will to do things that really matter to you, for your community, for the environment, and for life at all? If you are concerned about this, in any form, and you want to contribute in a meaningful way, you are probably aligned to the principle of lifefulness.

* *Awareness*: do you assess your work for the potential it has to bring you a personal and professional development and learning experience overall? If you are genuinely concerned about working on developing your personal skills and capabilities, cultivating a growth mindset in order to become a better version of yourself, you are probably on the virtuous path illuminated by the principle of awareness.

* *Bio-logic*: are you increasingly looking for new ways of making your own life more sustainable and nature-friendly? If you are willing to adopt a sustainability-driven and natural lifestyle, and you make your choices based upon that, you are probably applying the principle of bio-logic to different areas of your life—nutrition, exercising, housing, mobility, education, purchases, relationships, etc.

The Zen Business model as an adaptive design framework for Gaia startups

Once the Gaia entrepreneur dares to develop her Gaia-based startup project, the next question that emerges is: how am I going to do that? The Zen Business model provides an open and organic design framework to guide this entrepreneurial journey. It is open and organic because it adapts to the context, situation, personality and expertise of each entrepreneur, following the principle of *wuwei*, or natural action. This entails, on the one hand, departing from the level of awareness of each person, and, on the other hand, to leverage the in-built talents and strengths of the entrepreneur.

The approach to implementing the Zen Business model, guided by the five corporate stars, hinges upon two organic and complementary coaching methods. The first is the maieutic-based enquiry method.[4] This process starts with thought-provoking questions in each corporate star that help reveal the entrepreneur's underlying assumptions and mental models driving her own behaviour. They also probe, test and reskill the entrepreneur's ability to overcome these assumptions in order to make her own project a reality.

The second coaching method is T-Qualia, an enabling environment that facilitates creating the experiences that guide and accompany the entrepreneur's enquiry process. The main objective of applying this methodology is to help the entrepreneur connect with the Tao-based universal principles that drive her own genuine will, expectations and energy throughout the entrepreneurial journey.

The intention of combining these two methods—T-Qualia and maieutic-based enquiry—is to marry the absolute and intuitive knowledge that all entrepreneurs carry within themselves with the rational knowledge that is required to reflect and make sense of the experiences that brought the entrepreneur to put her own energy, knowledge and skills at the service of Gaia (see Figure 2.1 in Chapter 2).

The application of the Zen Business model follows the application of each corporate star, starting with the Human Leadership star, as explained in Chapter 5. In facilitating the coaching sessions, the facilitator uses a combination of the two methods described above. The intervention requires, under each star, to specify the concepts that frame the working sessions in that star, set up the tools that the entrepreneur will work with in utilising the concepts and discuss the implications derived from applying each star.

Human Leadership star: Fire

Conceptual work

Gaia entrepreneurs find they are often precluded from classic entrepreneurship approaches because these approaches are primarily focused on selling and maximizing the economic return of the entrepreneur's investment in the shortest time. This approach does not resonate well with them. The application of the Zen Business model to Gaia startups begins with an internal process of reflection and self-awareness guided by the Human Leadership star.

This internal work is essential for aligning the entrepreneur's motivation and expectations—related to her contribution to Gaia—with her own personality, talents and leadership skills—related to her role as change maker. When this internal–external balancing calibration happens, the entrepreneur naturally flows to a state of consciousness where she becomes self-aware of her power to act in line with who she is.

Ester Galindo is a Gaia entrepreneur who started Antum, a nutrition-based approach created with the purpose of reminding people of what they need to eat, how they need to move and in what environment they need to live, so that people's well-being improves in harmony with the planet. Previously to her work with the Zen Business model, Ester had been tempted by classic business as usual approaches that saw her potential and recommended her to directly scale up her project through content creation and intensive marketing through social media. However, she was not ready for that.

She underwent a process of self-awareness, making sense of her past experiences—a cumulation of crises and revelations—that brought her to create her dream project by following her intuition and the knowledge she gained from it. She reflected upon a fundamental question that helped her find balance between the potential of her business and her ideal of harmony in life: what does success mean to me? This question is critical in reflecting upon the *wuwei* principle of natural action.

She came up with five values that helped guide her life, business choices and behaviour: nature (what we really are); network (the ecosystem that hosts all living organisms); harmony (the defining feature of healthy living organisms that organically flow and prosper); intelligence (the capacity of sentient beings to connect with their own intuition); and communication (the act of sharing the knowledge learned in a clear, direct and understandable way). To Ester, the quest for meaning is what triggers the desire to make a better world.

Tools

The "purpose quest" is a powerful exercise to guide the work on the Human Leadership star. It consists of five steps.

1. Choose a T-Qualia practice you feel at ease with to activate your creative mind. Meditation and nature walks are among the most useful.
2. Identify the top five critical moments of life transformation that have led you to the place you are now. They can be key learnings based on experience, insightful crises-based learnings or inspirational learnings from people who have touched you and helped you with your own development process. Connect the dots.
3. Write the learnings down as your story and share them with a colleague or a friend. You can use visuals to help you guide the storytelling.
4. With her help, identify the recurrent patterns that underlie these takeaway points.
5. Based upon that, write your purpose statement.

Purpose, above all, is a question that connects us to life. This work on purpose allows us to channel the exploratory process of self-awareness. Who am I? Why do I exist? Why do I do what I do? Why do I want to do this now? These are essential questions, the heart of the matter. The purpose quest enables a suitable environment to provoke reflection and insight.

That was the case with Simona Galbiati, who asked herself those questions during the purpose quest. As a result, she became aware of the resistances she had as a Gaia entrepreneur. She associated them with the mental models she internalized due to her childhood's formal education. School taught her to associate intelligence to social sciences and mathematics, leaving arts and humanities aside. That mindset guided her to start a career as an economist, the formal way to earn a living, and she disconnected from her passion for arts for a while.

But that was temporary. She reconnected with that passion after moving to another country, by working on an illustration project that sparked her motivation to develop her artistic talents. That happened at a time when she was working on developing her ecological awareness of life. A learning journey in Bolivia awakened her desire to integrate arts and spirituality in her daily life, in all dimensions.

Simona's quest illustrates an underlying assumption—"you can't live from the arts"—that conditioned her behaviour as an artist and limited her potential as a Gaia entrepreneur. She was very brave in challenging this assumption. As a result, she liberated herself from those beliefs, inspired by her purpose to become a channel and use her artistry to help people connect with their own magic in order to live a more loving and harmonious life. She can no longer live without art.

Implications

Working on your human leadership is an inside job. Purpose is a big word. As such, it can both shine a light and cast a shadow. What if you do not find your purpose? Well, it can be frustrating. But that is all right. In the end, purpose is just a word. The important issue is the meaning you attach to the term "purpose". You can still follow a purpose you like above others, or just simply follow your passion. There can't be any purpose without passion. It's the energy that qualifies the purpose. If you identify passion-driven pathways, just pull that thread.

Another issue with purpose is the fear it may create. Some people feel repelled by the word purpose. My assumption here is that discovering and naming a purpose implies a choice. And any choice in life carries an opportunity cost. In other words, choosing a life path implies renouncing other life paths. And some people feel constrained when they are making that choice. It is like a sensation of vertigo, of losing some kind of freedom, of giving up some open possibilities that life may bring up later on.

But, to me, this is a rationalized misconception of the meaning of purpose. Purpose is an emotional work that reveals deeper illuminations of one's passions. The work on purpose is related to the limbic system of our brain. We are the ones that make it work—or not—for us.

Mònica Calderón is a multi-faceted Gaia entrepreneur who was initially reluctant to tackle the work on purpose. She felt limited by the concept, as every time she got closer to a concrete purpose statement, she felt she was renouncing other potential purposes. Furthermore, having a concrete purpose was in conflict with her values of freedom and autonomy.

But she did something inspiring. She let herself be touched and moved by this feeling of discomfort, a process that requires humility to alienate the ego from the observed stressful phenomenon. As she persevered, she was able to combine T-Qualia practices with the enquiry process in order to explore the concept of purpose from different angles and depths. Finally, she got her own personal "satori", or insightful revelation. She naturally resonated with an open purpose, wide in scope, which housed all her concerns and interests.

She started The Love Way, which is a project aimed at cultivating love in life by fostering women's self-esteem and self-love. She developed her own method by drawing on her own expertise as a psychologist while combining that with new interests and knowledge she learned from experiencing and getting in touch with other disciplines.

The Human Leadership star is about lighting the fire; fuelling and channelling our energy to the things we care about in life, for life. Leadership consists of being able to inspire and communicate this fire, the vision of the project aligned with how it is relevant for society. Despite the transcendence of this work, we should approach this process with lightness, naturally, and with a touch of humour. Purpose is also subject to the evolutionary state of our consciousness. As we change, as everything changes, our purpose may change too.

Stakeholders' star: Earth

Conceptual work

Having a guiding purpose and values is the personal and professional development work that allows the entrepreneur to have a clear value proposition to identify, attract and select key stakeholders (Fire $\longrightarrow$ Human Leadership generates Earth $\longrightarrow$ Stakeholders). Stakeholders nurture the Gaia project with knowledge, skills and resources. Purpose fitness is a critical attractor and a matchmaker of potential partners, the trigger of co-creation. This criterion applies for attracting the people that resonate with the project. It builds on the premise that people will be interested in the project if they resonate with its purpose. They feel identified with the intention that the entrepreneurial initiative has in serving Gaia (the mother Earth), in any life-creating and life-caring form.

This purpose-led intention, properly channelled and communicated, creates a vibration that captures the attention of other potential Gaia entrepreneurs. During the development of the Stakeholders' star, entrepreneurs often report, with amazement, how key people become interested in the project once the entrepreneur is clear about the purpose and starts communicating it with the objective of finding the right purpose-led partners.

That was the case of Betta Marzio, who initially started the Zen Business process on her quest to develop an observatory with the purpose of helping working mothers cope with mental health and other stress-related issues. During her work on the Human Leadership star, she connected with a different purpose. In general, connecting with a purpose that is not related to your initial idea or to the project you want to develop can happen when you are fully and openly immersed in your purpose quest. Sometimes we tend to fall in love with the idea behind the purpose, instead of the purpose itself with all its implications.

In this case, Betta developed a purpose-based value proposition connecting her background in communication with her passion for spirituality and conscious living. She connected with the need to help brands in becoming more conscious, to inspire a better society and planet. She persuaded her business partner, Piero Caterino, with a similar background and the same passion for design and spirituality to join her in setting up their own business to help conscious entrepreneurs. Piero resonated with Betta's trajectory, which mirrored Piero's (they shared similar professional and personal backgrounds in communication and conscious living). As both were inspired and engaged by the same purpose, they created MeteOro, an agency specializing in conscious design and communication.

Tools

The "Stakeholders' constellation" is a tool aimed at identifying a group of stakeholders that is motivated by a shared higher purpose. It consists of the following steps.

1. Identify the key stakeholders that you feel the project needs. Name them and assign a role-based typology to each of them: employee, supplier, business partner, investor, business angel, mentor, and so on. Write them as dots in a blank canvas.

2. For each single stakeholder previously identified, ask and reflect upon the following questions:

- Does this stakeholder share my purpose? And my values? In what way?
- What value does this stakeholder bring to the project?
- What value does my project bring to this stakeholder?

3. Link the stakeholders identified with bi-directional arrows (the dots written in step 1), including yourself, and describe the type of value-based relationship you would like to establish.

4. Armed with your purpose-based value proposition pitch, contact and inspire them.

This exercise also allows one to develop a mutually beneficial value proposition for each stakeholder, with a high degree of personalization depending on the roles and interests of each stakeholder. At an initial stage of development, the Gaia entrepreneurs need, above all, funding. Any project needs a lot of energy and commitment from entrepreneurs, who often find themselves struggling with the new project while personal finances shrink. They usually think of contacting traditional investors, such as banks or private equity investors, investors that often seek short-term profitability from the projects they invest in.

Ted Nozun and Sam Goldman were in that situation when they came up with the idea to set up D.light,[5] a social enterprise aimed at delivering affordable solar-powered solutions targeted to poor people without access to reliable energy in developing countries. They met at Stanford while studying a course on "Design for extreme affordability". They found they were passionate about social business and the Bottom of the Pyramid[6] and they discovered they shared the same values.

Initially, they sought seed capital ($10,000) mostly from family and friends who resonated with the idea and contributed to finance the first field trips and early prototyping. As the project advanced, Nozun and Goldman identified a set of advisers—mainly faculty—who provided feedback and guidance to the project. To attract more funding, they decided to look for impact investors, a group of investors that specifically target projects with high prospects of delivering social impact instead of short-term profitability.

In their case, they entered social impact project competitions. This process did not only allow them to raise funding for the project—$1.6 million from six venture firms and four business angels—but also enabled them to assemble the right ecosystem of stakeholders. They worked in partnership in order to develop and refine D.light products, with a long-term commitment to the entrepreneurs and to the project.

Implications

Working on the Stakeholders' star is an outside job. It is about finding the right partners and the right people for your project. It can be exciting, but also time-consuming and stressful. The entrepreneur spends a lot of time researching, pitching the purpose, designing and developing the project, networking and, often, investing in the acquisition of knowledge and skills.

Sustaining this process requires financing the transition until the project generates enough income. In some cases, the development of the Gaia project is conducted in parallel with the entrepreneur's current job, taking time outside the job to work on the project. In other cases, the entrepreneur devotes full-time to developing her project. In the former case, the entrepreneur enjoys more financial security but may lack time; in the latter, the entrepreneur has plenty of time but may lack financial support after a given time—normally until she runs out of savings or financial external support.

One way or another, this process is like crossing a desert. Along this dry journey, it is common that the entrepreneur finds herself tempted by external job offers and project proposals that deliver on the promise of solving her financial insecurities. The entrepreneur may wonder: what if I take that job, save some money and resume my project later on? This kind of temptation tests the entrepreneur's commitment and ability to shape the project's stakeholders ecosystem, which is a critical step for the success of the initiative (the chance of obtaining a more financially secure alternative to the project proves the strength of the entrepreneur's connection to its purpose, which is measured by the resilience she demonstrates when she experiences difficulties in engaging stakeholders).

In a situation of desperation, which I've seen in most Gaia entrepreneurs (and experienced for myself), the entrepreneur may recall her purpose and values again. Having the fire alive and connecting with it in harsh situations provides the impetus that helps pass the test, giving comfort and a sense of hope in difficult times. These times mould the resilience of the entrepreneur and bolster her real willingness to become a Gaia type of business.

The process of stakeholders' matchmaking requires networking and, therefore, a great deal of personal interaction. This interaction provides a wealth of information on the fitness and compatibility between the entrepreneur and the potential partner. Most often, this information is tacitly captured during the interviews and other encounters with potential stakeholders. This requires a strong sense of intuition and perception on behalf of the entrepreneur. Initial assumptions on compatibility can be validated by further rounds of interaction and initial steps of trial and error in preliminary collaborative work.

Marketing and Innovation star: Metal

Conceptual work

The entrepreneur and her stakeholders collaborate and use their knowledge and skills to serve Gaia, to deliver the value that has been identified and co-created in the previous corporate stars (Earth generates Metal). Value delivery is shaped through the development of products and services that are communicated and launched to the market. This is a tangible and visible process. It is when the entrepreneur can finally admire her baby, which goes out there seeking the social embodiment of Gaia. For any entrepreneur, this is the real moment of truth.

The work on the Marketing and Innovation star joins the innovation process of coming up with a differentiated product or service with the marketing process that elaborates a well-positioned sustainable value proposition targeted to a well-defined customer need. Market analysis is definitely helpful in identifying benchmark projects that may provide inspiration. But benchmarks are also especially useful for identifying niche market spaces or small "blue oceans"[7] where the possibility of differentiation exists.

Antonio Arco is a Gaia entrepreneur who redefined the concept of illness in osteopathy. As an osteopath, during years of practice, he explored the links between the patient's psyche, her emotions and her bodily organs. This holistic approach led him to create the concept of organic psycho-osteopathy, which precisely unifies the patient's psychology with her emotions throughout her organs. The body links the psyche with the organs, which act as communicating vessels that express illness and health through the body.

This process of research led Antonio to develop Empo, a clinic aimed at improving the well-being of individuals through this holistic understanding of health and illness. The value proposition hinged upon his brand-new concept, organic psycho-osteopathy, which led him to develop his own methodology. It was a unique methodology crafted by Antonio's own experience, which made it his differential factor. He targeted, on the one hand, patients looking for alternative holistic approaches to classical treatments and, on the other hand, health industry professionals interested in getting professional education and training on this new approach. He complemented the offering of treatments and educational programmes with a mix of personal growth activities that rounded out his portfolio of services.

Empo's higher purpose quickly attracted a group of highly motivated individuals that studied with Antonio. His vision was to develop a community of practitioners with his students. Some of them became Empo's professors and osteopaths, and, above all, brand ambassadors. Empo's business model is based on a systemic understanding and personalized approach to health that seeks to empower the individual. This model builds trust, which is the basis of Empo's word-of-mouth marketing strategy. The clinic's philosophy is to conduct as few treatments as possible, to honestly assess and constantly communicate the feedback to the patients and to have a group of highly skilled professionals that constantly challenge themselves in deepening Empo's approach.

Empo's case illustrates how Fire (Human Leadership) shaped Metal (Marketing and Innovation) while, simultaneously, Earth (Stakeholders) nurtured Metal: his higher purpose attracted clients that became his employees and jointly refined the clinics business model and delivered Empo's value proposition to the market.

Tools

The "brand brief" is an exercise aimed at guiding the entrepreneur in developing her differentiated value proposition, her brand positioning and her marketing mix.[8] It consists of the following steps.

1. Describe your ideal customer profile. Focus on the following segmented variables: problem/need, behaviour, lifestyle, and socio-economic indicators such as age, gender and income. Ask yourself: why may they contact me? Assign "personas" to their profile.[9]

2. Identify and benchmark your competitors (your admired competitors that inspire you and that could eventually become your collaborators). List five projects/brands in the same sector that you admire, that are competitors but that also have the potential to inspire you. Particularly check, for each of them: what is their product/service portfolio? What is their target market? What do you like about them? What can you—and your project—learn from them? What do you do differently?

3. Elaborate your brand positioning statement. Ask yourself: what differentiates what I offer from the rest? Focus on the brand's four dimensions: its sense of purpose (spirit), its authenticity (soul), its emotion (mind) and its functionality (body).

4. Design your marketing mix. Prototype a differentiated product/service portfolio, its associated pricing, the place(s) you are going to sell it (distribution channels), a targeted communication strategy with a mix of social media and identify the brand ambassadors and influencers.

5. Assign a budget for developing all marketing tools you need at this moment. Do you need a website? Do you need a corporate image? Do you need equipment to create your marketing-based content? Do you need a community manager? Do you need training?

Implications

Going through the process of the Marketing and Innovation star implies dealing with two interrelated phenomena: the level of exposure and the tolerance of criticism that the Gaia entrepreneur is willing to assume. These are two stepping-stones in the process of offering the project to Gaia. To what extent are you willing to devote time and energy to social media, with its concomitant exposure? To what extent are you willing to tolerate criticism of your work and branding?

This reflection is necessary in order to scope the outreach of the Gaia project. Some entrepreneurs want to reach a wide audience but they are not ready to give up some degree of privacy and to devote time to social media. The conscious entrepreneur reflects upon these issues in order to find a balance.

That was the case of Marta León. She found her own "blue ocean", following her passion for linking nutrition to help women in improving their health with a solid scientific basis. She developed a tailored methodology, adapting a woman's nutrition to her natural cycles of menstruation, which she applies in one-to-one consultations and trainings. She started sharing her knowledge in a blog, which was getting attention. While developing the Marketing and Innovation star, she realized that to reach a wider audience she would need to go deeper into social media. And that idea frightened her.

She is truly gifted in communicating, so she got pressure from peers and colleagues who noticed that talent and thereby recommended her to delve into developing and sharing audiovisual content. That pressure did not help. This notwithstanding, she found a lot of courage to connect with her purpose, to own her story and to speak her truth. She did this by connecting her scientific mindset to her deep intuition, grounded in her personal experience and background. She realized her story transcended her, and that her learnings could be of value to women. That helped her to become more confident about her project's value, and she started sharing her perspective and telling her story. She opened up about sharing her experience as an act of service to help women's health, which is her way to serve Gaia.

This is a vivid example of how the Marketing and Innovation star is guided by the Human Leadership star—Fire controls and moulds Metal. Purpose and values are like a lighthouse that guides Gaia entrepreneurs in difficult times. When the levels of energy are low, and when resistances manifest in terms of fear—of losing privacy, of opening up to criticism—it is wiser to pause. It is time to connect with one's purpose, reflect and make sense of it rather than losing oneself in the pressures of marketing. Without Fire, the world of marketing can feel quite cold, an unprotected territory that needs a conscious and timely approach.

Full Profit star: Water

Conceptual work

Once the value is delivered to the customer it is time for the Gaia entrepreneur to get the rewards from her service (Metal generates Water). At this point, the entrepreneur's main concern in developing her startup is to guarantee the financial sustainability of the project. This work encompasses designing a revenue model that best captures the value, fitting the purpose and values of the entrepreneur.

Alex Sicart understands technology and entrepreneurship as an opportunity to decentralize control and, therefore, foster citizen empowerment. His entrepreneurial agency is very much embedded in his DNA. At age 13, he set up FileNation, a digital platform for students to share content. At age 17, he co-founded Sharge, a sharing-economy platform of charging stations for electric car users.

His latest development is Shasta, a block chain, mobile-based financial infrastructure aimed at easing the transfer of large amounts of money between peers, without financial intermediaries and, therefore, without commission. Shasta's revenue streams are based on a freemium model with three membership plans, one of which allows some customers to enjoy a number of services free, while the other two available plans increase the apps features for a fee.

When I met Alex in the Zen Business workshops, I felt inspired by his ability to link his own quest and passion for self-awareness with his equal passion for entrepreneurship. To him, life is an entrepreneurial journey, a learning journey that has to make sense to oneself, in relation to others. He gave up a formal college education, as he believed that the real learning was to be found in the act of living and learning by doing, which for him embeds the very essence of the entrepreneur.

To Alex, money is a tool to raise awareness, to empower citizens to invest their money in their projects. He sees money as a way to democratize power relations and to allow people and entrepreneurs to use it at their service, without unnecessary intermediaries that slow down, control and make the flow of money more expensive. This example illustrates how the Full Profit star (Water) can control the Human Leadership star (Fire).

Tools

The "revenue model" is an exercise aimed at guiding the entrepreneur in identifying and describing her income streams associated with the selling of her products and services. The Gaia entrepreneur develops the revenue model after working on the Human Leadership, the Stakeholders and the

Marketing and Innovation stars (in traditional entrepreneurial develop-ments, it is common to start designing the revenue model first, which can jeopardize the Human Leadership star, as too much Water extinguishes the Fire). As a result (Metal generates Water), the revenue model exercise focuses on capturing the real value that the Gaia entrepreneur delivers to the market, taking into consideration the consciousness of the entrepre-neur and the co-creation of sustainable value with the right stakeholders. The revenue model consists of the following steps.

1. Understand the business you are in. Revenue streams are condi-tioned—but not limited—to the type of work you perform. For exam-ple, if you work freelance, or in consulting or coaching, you mostly earn active income, which means the income you earn in exchange for a service you have performed. If you are a published author, you earn passive income, as the work done in the past requires little continued effort to generate ongoing revenue streams.

2. Scope alternative/complementary revenue streams. Gaia entrepreneurs quite often start operating from a transactional, active income-based revenue model (it's a direct way of generating revenue, as custom-ers just pay for the service or product they get, such as in the case of a consultant who trades her time for a fee). However, income is associated to the level of fees and the time spent in performing the service. It is a difficult model to scale. To complement, entrepreneurs can explore asset-building passive income possibilities. These require quite an amount of investment in money and time upfront, but they may open opportunities to diversify the revenue streams. Alternatives include podcasting, books and articles, freemium-based subscription fees, online trainings, ads (they require a lot of traffic though) and affili-ate commissions, among many others.

3. Downsize your expenses and verbalize your expectations. How much do you need? How much is enough? These two issues are critical for designing revenue streams that you feel comfortable with, that allow you to live not only for your project but to enjoy living it, in harmony with the other aspects that are important in your life. Work–life har-monization is a key aspect for the Gaia entrepreneur. These questions are directly associated to your idea of success, which was dealt with under the Human Leadership star (Water controls Fire).

Implications

Most of the Gaia entrepreneurs I have met are not born entrepreneurs. They have come to that situation as a result of a life journey, inspired by the will to find exciting, purpose-driven approaches to contribute to building a healthier, fairer and cleaner world. In most cases, they previously earned their income as employees. This process shapes a pattern of behaviour and a work ethic built around the "trading time for money" assumption as a way to make a living.

As a consequence, the work on the Full Profit star implies a deep reflection around the personal meaning of abundance. Active income is an implicit incentive that allows the entrepreneur to give more time to the project in order to generate the desired income. The Gaia entrepreneur quite often feels pushed to become a workaholic,[10] because she is passionate about what she does and because she needs to secure an income that is not steady, as it does not come from a fixed salary.

Developing an abundance mindset goes beyond being ready and open to acquiring financial wealth. It also entails a self-enquiry process of continuous critical review of how the entrepreneur wants to enjoy the treasures that life on Gaia offers to all of us: nature, culture, relationships, and, above all, time. This enquiry is guided by the following question: what is my idea of success in life? This process allows the entrepreneur to harmonize the value she gives (to Gaia) with the value she receives (from Gaia). Without this process, the entrepreneur may get stuck in an obsession for delivering value, thus ignoring the rest of the treasures that life offers, which may result in imbalances in her overall well-being and satisfaction in life.

Once the entrepreneur approaches her project through an abundance mindset, it opens up to receive the fruits of her work. The Gaia entrepreneur feels worthy of the money that it captures (Water) after delivering value to the market (Metal). Money is not seen as a selfish accumulation of wealth (that is characteristic of a mindset of scarcity), but it is, rather, understood as an empowering energy that, consciously put at the service of Gaia, facilitates opportunities for regenerating the economy, society and the planet (the energy of Water).

Brand Impact Recognition star: Wood

Conceptual work

The social embodiment of the Gaia entrepreneur's products and services in the market is proof that customers appreciate her offerings and her work in general. This social recognition embedded in the Full Profit star fosters a culture geared to a corporate brand recognized by its impact (Water generates Wood).

Against this backdrop, the work in the Brand Impact Recognition star is twofold. First, the entrepreneur designs a model that captures the intended impact to Gaia. This intention was previously defined and stated under the

Human Leadership star. Second, the entrepreneur reflects upon the type of culture that she would like to apply to her project, in order to balance her needs with the needs of the project.

Ester Galindo set up Antum with the purpose of improving people's well-being. To learn about the impact Antum has on its clients, Ester developed her own impact evaluation model. She focused on the process of transformation after the clients start the Antumization (the process that allows the client to change her eating habits). Antum's theory of change is based on the assumption that the simultaneous introduction of healthy eating, moving and environmental habits in the person's lifestyle will positively contribute to the overall levels of well-being of that person. This theory of change was the result of a self-enquiry process grounded in her own experience as an athlete in constant search of high performance.

Ester decided to evaluate this process of transformation empirically, verified by her clients' own experience. She was guided by questions such as: Does my clients' well-being improve during and after the Antumization? How do they feel? What are the effects of the process? She captures that experience through direct feedback that her clients give her in two types of surveys: a symptomatic survey, where she monitors changes in the symptoms that indicate improvement or worsening of well-being conditions, and a habits survey, where she monitors the introduction of healthy habits that drive changes in behaviour. She compares the two data sources in order to identify correlation and causal links between habits and well-being.

In addition, she monitors Antum's activity with a set of indicators that allow her to have a quick overview of Antum's pulse in terms of services delivered and her own education: turnover, by income streams; number of people reached, by type of service; investment in trainings attended.

Ester's impact model illustrates the importance of knowing why and how the Gaia entrepreneur generates impact. It is precisely the knowledge that is generated during this process that allows the entrepreneur the social recognition of her brand (recognized by the impact generated) and the adaptation and development of the project based on the impact feedback received (the learning that is used in improving, adapting and developing the project according to clients' changing needs).

Tools

The "impact model" is an exercise that helps the entrepreneur (i) raise awareness of how it generates the desired impact; and (ii) reflect and learn about how to improve the effectiveness and efficiency of the project based on the impact knowledge raised, aligned with her professional and personal values. It consists of the following steps.

1. Define the type of impact of the project, in line with the intended impact stated in the purpose.

2. Describe how the impact is generated. You can start by designing the theory of change that underpins the transformation, and identify its dimensions and the variables that define it.

3. Design methods for collecting the data you need for monitoring and evaluating the impact. They can be quantitative and/or qualitative.

4. Reflect upon the impact generated on others and the environment, either positive or negative. You can use this information to design corrective and adaptive strategies and actions, as well as to communicate your impact in order to engage your stakeholders.

5. Reflect upon the impact the project is having on yourself. You can do it by assessing your own values against your personal entrepreneurial experience. Are you enjoying it? Are you learning what you expected? Are you accomplishing your own objectives? Can you balance your work with your other life activities? To what extent do you feel fulfilled? Are you missing something? These types of enquiries trigger an internal dialogue that feeds your Human Leadership star again (Wood generates Fire), and makes your purpose evolve and adapt to who you are in a particular moment. In other words, they guide you to live the life you want to live.

Implications

Gaia entrepreneurs are quite often charismatic, self-made; they are people that release positive energy given their passion and belief in what they do. They are driven by impact, and this passion to contribute (that sometimes leads to obsession) can create imbalances in developing a culture in the organization that is too dependent on the entrepreneur's leadership. This creates tensions in the organization, as decision-making concentrates on the founding entrepreneur, and also in the entrepreneur. She usually feels overwhelmed, as her presence, dedication and work are constantly required.

That was the case for Antonio Arco, who set up Empo and managed to attract a loyal community of employees that admired him for his knowledge, charisma and tenacity. At the beginning, that was not an issue, but, as Empo was growing, it was tacitly shaping a culture that was very much dependent on Antonio's leadership.[11] Antonio soon started to feel that issue as a burden.

He assessed the impact of his leadership on the rest of the team and on himself. For the rest of the team, he found his presence was not fostering a culture of autonomy and empowerment. For himself, his increasing dedication to lead and manage Empo was creating tension in his work–life balance, at a time that he was embarking on parenthood.

He identified the need to delegate, decentralize power and foster self-managed teams in order to become more agile and adaptive. However, in the attempt to apply this new governance structure, he found himself caught in the control trap. It was hard for him to let go of control, and now taking a step backwards was a big challenge. Despite the difficulty, he went ahead.

He started by openly sharing his concerns with the team, with the goal of finding a joint solution. He collectively facilitated the development of a shared purpose and values through team building creative sessions. In addition, by reducing his daily presence and trusting his colleagues' self-regulating skills, the team responded positively. He could free time for himself for personal life issues and for starting up other projects and working on Empo's scalability.

Working on the Brand Impact Recognition star entails reflecting upon the potential scenario of scalability. At some point, the entrepreneur will have to deal with the issue of power delegation. This will probably entail curating a team culture where the distribution of work and power is in balance with the project's agility to adapt, as well as the entrepreneur's personal capacity to harmonize life and career goals.

Notes

1 I have been facilitating Zen Business workshops since 2015 in universities and business schools at the executive level in Spain, the Netherlands, South Korea, Mexico, Brazil and Portugal, so far. Participants have mostly two profiles: they are entrepreneurs looking for purpose-driven approaches to design their business projects, or they are executives looking for new sustainability-driven methods to help their organizations generate impact-based growth.
2 According to a Gallup global study, 85% of employees do not report being engaged at work.
3 According to Intuit, the percentage of Americans in the gig economy was 34% in 2016, and is expected to grow to 43% by 2020
4 This method is also known as the Socratic method. According to the *Unabridged Dictionary*, its aim was to "elicit a clear and consistent expression of something supposed to be implicitly known by all rational beings".
5 This case is based on desktop research, and data is sourced from Stanford's Global Health Innovation Series entitled "D.light: securing early funding" (February 2012).
6 Bottom of the Pyramid, a concept popularized by Professor C.K. Prahalad, refers to a market-based model of economic development that promises to simultaneously alleviate widespread poverty in the people living at the bottom of the income pyramid while providing growth and profits for multinational corporations (Prahalad, C.K., 2004. *The Fortune at the Bottom of the Pyramid*. Wharton School Publishing).
7 According to authors Kim and Mauborgne, a "blue ocean" refers to a market for a product where there is no, or very little, competition (*The Blue Ocean Strategy*, Harvard Business Review).

8 The marketing mix is a set of actions to launch and promote a brand in the market. It is aimed at attracting and building customer loyalty through satisfaction of customer needs. Philip Kotler defines it as a classic tool to develop what to offer to consumers and how to offer it to them (*Marketing 4.0: Moving from Traditional to Digital*, Wiley).

9 Personas are fictional characters, which you create based upon your research in order to represent the different user types that might use your service, product, site, or brand in a similar way. Creating personas will help you to understand your users' needs, experiences, behaviours and goals (source: www.interaction-design.org /literature/article/personas-why-and-how-you-should-use-them).

10 A person who compulsively works excessively hard and long hours; who works most of the time and finds it difficult to stop working in order to do other things.

11 As renowned organizational culture scholar Edgar Schein points out, "the leader's values and preferences are the first ways that a group or organization does things and if that works it becomes eventually the culture of that group. So in a very real sense, founders and leaders create culture".

Chapter 8

Managing abundance beyond the triple bottom line

In 1994, John Elkington introduced the triple bottom line as a sustainability framework that examines a company's social, environmental and economic performance. It was a new management concept that was widely adopted for transitioning organizations "to measure the financial, social and environmental performance of the corporation over a period of time".[1] It is applied as an accounting tool for measuring the full cost involved in doing business.

But this is not what Elkington expected. In a self-assessment article published in the *Harvard Business Review*,[2] he makes a pledge to recall the meaning and practice of the triple bottom line as a concept: a critical exercise that does him credit. He acknowledges that the

> TBL's stated goal from the outset was *system change*—pushing toward the transformation of capitalism. It was never supposed to be just an accounting system. It was originally intended as a genetic code, a triple helix of change for tomorrow's capitalism, with a focus on breakthrough change, disruption, asymmetric growth (with unsustainable sectors actively sidelined), and the scaling of next-generation market solutions.

Despite the growth and positive forecast for sustainable market opportunities,[3] he feels quite disappointed when he assesses the progress achieved on people well-being and planetary health attributed to the corporate sustainability sector. Elkington concludes his essay with a (re)calling. He urges using the triple bottom line as a "triple helix for value creation, a genetic code for tomorrow's capitalism, spurring the regeneration of our economies, societies, and biosphere".

I'm fully in accord with the spirit of his message. But I think his assessment misses an important point. To truly change capitalism, our economic system, we need to change the power relationships between the components

153

of the system. The underlying assumptions that spur the practice of capitalism today, as mentioned in Chapter 1, are based on an egocentric and narrow understanding of freedom and abundance in a world incentivized by competition and conditioned by the fear of scarcity, two of the system's components.

The following Taoist story illustrates how the fear of scarcity restrains our behaviour and capacity to adapt.

> Long ago, a monk set out on his travels across a faraway land. Night was falling and he needed somewhere to shelter. Eventually, he found a humble shack, in the middle of nowhere. A poor family lived there and the mother, father and children were dressed in rags. The monk asked if he could spend the night there. "You are most welcome to spend the night," said the father. They prepared a simple meal consisting of fresh milk, cheese and cream and the monk appreciated their simple generosity greatly.

When they finished eating, the monk asked them how they managed to survive in such an isolated place, so far away from the nearest town. The wife told him. "We have one cow. We sell her milk to our neighbours who do not live too far away. We keep enough for our needs and to make some cheese and cream—that is what we eat."

The next morning, the monk said his goodbyes and set out to continue his journey. Not far from the family's little hut, he came across the cow. The monk pondered for a moment before leading the cow to the edge of a nearby cliff and pushing it over the edge.

Several years later the monk again passed that way and found himself on the same road where he had found lodging so many years ago. Driven by a sense of curiosity, he decided to visit the family. He rounded the curve in the road and, to his surprise, he saw a splendid mansion, surrounded by landscaped gardens, in the place where the little hut used to be. The monk knocked on the door. The father of the poor family answered, now well-dressed and looking healthy. He recognized the monk immediately and invited him in, inviting him to stay as a guest.

While they ate, the monk asked what had changed in the years that had passed. The father explained how the family's fortune changed. "You know, we used to have a cow. She kept us alive. We didn't own anything else. One day she fell down the cliff and died. To survive, we had to start doing other things, develop skills we didn't know we had. We were forced to come up with new ways of doing things. It was the best thing that ever happened to us! We are now much better off than before."

The capitalist system is actually our "cow". It is the comfort zone that frames our playing field. There is no other system out there. The difference is that we do not have a monk to get rid of it. We are the monks. And in order to become aware of the need to push the cow off the cliff, or, in other words, to truly transform the system, we need to understand the complexities of the current system dynamics and approach the transformation from a new viewpoint of abundance. Let's see.

The neoliberal economic system was built on the premise of individual freedom and choice. But, in the end, we spend most of our time on securing a living; time we take away from other things we truly value—relationships, culture, healthcare, education. This is one of the paradoxes of capitalism: the system sells you freedom and it steals it from you. To spur the regeneration of our systems—social, economic and ecologic—we need to see the world through renewed lenses of abundance. But, what does abundance mean? What does it imply?

Abundance in capitalism system dynamics

What is the first thing that comes to mind when you hear the word "abundance"? In the context of capitalism, society's neoliberal market-based economic system, the concept of abundance is biased by the concept of money. Here, money refers to the self-accumulation of capital, properties or any kind of material possessions. Why do we work? For many, we work to earn a living.

Our ancestors built a life organized around the idea of work, wealth generation and consumption. A work ethic is a cultural principle that is often associated with the idea of success understood as individual accumulation of wealth.[4] This idea of progress is a fundamental underlying assumption of our economic system. There are, furthermore, three other fundamental underlying assumptions that help us understand abundance in the current capitalist context.

One is the idea of infinite corporate growth as the main engine for wealth generation. This assumption is, in turn, a consequence of another fundamental assumption: the Earth has endless natural resources that can be used as means of production. And the third fundamental assumption is to believe that competition[5] is the primary foundation of innovation, productivity, growth, employment and progress.

These assumptions have a profound impact on how the dynamics of the economic system work, or, in other words, have a profound impact in shaping the rules of the game. Let's consider Figure 8.1. Corporations, who have the ownership of the means of production, invest in securing the provision of labour, technological equipment and natural resources. They use their own funds, capital coming from private equity, or public funding in the form of research and development grants, tax deductions, industrial subsidies, advantaged loans or any other kind of public support.

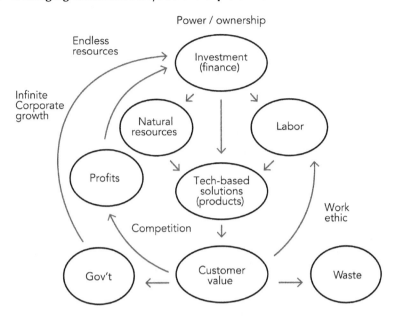

Figure 8.1 Economic system dynamics

With money, technology, labour and nature, called resources or inputs (we have normalized the fact that nature and people are considered resources, when they should be the beneficiaries of the outcomes of the economic system), corporations design and develop technological solutions in the form of products and services that create value for the customer. This value generates consumption, either for the satisfaction of a need or the improvement of customer experience.

Companies trade this value in exchange for revenue. Part of this revenue is distributed in the form of wages to employees, dividends to shareholders and taxes to government. In some cases, part of the income is reinvested in the company. And also, part of this value has an externality, which is the waste that generates ecological costs.

The incentive of capital owners and investors to become wealthier drives the dynamics of the current economic system. The rate of accumulation of capital is far higher than the rate the economy is able to grow. It is also much higher than the increase and distribution of wealth that goes to employees, the largest part of society.[6] This results in higher levels of inequality that, together with the wage–productivity decoupling (meaning that increases in productivity do not translate to higher salaries), are squeezing the middle class. Squeezing the middle class, the fundamental pillar of the economic system,[7] happens simultaneously with inflating the wealth of a super-rich elite. These capital owners and investors, also called winners, increasingly concentrate more power, ownership and technology in their hands.

Sustainability, in theory, is an attempt to rebalance some of these dynamics. The United Nations Sustainable Development Goals, officially adopted by 193 countries in 2015, has, for example, a specific goal aimed at reducing inequalities. Other goals, such as ending poverty and hunger, increasing quality education, and health and well-being are also related to reducing social and economic inequalities.

As a concept, sustainability introduced, in the 1980s, the idea of doing less harm to the environment, but with a focus on reduction. Reducing carbon emissions, reducing water consumption, reducing fossil-fuel energies, reducing the use of plastics, and so on. These reductions were captured and reported in triple bottom line-based accounting systems. This reflects what Elkington said: "many early adopters understood the triple bottom line as a balancing act, adopting a trade-off mentality".[8]

Corporate social responsibility, philanthropy, or inclusive business, to name some social business approaches, have primarily focused on improving living conditions but within the frame of the current economic system. Traditional sustainability practices, as currently approached, have not changed the rules of the game. There was no explicit call to change the incentives. In corporate terms, abundance is still perceived as profit maximization. It is what is sought.

This notwithstanding, there is a growing group of techno-optimists who believe in the power of technology to free resources as a way to solve Anthropogenic challenges. This assumption is grounded on a positive outlook on the progress achieved since the first industrial revolution, and especially after the Second World War. There is a strong wealth of evidence that supports this view, as mentioned in Chapter 1.

Peter Diamandis, co-founder of Singularity University, is a proponent of this vision. In the book *Abundance: The Future Is Better Than You Think*, he makes a compelling case—with Steven Kotler—of how technological disruption is a resource-liberating mechanism that can make the once scarce now abundant. Solar-powered energy or closed water cycle loops are examples that support this thesis. But, will technology be enough?

The crossroads: what technology does and what could do but does not do (yet)

We live in a world of abundance, in absolute economic terms. If we distribute the wealth that human beings are capable of generating equally for each individual on the face of the Earth (the gross world product per capita), there would be no poverty.[9] We would all have sufficient resources to live with dignity. However, we live with poverty, inequality and precarious work in a dual world. And at what price? The system is smart at generating economic wealth, but inefficient at creating natural wealth and fostering the well-being of people while leaving no one behind.

Technology is the main explanatory factor behind economic abundance. And this trend has only just begun. Robotization and automation, the internet of things, artificial intelligence, genomics, nanotechnology, 3D printing, quantum computing, new materials or biotechnology, fields powered by accelerated digitization, are exponential technologies that will end up generating incredible wealth without creating jobs. It is the theory of zero marginal cost.[10] Today, Uber already beats General Motors in stock market value. The digital economy beats the industrial economy in economic value, but loses in job creation.

The wealth generated is concentrated in a few technology companies that rise up like new monopoly empires. Google, Apple, Facebook, Amazon and Microsoft—the so-called GAFAM—are already large ultra-diversified holdings with huge amounts of cash reserves.[11] With these reserves, these companies acquire the most promising startups from all over the world. We are seeing a huge process of capital, talent and technology concentration in the hands of a few companies. Power dynamics concentrated in the hands of a tech-based elite that generates and concentrates a lot of wealth.

Technology has also the potential to free resources. It may replace—and it actually has—labour. This phenomenon has two interpretations. On the one hand, automation of repetitive and non-creative tasks conducted by low-paid workers, in most cases under precarious conditions—the so-called bullshit jobs[12]—can be positive. It is so if these workers are socially protected or have the ability to find better jobs or create their own. Who wants to have a bullshit job?

On the other hand, technology creates new jobs. It can create highly specialized jobs—mostly STEM (science, technology, engineering and maths)—but also bullshit jobs such as platform economies' jobs. The issue is whether the pace of new job creation can fill the void of the unemployed, disrupted by job automation.

Technology is also a powerful force for liberating natural resources and making them available to consume renewable energies, water and food (the so-called nexus for its interconnections), to improve living standards and to regenerate the environment. Energy is probably the main trigger of abundance. With energy, we would be able to solve the issue of water scarcity, which would improve many health issues that are related to water, and tackle food security. It would also make electricity accessible, which would facilitate education, and, therefore, reduce poverty. And we could continue identifying more interdependencies.

The technologies that liberate resources are already there. The problem is that they are not profitable enough to scale and make them widely available. This problem, approached only from a business model perspective, has not yet been solved. This is, fundamentally, a financial issue. Do you imagine what these technologies could do if they could be brought to all people in need?

Technology can also be harmful to society. The concentration of tech-based power is an incentive in itself for digital companies that commodify personal data for a profit. This surveillance capitalism works in favour of the big tech corporations that control data and, thereby, have also a big influence on the political system. Democracy's crisis is, in part, a consequence of the manipulation through fake news that alter election results, as the case of Cambridge Analytica unveils, popularly portrayed in the Netflix documentary *The Great Hack*. Politics is getting polarized at both ends of the ideological spectrum, right and left, with populist propaganda spreading fear across the population.

This process has been accelerated with the Covid-19 crisis, as people gave up individual freedom in exchange for safety. Data obsession calls attention to consumers. Data/attention has become the new oil. A scarce resource for which digital platforms fight. User interfaces are designed to capture human attention, which make people more prone to consume the information that algorithms are designed to push. It is a strategy for conditioning the focus of people's perception.

All in all, it feels as if we are at a crossroad, a turning point. On the one hand, we have the engine of abundance: sufficient resources for all thanks to a technology that liberates us from precarious work and frees natural resources. A technology that helps democratization, simplifies problems and improves experiences. On the other hand, we have the engine of technological neofeudalism: great inequality, poverty and precariousness in a world governed by the excessive power of technological ultra-capitalism. Both lead to a world in which we are going to live with ubiquitous technology, with robots, sensors, tech implants, wearables and algorithms everywhere. But, in the engine of abundance, the machine is at the service of the human being and in the other man has lost his identity in a bionic world subjugated by the power of techno-economics. Which engine do you want to board?

Houston, we have a management problem

In order to reflect upon the above question, we need to frame the real problem. Back in the industrial revolution, when the vast majority of people lived in poverty (around 90% of the population),[13] the problem of the economy was a problem of resources. People needed to meet their basic needs: food, housing, clothing, and sanitation. Fewer people could afford education.

Today, we still have many people in extreme poverty, but "only" 10% of the population in relative terms. The cost of ending extreme poverty is estimated by economist Jeffrey Sachs at \$175 billion per year for twenty years. A sum that could be fully covered by the corporate tax revenue losses, which are estimated by the International Monetary Fund at \$500–600 billion per year. In an economy of abundance, the real problem today is a management problem.

As a species, humans have demonstrated a remarkable capacity to create wealth. We have moulded and adapted this capacity to the ups and downs of every situation and every epoch. Even during the twentieth century, the bloodiest in the history of our civilization, humans have seen the most unprecedented levels of creativity and innovation (e.g., humans have stepped on the moon and have invented the world wide web). We witnessed the exponential waves of global technological disruption that have led us to the highest gross world product ever (the total amount of goods and services produced in the twentieth century is estimated to have exceeded the cumulative total output over the preceding recorded human history[14]).

But, unfortunately, we have not learned how to share and manage these resources fairly and inclusively among us. The economic system does not help. As Warren Buffet puts it, "the natural function of a more specialized market economy is to divert more and more rewards to the top. That's something I don't think we've fully addressed in this country". This system has left so many people behind. So, we have, fundamentally, a management problem. We are running an economic system in the twenty-first century with the mental software of the nineteenth century.

Sustainable business is definitely one of the major advancements in microeconomics that we have seen during the past three decades. It is an entry point to changing the system from the inside; a breakthrough if done with authenticity, rigour and perseverance. But it is probably not enough if left alone, if not grounded to a systemic thinking that can identify the interdependencies between the individual, the organization and the economic system dynamics and behaviours.

Buddhist and Taoist systems thinking provides this ground. It is a "software for the mind" to address the challenges of the twenty-first century by connecting the interdependencies within the economic system and between the economic and the social, political and ecological systems. As a way of liberation, Buddhism and Taoism offer a renewed analytical framework for understanding sustainability in the context of abundance. This concept needs a revisited definition for managing the transition to the new business paradigm.

Abundance revisited: a lifefulness approach

The gateway to managing abundance is perception. Our perception of the world is a function of how we see ourselves in relation to our experiences, which includes our reactions to the information we are exposed to. As such, perception is conditioned by how we experience the world. Buddhism and Taoism converge again in identifying the principle that leads to developing a universal ontological outlook of the world: emptiness.[15]

If we want to develop a universal worldview, a view that is grounded on universal natural laws and values, we can empty our minds (see Chapter 2 for an explanation of emptiness). It is then when we open up to everything, to the whole, to a world of possibility, of opportunity. It's called empty when it is a separate being or existence. A person is empty of a separate self. As Zen master Thich Nhat Hanh puts it, it is full of everything, full of life.

Emptiness causes us to feel and operate from oneness, in which we see the interdependencies of all things. It is in such state that we can find new meanings and new relationships in the things that surround us, that concern us. It is in this condition when our embodied mind perceives nature as abundance, lifeful as it is, and is able to trace the interconnections between, within and across systems.

Perceiving nature as abundance is a common trait of the indigenous cultural approach to sustainability. Demarus Sandlin, who studied the relation between indigenous knowledge and Western science, affirms, "indigenous sustainability is more than sustaining resource use for human benefit, it is about creating abundance in nature for the health of ourselves and our animal and plant relatives".[16]

In current times, managing abundance implies revisiting this concept in relation to our place in the world. Buddhism and Taoism, in order to set perspective and reflection, provide an analytical framework with three dimensions that are the building blocks for the study of life: time, space and being. These three dimensions are explored through two subjects that construct the meaning of life in the present moment: the individual and the collective. In our current economic system of scarcity, managing abundance implies redefining how we manage our time, our space and our way of being, at both the individual and collective levels (Figure 8.2). Seeing the world through this renewed lenses of abundance leads to a prosperous, healthy and harmonious understanding and experience of life.

Time and freedom

Time is an essential component in the study of Buddhism and Taoism. Buddhist philosophy acknowledges time as a subjective construct that appears in our consciousness during the process of knowing. Hence, time is relative to our consciousness through the perceptions we have of the world. These perceptions are captured by our experiences in our embodied

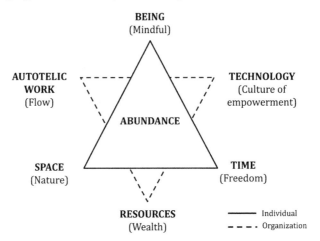

Figure 8.2 An analytical framework for managing abundance

mind.[17] The cycle of rebirth, a central concept in Buddhism, is a product of understanding time from a metaphysical point of view. This understanding of time opens the door to life beyond the physical experience, a possibility that exists in our consciousness. This possibility engenders abundance, the opportunity to experience life in many forms, even beyond the physical realm.

Taoist philosophy channels the study of time through *Bazi*, or *Saju*, a discipline that belongs to the Studies of Life, as explained in Chapter 5. *Bazi*, or *Saju* approaches time in two ways. First, by analysing the metaphysical imprint that the moment of birth has in the different areas of a person's life; and second, by relating the astrological cycles—that change with time—to the different areas of the person's life as it evolves. Time is, therefore, an essential element for understanding the process of transformation and how a person constantly changes in relation to their environment, both physical and metaphysical. Time, through this lens, is an opportunity for growth and transformation, to experience different lives within this life.

At the individual level, time relates to the concept of freedom, the power or right to act, speak, or think as one wants. In this context, approaching time through abundance requires going through a process of self-enquiry about how we experience time. Do we have enough time to do the things we truly value? Why? Why not? What is impeding me from having more free time for these things? To what extent am I free to do what is important to me? To what extent am I enjoying my time?

In the economic system, freedom is highly constrained by the pressures to earn a living and the work ethic principle. In a situation of poverty, this is a major constraint for development. The economist and Nobel Prize winner, Amartya Sen, made an important contribution in linking the concept of freedom to economic development. To him, freedom is both the primary objective of development, and its primary means. Sen sees development as the process of expanding human freedom: "It is the enhancement of freedoms that allow people to lead lives that they have reason to live".[18]

In the context of the economic system, the relation between time and freedom needs to be explored by revising how we use our time in the cycle of production and consumption. This implies the need to qualify our time, beyond the traditional economic valuation of time. That is, to assign a qualitative meaning to how we spend our time. Qualifying our time is essential for our own development, for spending that time in doing what is joyful, interesting, useful and meaningful to us. This has huge implications for entrepreneurs and organizations.

Gaia entrepreneurs and organizations, motivated to dedicate their professional time to contributing to Gaia by creating life-nurturing projects, need to redefine how they understand and use time. The first implication of this redefinition is the development of autotelic work, which is performing a rewarding job that provides meaning, that allows the fulfilment of a sense of purpose and curiosity and that is internally driven, producing a state of flow while performing the activities.[19]

The opposite of autotelic work would be bullshit jobs. In a context where precarious work is widespread, the real issue here is to advocate for, and create, an enabling environment for decent work, a human right outlined in the Universal Declaration of Human Rights. The declaration states that decent work is not only the right to work; it includes enforcing just and favourable conditions of work, protection against unemployment, equal pay, social protection, and the right to form and join trade unions.[20]

The problem arises when the actual economic context is at odds with such an environment. How do we get rid of bullshit jobs and foster autotelic work when job automation, economic recession and the pressures of fierce competition disrupt the labour market? In such a situation, entrepreneurs and organizations can form links with political economic policies or social innovation measures to correct these market failures.

A prominent example that is gaining traction across the world is the implementation of a Universal Basic Income. A basic income is a periodic cash payment unconditionally delivered to all on an individual basis, without a requirement for means-testing or work.[21] The direct benefits of such a policy would allow the ending of poverty, and give people more freedom of choice. With this freedom of choice people could end precarious work, and instead find autotelic work or start up their own entrepreneurial project.[22]

The second implication of qualifying our time lies in relation to balancing the different areas of our life that are important to us. Gaia organizations that aim at fostering well-being at work are aware of the importance of work–life balance. But where to start? Remote working and flexible scheduling, for example, do certainly contribute to fostering employee autonomy and engagement. Nonetheless, companies are still tied to the competitive pressures of the markets. Some proposals include a reduction of the weekly work schedule to thirty or thirty-five hours, or from five to four days a week. This debate is already on the table, but it requires collective action and advocacy on behalf of all actors involved.

Space and nature

The experience of time is inextricably linked to the experience of space. Any time event occurs in a particular environment. These are the dimensions of physics for the study of nature, where we find all the resources we need to live an abundant life. Buddhism and Taoism both study space through different, but complementary, approaches. Buddhism explores the internal space that occupies the mental state of being understood as the direct observation of one's own consciousness. When the mind enters a state of infinite consciousness is when the human being realizes the spatial whole.

This space of infinite consciousness can be accessed through the subtle mind—a concept called *namshe tramo* in Sanskrit. According to Buddhist monk Lama Wangchen, director of the House of Tibet in Barcelona, the subtle mind is an advanced state of consciousness experienced in the transition between lives, in which the mind experiences wholeness as a state of space and time infinity. Wangchen affirms that "space is limitless; without space nothing would exist. Without time our motivation does not make sense. We do things for a happier future. So the concept of future is key to act, to start moving now".[23]

Taoism developed a specific discipline to study space from a pragmatic point of view: Feng Shui. According to Taoist metaphysics master Raymond Lo, Feng Shui—which literally means wind and water—is a body of knowledge created by ancient Taoists about how the natural environment affects human well-being. Inferring from both philosophies, human well-being is conditioned by how we experience nature, our own nature in relation to the surrounding environment.

At the individual level, our experience of nature—and, therefore, our relationship with her—is very much dependent on where we live and how we live. It depends on the balancing (or unbalancing) presence of the Five Elements—Wood, Fire, Earth, Metal and Water—and our interaction with them and with other sentient beings. We can interact with them by (inter)being with them, and by nourishing from them.

The fact of the matter is that as we have progressed to the rhythm of globalization under the current economic system, we have gone far from nature. We have split. The majority of people live in big urban areas, most of the food consumed comes from abroad and most of the energy we use is still sourced from fossil-fuel materials.

Going back to nature and taking advantage of her potential implies connecting with our natural environment with a mindset of possibility, of life-fulness. At the organizational level, this connection can be empowered by technology. The Gaia organization understands and uses technology as a way to liberate resources and create life. This approach can be anchored through design-for-life frameworks.

Cradle-to-Cradle is one of these. According to its creators, William Mcdonough and Michael Braungart, a key concept is that materials can be designed to differentiate between the biosphere—the ecological system—and the technosphere—the technological system—and become nutrients forever.[24]

They distinguish the circularization of biological nutrients, in which the waste of an animal becomes nutrition for other animals, including humans, from technical nutrients, in which non-natural materials such as metals and plastics can nourish other products. And that new product can become "food" again for other products, endlessly, becoming part of the natural cycle of regeneration on the planet.

This approach builds on abundance, as it takes the viewpoint of opportunity. It transcends scarcity-based sustainability. The authors illustrate this idea with an example. Many people enjoy taking long showers. In most households, when the water runs too long, one might assume that water, money and energy are being wasted. But if water in a house or a hotel is filtered, recirculated, and solar-heated, people can shower guilt-free for as long as they like. No one is worried that he or she needs to waste less water, energy or money. The design is optimized around lifefulness.[25]

Mcdonough and Braungart call this approach "upcycle". It is aimed at creating a culture of technological-based empowerment, in which natural (energy, water, food/nutrients) and technical resources (materials) are symbiotically used for making nature available and accessible. This approach implies that organizations invest in research and development of "upcycle"-based technologies, and for governments to incentivize these mission-orientated innovations.

Being and mindful

Being is the core subject of Buddhist and Taoist philosophies. It is, in fact, our quest as the human species. Who are we? Where do we come from? Why do we exist? What are we supposed to do in this life? Why are we doing this? Both Eastern philosophical streams have long enquired about our own nature, and they also provide a roadmap for harmonious living. As perennial philosophies, their indigenous knowledge is grounded in natural living, in harmony with nature.

It is in finding answers to these questions that the seeker can find her place in the world, in the context of interbeing. When this happens, the seeker experiences a profound feeling of abundance; a state of being that makes her peaceful, grateful and appreciative of all things in life.

Buddhism conceives being at the intersection of time and space. Being is precisely related to our existence here and now. This is the central tenet of Zen practice, the development of a lifestyle that concentrates on being fully present in the moment. This mode of existence can be attained through the practice of mindfulness, which is an ancient meditative-based technique that purposefully consists of being non-judgementally aware of the present moment of one's body, mind, feelings and surrounding environment.

Taoism understands being as *wuwei*, the state of natural flow, or natural action, as described in Chapter 2. The practice of *wuwei* requires the activation of the Tao principles of oneness, emptiness and impermanence, which embeds a lightful approach to the art of living.

At the individual level, living mindfully in a state of natural flow is a challenge in a world driven by materialism. It implies adopting a lifestyle based on the premise that less is more, a common premise in Zen. This explorative journey starts with the question: how much is enough? This enquiry is an opportunity to cultivate an appreciative mindset of the material and non-material things that surround us. Of the things we truly need, the ones that are superfluous and we don't need, and the ones that bring real joy to our life. Appreciation is the basis for feeling abundance as a mental state of being.

Beyond Zen, this lifestyle is gaining traction in current times, in the form of minimalism. The movement started in the mid twentieth century, with arts and design movements characterized by the use of simple forms. Decluttering, tiny houses, co-working, co-living, etc., are some of the emerging minimalist initiatives that are becoming popular as a way to counteract materialism.

In an increasingly complex world, simplicity is a value. Yvon Chouindard, co-founder of Patagonia and a Zen practitioner, applied this mindful life principle also to business, as he makes no distinction between business and life. In his book *Let My People Go Surfing: The Education of a Reluctant Businessman*, he states

> going back to a simpler life based on living by sufficiency rather than excess is not a step backward; rather, returning to a simpler way allows us to regain our dignity, puts us in touch with the land, and makes us value human contact again.

The application of the "less is more" principle is grounded in the individual. It represents a personal choice that starts with questioning how we manage our material abundance and wealth as individuals. But this choice does not lead to a reflection on how less can be more as a society, as a whole. One can be a minimalist operating from the ego-system. If we want to leverage this principle to the collective, from an eco-systemic point of view, we need to think about how the overall wealth is distributed across the entire population. And, especially, including the people that live in a time and space of material scarcity and deprivation.

How do we make this connection? How do we balance the world's resources? As happens with natural resources, we also need technologies that can liberate resources from the wealth that is collectively created but concentrated in few but super-rich elites. These technologies I'm talking about here are social technologies. There is a need to inclusively design more equal and fairer policies that can distribute the wealth to the whole population, especially to those left behind. Less concentration of wealth is more well-being for all. This is like the principle of oneness applied to the collective state of mindful being.

Distributive policies are an opportunity to make material abundance available to more people. A matter of social justice. For business organizations, this kind of corporate activism—lobbying for fair wealth distribution—is uncharted territory, although some are becoming aware of the problem of inequality and its association with the power dynamics of the economic system.

The current economic system's dynamics do not incentivize wealth distribution fairly. An example of that is the issue of taxation. Taxation matters. It not only helps to fund essential public goods, services and social safety nets, it also ensures a level playing field for all types of businesses, large and small. In order to raise awareness of this issue, Fair Tax, a UK-based non-profit organization, set the Fair Tax Mark in 2014. The Mark is a certification scheme aimed at encouraging and recognizing organizations that pay the right amount of corporate tax, at the right time and in the right place.

What engaged my curiosity is seeing some millionaires, the direct beneficiaries of the current economic system, being aware of the problem of unfair taxation. In the context of the deep Covid-19 economic recession, 83 millionaires from different countries, including people such as Abigal Disney, Ben & Jerry co-founder, Jerry Greenfield, and former BlackRock managing director, Morris Pearl, demanded higher taxes on themselves. This group, self-named "Millionaires for Humanity"[26] signed an open letter asking their governments to "raise taxes on people like us. Immediately. Substantially. Permanently. [...] It is the right choice. It is the only choice."

Another group that is becoming interested in wealth distribution is a growing number of high-profile tech entrepreneurs[27] that are endorsing and pushing for the need to introduce a Universal Basic Income. Their primary motivation stems from their concern about the negative impact of robotization and automation (a technological disruption they lead) on the job market and the economy at large.

Concluding remarks

Managing abundance requires a systemic approach to understanding the dynamics of the economic system and identifying the leverage points. These points are areas of change and potential (activities, initiatives, solutions, incentives) where small shifts can produce large improvements in the system. In an economic system of scarcity, managing abundance implies redefining how we manage our time, our space and our way of being, at both the individual and collective levels.

For individuals, managing abundance is about developing the way to liberate oneself from the harmful *samsaric* dynamics of the economic system that constrain our freedoms and capacities to reach our full potential. For the organization, managing abundance is about developing new ways to liberate natural, technical and economic resources that create and nurture a meaningful and flourishing life for all.

The management of abundance, as we saw in the Zen Business model (Chapter 5), starts with intentionality (the purpose principle). We can have good intentions that guide our actions as we expect them to contribute to transforming the economic system. But, how do we know our intentions have come to fruition? In other words, how do we know our actions have contributed—or not—to transforming our economic system? These questions are explored in the next chapter.

Notes

1 "Triple bottom line", *The Economist* (17th November 2009).
2 25 years ago I coined the phrase "triple bottom line." Here's why it's time to rethink it, by Elkington (*Harvard Business Review*, June 2018).
3 Markets for sustainable products and services expect to grow over $12 trillion a year by 2030, according to the UN Sustainable Development Goals.
4 In *The Protestant Ethic and the Spirit of Capitalism*, one of the most influential books of the twentieth century, Max Weber correlates the Protestant work ethic with entrepreneurship and higher levels of wealth, which set the foundation of the idea of progress in industrial Western societies.
5 Competition is defined as "the activity or condition of striving to gain or win something by defeating or establishing superiority over others", according to Lexico.

6 These are the central theses of Thomas Piketty, developed in his popular book, *Capital in the Twenty-first Century* (2013).

7 The OECD warned about the perils of wages decoupling from increases in productivity. "Several OECD countries have been grappling not only with slow productivity growth but have additionally experienced a slowdown in real average wage growth relative to productivity growth, which has been reflected in a falling share of wages in GDP" ("Decoupling of wages from productivity: what implications for public policy", OECD 2018).

8 In 25 years ago I coined the phrase "triple bottom line." Here's why it's time to rethink it, by Elkington (*Harvard Business Review*, June 2018).

9 The gross world product per capita in 2017 was approximately Int$17,500 according to the CIA World Factbook. The international extreme poverty line is set at $1,9 per day according to the World Bank (with more than 730 million people, around 10% of the world's population, still living in extreme poverty). In the US, for example, the poverty line is set at $12,760 annually.

10 Jeremy Rifkin argues, in *The Zero Marginal Cost Society*, that we are about to enter an era when the Internet of Things, "free" energy, and what he calls "the collaborative commons" will make anything and everything available for practically nothing.

11 GAFAM companies alone jointly possess $454.4 billion in cash reserves (source: FactSet via CNBC, 7th November 2019).

12 Graeber, D. (2018). *Bullshit Jobs: A theory*. Simon & Schuster.

13 Martin Ravallion's seminal book, *The Economics of Poverty: History, measurement and policy* (Oxford University Press, 2016), offers a detailed historical perspective on the evolution of poverty across centuries.

14 International Monetary Fund, "World Economic Outlook: asset prices and the business cycle" (May 2000).

15 In Buddhism, the concept of emptiness is originally translated from the Sanskrit term *sunyata*; in Taoism, emptiness corresponds to the translation of the Chinese term *Wu*.

16 Sandlin, D.T. (2019). *Ethical Science and Indigenous Sustainability* (Internship Report for EPA Region 10). Washington, DC: Office of Environmental Assessment, Environmental Protection Agency, in *Blue Marble Evaluation* (Patton, M.Q., 2019).

17 Bunnag, A. (2017). The concept of time in philosophy: A comparative study between Theravada Buddhist and Henri Bergson's concept of time from Thai philosophers' perspectives, *Kasetsart Journal of Social Sciences*.

18 Sen, A. (2001). *Development as Freedom*. Oxford University Press.

19 Mihaly Csikszentmihalyi introduces the concept of autotelic personality in his book *Flow: The psychology of optimal experience* (Harper Perennial, 2008).

20 International Labour Organization Statement to the Third Committee of the 68th General Assembly, 23rd October 2013.

21 This is the definition developed by the Basic Income Earth Network, widely shared by the academic community.

22 I have long advocated the need to introduce a Universal Basic Income as a way to dignify human life. I understand it as an empowering measure that, despite not being the solution to all the problems, would facilitate the transition to the new business paradigm. In the book *Economía de la Felicidad* (Plataforma, 2017), together with Xavier Ferrás, we propose to name it a Universal Decent Income to precisely emphasize the human right component that entails liberating the human population from the threats of poverty and deprivation, in line with Sen's approach.

23 Based on a personal interview with Lama Wangchen in Barcelona during August 2020.
24 Mcdonough, W. & Braungart, M. (2013). *Upcycle: Beyond sustainability, designing for abundance.* North Point Press.
25 Ibid.
26 www.millionairesforhumanity.com.
27 According to Business Insider, entrepreneurs that have publicly endorsed UBI include Elon Musk (Tesla), Ray Kurzweil (Singularity University), Sam Altman (Y Combinator), Sam Gross (Pacific Investment Management), Chris Hughes (Facebook), Andrew Ng (Baidu), Albert Wenger (Union Square Ventures), and Tim O'Reilly (O'Reilly Media).

References

Bunnag, A. (2017). The concept of time in philosophy: a comparative study between Theravada Buddhist and Henri Bergson's concept of time from Thai philosophers' perspectives, *Kasetsart Journal of Social Sciences*.

Coll, J.M. & Ferràs, X. (2017). *Economía de la Felicidad: las claves de la tecnología, la desigualdad y el trabajo en el poscapitalismo*. Plataforma Editorial.

Elkington, J. (2018). 25 years ago I coined the phrase "triple bottom line." Here's why it's time to rethink it. Harvard Business Review, June.

Graeber, D. (2018). *Bullshit Jobs: A theory*. Simon & Schuster.

Mcdonough, W. & Braungart, M. (2013). *Upcycle: Beyond sustainability, designing for abundance*. North Point Press.

Piketty, T. (2013). *Capital in the Twenty-first Century*. Harvard University Press

Ravallion, M. (2016). *The Economics of Poverty: History, measurement and policy*. Oxford University Press.

Rifkin, J. (2014). *The Zero Marginal Cost Society: The Internet of Things, the collaborative commons, and the eclipse of capitalism*. St. Martin's Press.

Sen, A. (2001). *Development as Freedom*. Oxford University Press.

Weber, M. (1930). *The Protestant Ethic and the Spirit of Capitalism*. London: George Allen & Unwin.

Chapter 9

Business mindfulness

Evaluation for systems transformation

Can we capture reality?

Once upon a time, there was a Chinese farmer whose horse ran away. That evening, all of his neighbours came around to commiserate. They said, "We are so sorry to hear your horse has run away. This is most unfortunate." The farmer said, "Maybe." The next day the horse came back bringing seven wild horses with it, and in the evening everybody came back and said, "Oh, isn't that lucky. What a great turn of events. You now have eight horses!" The farmer again said, "Maybe."

The following day his son tried to break one of the horses, and, while riding it, he was thrown and broke his leg. The neighbours then said, "Oh dear, that's too bad," and the farmer responded, "Maybe." The next day the conscription officers came around to conscript people into the army, and they rejected his son because he had a broken leg. Again, all the neighbours came around and said, "Isn't that great!" Again, he said, "Maybe."

This is the story of the Chinese farmer,[1] which is often portrayed in Taoism to showcase the complexity of evaluating the nature of events occurring in a specific context. In Alan Watts's words,

the whole process of nature is an integrated process of immense complexity, and it's really impossible to tell whether anything that happens in it is good or bad — because you never know what will be the consequence of the misfortune; or, you never know what will be the consequences of good fortune.

Capturing reality seems an impossible enterprise, as perception is a matter of subjectivity, time and space. What is a reality for one may be a different reality for another. Judgement is, thereby, relative to the level of perception of the participators. Perception directly influences how we interpret the events that we call reality.

The relativity of reality makes it hard for organizations to evaluate transformation. Imagine a company that has reduced its greenhouse gas emissions by 20% during the last five years. Is that good enough? It depends on how we look at it. Perhaps the bottom line is still high, and the company could have reduced it much more. Maybe its competitors just cut the emissions by 10% and this gave the company a competitive advantage. Or maybe the reduction of emissions has been done at the expense of other environmental or social costs, like cutting jobs, reducing salaries or using more polluting materials.

Buddhism, through Nagarjuna's two truths doctrine, defines this relative reality as conventional reality. Conventional reality is the interpretation of the daily experience of concrete phenomena (events, facts, data or any kind of evidence). It is a *samsaric* reality, approached through the lens of the self. Conventional reality is opposed to ultimate reality, which is related to the *nirvanic* state of consciousness. This reality is the universal, or absolute, reality, where one has attained enlightenment as it experiences the full immersion with the oneness of the Tao (as was described in Chapter 2). In this reality, the self no longer exists, one is empty of a separate self. One is everything.

Conventional reality is, therefore, the starting point that frames any process of transformation. To analyse and understand that reality, Buddhism applies the principle of mutual causality. Causality, according to Joanna Macy (1991), is

> usually defined as the interrelation of cause and effect, is about how things happen, how change occurs, how events relate. The Buddhist term Dharma carries the same meaning. It also refers to the Buddha's teachings as a whole ... for the ways that life is understood and lived are rooted in causal assumptions.

Shen and Midgley[2] emphasize that mutual causality, in Buddhist philosophy, emerges in a specific context or under certain conditions. They point out

> the belief is that everything, mental and physical, comes into being owing to certain conditions, and disappears when the conditions disappear, so nothing is independent. Reality is viewed as a dynamically interdependent process. Everything exists in a web of mutual causal interaction, and nothing, whether mental or physical, whole or part, is immutable or fully autonomous.

Organizations transitioning to the new business paradigm—that is, Gaia organizations—seek to transform conventional reality. These types of organizations are initiates in the art and science of transformation. They would like to get closer to the ultimate reality, where organizations liberate from the extractive and degenerative economy and instead contribute to building harmonious economic, ecological and social systems. In doing so, they operate in the context of an economic system that determines the contribution that organizations can do to transformation.

The fact that the economic system operates in the realm of conventional reality has an important implication: reality is relative and, therefore, subject to the principle of mutual causality, or cause–condition–effect. In this context, one of the biggest challenges for transitioning organizations is to rigorously monitor and evaluate the impact they have on the transformation of that system. Can we say that we transformed anything? Have we achieved our expected results? How have we contributed to transforming the system in which we operate? Which factors and mechanisms play a role in the process? Are we doing and measuring the right things? What can we learn from this entire journey? This exploratory process requires a systemic frame of analysis (an enquiry framework), which is subject to the principle of mutual causality because reality is rooted in causal assumptions.

Furthermore, enquiring about the nature of the process of transformation also requires the practice of business mindfulness. Business mindfulness, I posit, is the cognitive process by which the organization becomes aware of the impacts generated by its business activities, positive and negative, intended and unintended, and internal and external to the organization. Business mindfulness triggers a process of organizational awareness that is not only focused on throwing light on the intended positive impacts, which is the target for most organizations; it also focuses on challenging the assumptions that drive behaviour, in all the aforementioned impact areas (negative, positive; intended, unintended; and internal and external).

Evaluating the process of systems transformation, from an organizational perspective, is about understanding why and how a system's behaviours change in the context of the contribution of the organization. Evaluating this transformation has two overall implications. The first is related to the organizational behaviour that drives the business model. In this regard, I had an insightful conversation with my colleague and world-class evaluator Jordi del Bas about the concept of business mindfulness. Del Bas highlighted the importance of identifying and testing the underlying assumptions that drive any business model. "A mindful organization operates in the present, but business models are built from past assumptions", he affirms. "Evaluation tests and shakes these assumptions to make sure that the organization operates on present assumptions. When this happens, the organization organically adapts".

The second implication requires adopting the principle of global thinking, given that systems—organizational, economic, social, and ecological—are all interconnected. Michael Quinn Patton, in his book, *Blue Marble Evaluation,* highlights the importance of how we see things and think about them, inviting us to think, engage, design and evaluate with global consciousness. The premise of the global thinking principle is that global problems that require systemic change, like most sustainability-related issues, require global interventions and, correspondingly, globally orientated and world savvy evaluators.

When I first read the approach outlined in *Blue Marble Evaluation,* I thought it was grounded in Buddhist and Taoist philosophies. Implicitly, it is. Blue Marble principles, such as transformation engagement, integration, global, Yin–Yang and time, for example, illustrate the importance of approaching evaluation with an adaptive mindset of interdependence and impermanence, taking into consideration the paradoxes that characterize the complexity of reality.

Evaluators Craig Russon and Karen Russon have been pioneers in exploring an Eastern paradigm of evaluation in order to enrich the current evaluation praxis, building upon the interdependent nature of reality, from an ontological,[3] epistemological[4] and methodological[5] perspective.

The objective of this chapter is precisely to incorporate a systemic evaluative mindset as a process of critical reflection into transitioning organizations committed to creating a positive impact on the regeneration and, *ergo*, transformation of the economy.

The evaluative mindset

Evaluation as a professional practice developed especially during the 1970s in the public sector. Evaluation is driven by the need of organizations to demonstrate the achievement of results in order to be accountable to the funders. Five decades later, the function of evaluation has become highly technical and specialized, indispensable in the development cooperation industry.

With the emergence of purpose-driven business organizations that seek to generate sustainable impact comes the need to capture that impact. Most organizations start by measuring impact, which is a critical step, but without evaluation it may not be enough (as discussed later in the section titled "Measurement is not evaluation").

Evaluating essentially entails setting up a deep reflective enquiry process based on the collection of evidence about what worked, what did not work, for whom and why against the achievement of the higher purpose. As mentioned in the Zen Business model (see Chapter 5), the knowledge provided by an evaluation allows the organization to become aware of its impacts, and to use this knowledge strategically for learning, innovation and adaptation.

For evaluating, you do not need to be a professional evaluator. Besides the technical capacities and professional competences characteristic of the practice of evaluation, what emerges as critical for the use of evaluation in mindful, purpose-driven organizations is to count on a widespread evaluative mindset. Any entrepreneur, executive and manager can evaluate if she or he has an evaluative mindset. Such a mindset is the gateway to applying business mindfulness, to being aware of the impact the organization is generating on the larger systems (economic, social, ecological). This type of mindset works for evaluating impact in private and public organizations.

For developing an evaluative mindset, you need to apply the fundamental Buddhist and Taoist principles that guide evaluative behaviour. These principles form a competency framework that characterizes the evaluative mindset and that broadly defines the blueprint for evaluative performance within an organization (Table 9.1).

Why do we need to evaluate?

Still, very few organizations evaluate. Why bother? Most of them are rooted in the old business paradigm, where organizations' overall objective is to maximize shareholder value. These organizations mainly focus on measuring financial performance and the factors that correlate with that.

Purpose leads to impact

When organizations state a purpose, the door to evaluation opens up. When the purpose genuinely drives behaviour, these organizations become transitioning organizations. A clear and concise purpose statement is usually formulated in terms of contribution to impact.[6] As soon as an organization has a sustainability-based purpose, it implicitly expects to create a sustainable impact.

Take the example of Walmart. Its purpose statement is "to save people money so they can live better". It assumes that Walmart's purchases make people save money—contribution—and that this contributes to a better life—social impact. How do you know that this is what actually happens? Tesla's purpose is "to accelerate the advent of sustainable transport—environmental impact—by bringing compelling mass market electric cars to market as soon as possible—contribution". How do you know how Tesla is contributing to sustainable transportation? Sustainable transportation is

Table 9.1 Competency framework for an evaluative mindset

Competency	Description of behavior
Oneness and inter-being	Be aware of the whole system, its context, its purpose, its boundaries, the interdependent relations between all stakeholders (including your relation to/intervention with the system), processes and dynamics in the system and of the events that emerge as a result of the interaction between these elements. Pull the thread of mutual causality in capturing reality.
	Approach your work with compassion and appreciation: empathize with the situation, roles and opinions of stakeholders and people with whom you interact. They want to lead a meaningful and fulfilling transformation too, and they want to enhance their capacities to do so. Avoid blame and start with gratefulness.
Emptiness and the Zen mind	Focus on identifying and assessing the quality of patterns, relationships, processes and networks that define the harmony or healthiness of the organization. Do it in a way that your assessment is not conditioned by your previous experiences. Approach evaluation and ask questions with a Zen mind: a calm state alienated from the ego, an empty mind that is ready and open for active listening and unconditioned learning.
	Approach your enquiries with humility. Ask questions with a beginner's mind. When asking for and collecting data, you are not trying to corroborate or validate your own assumptions and mental models, but to provide evidence and context on the causal effects you are observing and analysing.

(*Continued*)

Table 9.1 Continued

Competency	Description of behavior
Impermanence	Adapt to changes in the context in which the evaluation takes place, to the emergence of unexpected events that may alter your plans and work schedule, to the introduction of new information that may change the course of your evaluation. Review and re-adapt your expectations accordingly and do not forget to contextualize, justify and communicate these adaptations.
	Focus on the aspects of the evaluation you can directly control and monitor through your work. Let go control and expectations that do not depend on you (e.g., such as having all the answers), and replace this desire for control with a positive influence for evaluating the transformation.
Wuwei	Go with the flow, do not try to force events to make them fit your plans. Follow the natural action, the natural path. This process of natural adaptation often requires making real-time decisions as events emerge during the evaluation, as things change. Feel and sense the situation. Channelling your actions to the flow of the evaluation requires intuitive and spontaneous decision-making. Trust it and link it to the purpose of the evaluation, the enquiry process and the collection and interpretation of evidence.
Yin–Yang	Identify the tensions that hamper the transition of the organization to the new business paradigm. Spot the opposites. Illuminate the possibilities that are hidden in the opposite direction of the Yin–Yang creative tension. Release the creative energy that is seeking to be resolved and, thereby, facilitate the harmonization of opposites.

(Continued)

Table 9.1 Continued

Competency	Description of behavior
Five Elements and Zen Business	In the context of conventional reality, focus on capturing the generators of that reality: drivers, forces or mechanisms that generate the impact (do not only focus on the outcomes, which sometimes are very difficult to capture!): use the Five Elements' dynamics of the Zen Business to identify what generates or blocks the value in the process of transformation.

Tesla's desired impact, its expected final result, but how do we know that is actually the case?

Organizations can only start knowing and understanding whether, how and why they have achieved their desired impact if they start evaluating the process of transformation stated in their purpose. That means initiating an evidence-based process of reflection driven by critical impact-focused enquiries. As del Bas stated in a conversation, "Purpose reflects the intention of the organization, and impact reflects the results of implementing that intention through its strategy and business actions". When transitioning organizations state a purpose that reflects a sustainability-based impact, then evaluation becomes an essential tool for organizational development and transformation. Evaluation is essential for understanding what, why and how the organization achieves the expected impact.

Accountability leads to impact

Incorporating evaluation as a common practice in transitioning organizations can be justified for multiple reasons: for reporting to investors, for marketing and communication, for learning and for adaptation. Or it can be simply for all of these reasons. In any case, the will to evaluate responds to a critical question: to whom am I accountable? What for? Transitioning organizations, as living systems, are, first and foremost, social agents. As such, they are accountable to the stakeholders that form the ecosystem in which they operate and generate impact (including the environment).

Accountability is an exercise of the responsibility that the organization has in achieving its purpose. It's a management tool for holding employees and executives responsible for accomplishing its goals, in collaboration with stakeholders, so that they can define their roles and make their decisions in line with the organization's expectations.

I learned about the Mountain of Accountability[7] from Michael Quinn Patton (Figure 9.1) in a working session we had in New York, together with Jordi del Bas and Valeria Carou-Jones, during our work in designing the developmental evaluation of results-based management at UNFPA back in 2018. The Mountain of Accountability provides a holistic accountability framework that captures the multiple levels of accountability that a transitioning organization can be accountable for.

Overall, there are three complementary levels of accountability. They can all exist in an organization, and the level of complexity increases as the level of accountability increases. The first level is basic accountability, which is mostly used for management processes and reporting to shareholders. It answers the questions: did we implement our work as planned

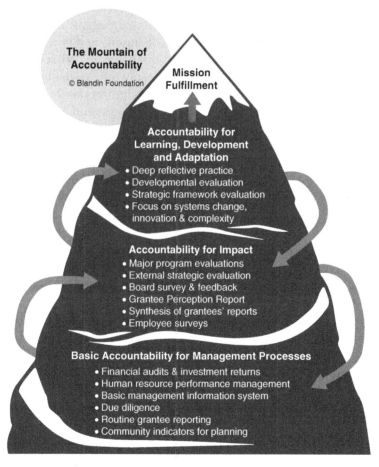

Figure 9.1 The Mountain of Accountability. Source: the Blandin Foundation

and authorized? Did we meet basic quality and sustainability standards in carrying out work? Classic sustainability reporting would fit at this level.

The second level is accountability for impact. This level carries an assessment of the organizational outcomes and impacts with the goal of assessing the effectiveness of the organization in meeting its desired impact. The organization asks three critical questions: to what extent are we building strong, positive relationships with key stakeholders and partners? To what extent and in what ways are we attaining desired and intended programme outcomes and impacts? What are we learning, and in what ways are we applying what we are learning to improve effectiveness? Impact-based reporting and feedback-based organizational learning would fit at this level.

The third level is accountability for learning, development and adaptation. This level takes on complexity and dynamic systems change to bring transformation. The focus is on learning to adapt purpose, strategy, innovation, culture and systems transformation. Here the organization asks: how are the world and the systems we work in changing, and how do we understand those changes so as to learn, adapt and develop? What does it mean to take our strategy seriously and enquire deeply into its elements and their implications for how we do our work and the impacts we have? What are the interrelationships and interconnections between and among our stakeholders and partners? To what extent do the many and diverse parts of the organization constitute a coherent and aligned whole? Systems-based evaluation and feed-forward learning would fit at this level (see Chapter 4, section titled "Systems learning and transformative adaptation").

The myth of attribution

When stakeholders' decisions to support a purpose-driven organization are based on impact reports—especially financial decisions—there is a tendency for organizations to establish a direct causal link between their actions and the results they observe. When this happens, these organizations tend to attribute the expected achievements or results to their work. This is a recurrent issue in the development cooperation sector, where most agencies and organizations compete to attract funding for their sustainability-based programmes. It is also becoming a standard practice in the impact investment domain, where financial decisions follow ESG (environmental, social and governance) criteria—stated in ESG reporting mechanisms.

This pressure to attribute impact is exacerbated by the confirmation bias, which is the tendency of organizations to select information that confirms its existing assumptions or hypotheses. The focus of organizations on the intended positive impacts (they have to justify) incentivizes and exacerbates confirmation bias, because they only look for evidence of what they have to justify (positive impact).

In evaluating systems transformation, the attribution analysis does not only distort the conventional reality; it hampers the organization in truly understanding how it is contributing to achieving its expected impact. How do you know, then, the direct difference that you have made? In systems change, it is very difficult trying to link your actions to a result, especially in complex contexts where multiple factors affect the same issue at the same time.

A more reliable alternative approach to understanding the difference you made is to assess your contribution. Contribution analysis, according to John Mayne,[8] offers an approach to make credible causal claims the organization is making to the observed results. It does so through an increased understanding of why the observed results have occurred and the roles played by the organizations' activities, stakeholders and other internal and external factors. Assessing contribution implies testing the underlying assumptions of the organizations' theory of transformation and business models. It requires, though, a collective effort from all stakeholders to see and understand the complexity in evaluating transformation, and, therefore, to set standard criteria based on contribution and alienated from the myth of attribution.

What do we need to evaluate?

The process of transformation

Once the purpose is defined and framed in the accountability of the organization, with all aforementioned implications, the organization can focus on evaluating its contribution to the process of transformation it is committed to.

Evaluating the process of transformation implies testing the underlying assumptions and mental models that drive the systems that are involved in the transformation. Think of Unilever. Its overall purpose is "to make sustainable living commonplace".[9] The Anglo-Dutch organization aims to do so by assuming that "brands with purpose grow, companies with purpose last and people with purpose thrive". The brand component aims, for example, "to improve the health of the planet with brands that regenerate nature, fight climate change, and conserve resources for future generations".

This purpose involves linking the economic and ecological systems. Unilever assumes that their brands are regenerating nature and fighting climate change. Evaluating this process of transformation means asking questions such as:

- Are our brands regenerating nature? How? In which ways?
- What are the links between our brands, our stakeholders, our business operations and processes, and their impact on nature's regeneration?
- To what extent are we driving change in our stakeholders' behaviour? To what extent and how?
- Are we changing the dynamics of our business operations and processes? If so, how? To what extent are these new dynamics changing the economic and ecological systems' dynamics?
- Are we doing it the right way? What are the tradeoffs? What are the difficulties?
- Are we generating any unintended negative and positive impacts? Which ones and how?
- What are we learning? What can we improve, stop, reduce, scale or develop in order to be more effective and efficient?

These questions are just an example of a hypothetic evaluation enquiry framework. They trigger the gathering of evidence that allows rigorous testing of the assumptions. Evidence provides input and informs the developmental process of reflection and learning, a process where the organization uses the evaluative evidence to validate its purpose and to make decisions for adaptation and transformation.

The lens to mindful business

Evaluating the process of transformation, for a mindful organization, means enquiring into the process through the lenses of business mindfulness. This observation focuses on three impact lenses that concern the process of transformation. The first lens refers to the intention of the impacts generated. Organizations normally intend to influence and control the desired impact. However, in systems transformation that operates under complexity, impact is also generated unintentionally. Imagine that you are developing a new eco-friendly product that requires extra dedication from your workforce. On the one hand, you have intentionally reduced the energy consumption, but, on the other hand, you have stressed your employees.

The second lens refers to the judgemental quality of the impact. Have your activities contributed to generating a positive or a negative impact? Organizations expect to generate positive results, but impacts can also be negative. The above example also applies here. The organization did not intend to stress the workforce, but the generation of a positive impact also carried the generation of a negative one.

The third lens refers to the space where impact takes place. Setting up a process of transformation may impact the organization internally (the organizational culture of the living system), or externally (the nested systems that mutually influence the organization). As a result of the transformation, for example, an organization may see internal changes in people's behaviours (i.e., employee engagement), processes (i.e., circularization of the supply chain) and structures (i.e., self-managed teams). External impacts may hinge upon changes in the systems' dynamics (i.e., corporate policies that become a standard in the industry and society), external stakeholders' behaviour (i.e., ecological and socially driven consumers), environmental degradation or regeneration and changes in structures (i.e., new governance mechanisms, Figure 9.2).

These lenses illuminate the impacts that the organization generates in different possible domains. In an honest exercise of business mindfulness, the organization—and its stakeholders—require the humility and the courage to acknowledge that impacts may be generated in all those multiple dimensions, even if some of them are negative and non-intended.

Measurement is not evaluation

One of the main caveats when considering evaluation as an organizational development tool is the confusion between measurement and evaluation. This is a recurrent pattern of behaviour that I observe in countless workshops, conferences, lectures and working sessions with managers and executives. Let me explain. Organizations are used to measuring performance. As Peter Drucker popularized, "if you can't measure it, you can't manage it". Measuring helps you monitor and manage what you care about. The majority of organizations—whose purpose is profit maximization—tend

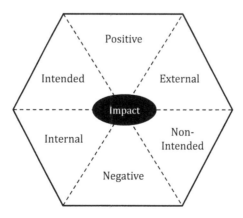

Figure 9.2 The lens to mindful business

to focus measurement on the financial performance and the related factors that conduce to financial performance.

These organizations use the famous KPIs (key performance indicators) to measure the performance of a particular activity. Organizations mainly focus on evaluating the success or failure of their activities by comparing defined KPIs against a baseline, a target, or a benchmark. A baseline is the value of the indicator before the implementation of the activity; it is the starting or departing point. A target is the expected level of result to be achieved within a specific timeframe—the destination. And a benchmark is the average result or standard achieved in the industry or sector where the organization operates.

Have we achieved the growth we wanted in increasing our turnover? Are we above the industry standard in customer loyalty? Are we reaching our target in employee satisfaction? Have we reduced the greenhouse emissions as expected? Have we helped the number of households expected? These are examples of classic KPIs that may let you take the pulse of how the organization is performing.

In general, there is an obsession with KPIs. Having a dashboard full of fancy KPIs and infographics is the dream of any controller. And that's all right. But they are not enough if what you want is to evaluate the impact of your purpose. What if you are measuring the wrong things? Data collection—and, therefore, measurement—is very much needed and useful if you are only measuring the things that matter. And for making sure they are measuring the right things, organizations need to ask the right questions. And this is precisely the spirit of evaluation; a deep process of evidence-based reflective enquiry. So yes, to inform results and decision-making so that the organization can assess the value and impact of its activities does include measurement. But evaluation is not just measurement.

Mind Campbell's law

I also learned from Patton a common law that exists in the evaluation field. It's called Campbell's law of corrupt indicators in honour of Donald T. Campbell, a social scientist who studied the effect of high-stakes indicators in the education sector.[10] This law states that

> the more any single quantitative social indicator is used for high-stakes decision making, the more subject it will be to corruption pressures and the more apt it will be to distort and corrupt the social processes it is intended to monitor.

The danger appears when transitioning purpose-driven organizations start practices proper of the new business paradigm but still have high-stakes strategic goals measured by quantitative indicators. Let's look at an example. Imagine an organization in the education sector whose purpose is to acquire and transfer knowledge in order to increase social mobility and cohesion through employability. This organization has its first and foremost strategic goal to increase the turnover by 20% in three years (this is a quantitative indicator).

Employees are incentivized with bonuses if they achieve this goal. As a consequence, employees' behaviour tends to focus on attracting the clients that can bring more income to the organization. This behaviour narrows down the scope of clients that can access the knowledge offered by the organization, which will be clients that can afford to pay for such services. This results in fewer opportunities to increase social cohesion and mobility, which is precisely detrimental to achieving the purpose of the organization.

At the beginning, the quantitative indicator set in the strategic goal was supposed to help the organization achieve its purpose, but, in the end, the indicator has corrupted the purpose itself. This is what Campbell refers to as the corrupting effect of the indicator.

To mitigate Campbell's law, it is recommended not to use high-stakes quantitative indicators, of any sort, linked to high strategic objectives. That does not mean that they should not be measured. Rather, it implies framing the measurement in an evaluation context, where the most important thing is to decide what are the most critical things to measure. In this context, evaluation emerges as a trans discipline that needs to be embedded in the strategic reflection and design of the business model and activities, from its inception.

How should we evaluate?

Now that we know why and what we need to evaluate in the frame of our perception and interpretation of the conventional reality, it is time to figure out how to evaluate. Evaluating systems with multiple, complex and changing human and non-human interactions does not feature a "one-size-fits-all" methodology. The section that follows does not aim to provide an exact "to-do list" to evaluate systems. Rather, its intention is to provide an approach, general guidance and food for thought, in the form of steps, that may help organizations think about, design and set up an evaluation for systems transformation.

The following steps are organized according to a time-sequence logic. However, they do not necessarily need to be undertaken one after the other. You can combine, alter, add, cut, fine-tune and adapt according to the situation, context and utility to your organization. Evaluating systems transformation relies on the capacity of the organization and its evaluators to identify and apply the most suitable tools to fit with the purpose of the evaluation.

1.   *Define the purpose and context of the evaluation*

Start with the why. You can frame the evaluation by defining the purpose—of the evaluation, not of the organization—and the context that describes the current situation, the background and the circumstances that trigger the need to evaluate. You should also include the utility of the evaluation, that is, how you expect to use this evaluation (intended uses) and who will use it (intended users).

2.   *Understand and visualize the system (in the context of the intervention)*

Evaluating the transformation of a system requires a thorough identification, examination and understanding of its dynamics, its elements, components, stakeholders, its boundaries and relations with other systems and all the interdependencies generated under the principle of mutual causality. This is a scoping exercise that can be undertaken by an interdisciplinary team, combining multiple perspectives with systems thinking tools that allow analysis and visualization of the system.

The Global Alliance for the Future of Food is a principles-focused strategic alliance working to transform global food systems. Its purpose is to build resilient, inclusive, healthy, equitable, renewable, interconnected and culturally diverse food and agriculture systems shaped by people, communities and their institutions. Food, along with energy and water, is an essential component of sustainability.

The Global Alliance is pioneering systems evaluation as a transformative practice for the organization. It applies the Blue Marble Evaluation approach developed by Michael Quinn Patton, which is utilization-focused, principles-focused and developmental. This approach conceives systemic evaluation as a trans-disciplinary intervention that is directly linked to design, implementation, learning, adaptation and evaluation.

The global food system is a diverse, complex and dynamic system comprising a multiplicity of interactions among many factors and stakeholders with different, and often diverging, interests. Food systems are shaped by—and impacted by—global issues, from climate change to economic disruption and migration.

The Global Alliance developed, together with other partners and stakeholders, a Food Systems Evaluation Framework—TEEB AgrioFood[11] (Figure 9.3) aiming at forging pathways towards more sustainable food and agriculture systems by bringing system thinking to understanding the production, distribution and consumption of food across various system types and scales when environmental, health, social and cultural externalities and impacts are taken into account.

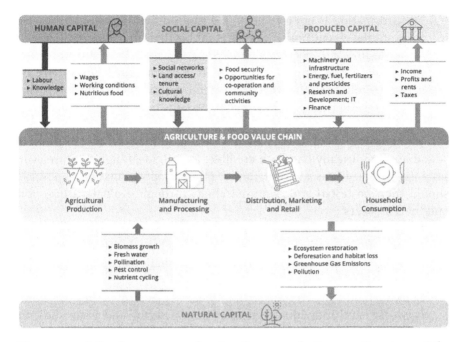

Figure 9.3 A food systems evaluation framework. Source: Courtesy of the TEEB Agri-Food Initiative—UNEP

3.   *Explain how you expect to transform the system*

In the context of the Anthropocene, an organization transitioning to the new business paradigm expects to transform the system. The formulation of an organizational purpose, as mentioned above, incorporates the desired impact for this transformation. It is a forward-looking exercise. In this phase it is essential to thoroughly explain how the organization expects to transform the system. In other words, the organization needs to define its theory of transformation. This is a breakthrough in itself, for the following reason.

Organizations that evaluate are usually designing their results framework following a linear logic of thinking (inputs $\longrightarrow$ activities $\longrightarrow$ outputs $\longrightarrow$ outcomes $\longrightarrow$ impact).[12] This is often the case in business organizations where they are used to understanding the process of transformation as a supply chain. However, this linear approach does not fit complex environments where unexpected changes and a high degree of uncertainty condition the implementation and, therefore, the results of the intervention.[13]

In this context, a theory of transformation transcends the linear logic and adopts a systems approach instead, in order to capture the complexities that surround global systems change. According to Patton,[14]

> Transformation is not a project. It is multi-dimensional, multi-faceted, and multilevel, cutting across national borders and intervention silos, across sectors and specialized interests, connecting local and global, and sustaining across time. A theory of transformation incorporates and integrates multiple theories of change operating at many levels that, knitted together, explain how major systems transformation occurs.

The explanation of the theory of transformation should be theoretically sound and empirically based on credible, useful, meaningful and relevant premises, propositions and hypotheses. These propositions and hypotheses should then be tested and enquired about through evaluation questions and their answers.

One of the Blue Marble evaluation principles deals with the application of a theory of transformation. This is central to the Global Alliance's strategy, which describes its own theory of transformation as follows:

> Genuine food systems transformation takes place when diverse actions, networks, and individuals intersect across sector and issue silos, the global and local, the macro and the micro. These intersections facilitate convergence around shared visions and values and, ultimately, build critical mass and momentum behind tipping points that lead to healthy, equitable, renewable, resilient, and culturally diverse food systems that dynamically endure over time.

As Global Alliance's Blue Marble Evaluator, Pablo Vidueira, and Senior Evaluation Advisor Michael Patton state, the Theory of Transformation provides enhanced strategic direction and evaluation criteria for taking the scale and scope of needed systems transformations seriously and contributing to transformational trajectories. It gives new meaning to, and opens new areas for, Global Alliance's role, purpose, niche, and strategy in support of transforming food systems with others.

4.   *Discover, identify and illuminate the Yin–Yang creative tensions*

An intentional transformation is grounded on the journey between an uncomfortable conventional reality (X) and a desired future scenario, or vision, that is yet to come true (Y). The transition between X and Y is often hampered by systemic tensions—structural issues and recurrent problems and challenges—that prevent the system from behaving the way we feel it should.

Articulating the transition through apparently opposing, contrasting yet complementary, and interdependent Yin–Yang creative tensions helps to focus on the analysis of root causes behind the problems (see Chapter 3 for a conceptual explanation of the Yin–Yang creative tensions). This way, the organization can understand the current patterns of behaviour and start a creative enquiry that leads to the identification of leverage points for change and transformation.

5. *Design an evaluation inquiry framework with evaluation questions*

Formulating questions is the natural approach to evaluation. Evaluation questions open up the exploratory- and explanatory-driven enquiry process around the journey of transformation (see the fictional enquiry framework I develop to evaluate Unilever's purpose, above). The tool that guides this step is called an enquiry framework, which encapsulates the critical questions that lead the evaluation.

Designing questions calls for three important prerequisites. First, questions should be grounded in illuminating the blind spots along the transformation journey. One way to do it can be by testing the intentional hypotheses that drive the actions. That is, to explore the mutual causality linkages that might lead to the desired results. Another way to do it is by evaluating principles.[15] Principles guide behaviour, and transformation is about behavioural changes. Identifying those changes, understanding why they happened, how they were produced and which mechanisms produced them is of the essence. If there are no changes, then we should explore why they have not been generated.

The second design prerequisite is related to whom you enquire of and observe and how you do it. It is important to capture multiple perspectives on the transformation process. In this regard, the organization can review the stakeholders' map, identify their different roles and interests and select the ones that may enrich the process of enquiry with multiple points of view.

The third prerequisite crosscuts all enquiry areas. It is about ensuring that questions are mindful, that is, that they allow the exploration of the positive and negative, the intended and unintended and the internal and external impacts of the transformation process.

6. *Set the methodological mix*

Evaluating systems transformation—as well as designing it—can only be approached through flexible methods. What does this mean? Most often, organizations seek gold standards or benchmark best practices in order to find straightforward and cost-effective solutions to solve their problems. When the problem is "how to evaluate", organizations usually look at what is available on the market. It is typical here to confuse evaluation methods with measurement frameworks.

However, this behaviour does not fit with evaluating systems transformation. Evaluating in highly complex and challenging dynamic environments requires the adoption of flexible tailored-made approaches that consider the combination of multiple methods along the course of the evaluation exercise. This adaptive approach requires developing a methodological mix[16] that fits the purpose of a systemic evaluation. This implies,[17] for the evaluation team, (i) to access and create a mix of methods, measurements and analytical approaches; (ii) to use a mix of qualitative and quantitative methods to capture the complexities of the transformation; (iii) to combine the use of data aggregated and synthesized at the global system level and data disaggregated within sub-systems; (iv) to apply longitudinal designs to capture the process of transformation over time; and (v) to design an emergent and adaptive methodological mix.

7.   *Collect data*

A major challenge in evaluating systems transformation is the availability and reliability of data. When the destiny of the system depends on a growing and changing multiplicity of factors and actors, assessing the contribution of the organization to the transformation of the system requires collecting data from myriad sources and methods. These may include emerging data collection methods, such as qualitative impact-based storytelling.

The application of new technologies (i.e., blockchain, artificial intelligence, big data, geographic information systems, remote sensing, the Internet of Things, among others) is bringing newer and wider possibilities for collecting more relevant and reliable data. Business and people analytics, for example, provide a wealth of data that can be used to evaluate impact.

8.   *Data analysis, visualization and interpretation*

A major challenge once data is collected is to structure, organize, relate, summarize and recognize patterns in the analysis of the evidence collected, mixing quantitative and qualitative data. Given the vast amount of data that can be gathered, presenting the data in visual formats can help guide the discussion and interpretation of the findings.

In this regard, there are some approaches that claim the need to simplify data collection in a cost-effective way to shed clarity on complexity. This is the case of lean data, a term popularized by Acumen, that refers to collecting high quality data related to social impact in order to demonstrate social change. It does so with an extremely efficient use of resources, employing the latest available technologies.[18]

9.   *Synthesizing the transformation of the system*

Synthesis is the process by which the complexity of the system is dissected into manageable components to make sense of the whole. The goal is to find organized patterns of behaviour that structure the process of transformation in a way that makes sense to the organization. Synthesizing implies having a big-picture view of the whole and the parts, including all the interdependencies between the contributing factors and the connections that shape the dynamics of the whole system.

Applying systems archetypes,[19] which, in systems thinking, are classic stories that describe common patterns of behaviour and structures that occur repeatedly in organizations, can be a tool to do this. Undertaking the synthesis of the system collectively can be a powerful organizational exercise that puts the findings into the perspective of the whole organization and its stakeholders. It is a tool to collectively define the conventional reality, beyond whether that reality is good or bad. It is about jointly discussing how and to what extent findings are meaningful to the organization. Organizational sense-making allows people to deal with uncertainty and ambiguity by creating rational accounts of the world that enable action.[20]

10.   *Learning for transformation*

The ultimate objective of an evaluation is to learn in order to adapt, anticipate and transform the system. In order to facilitate this type of organizational learning, it is of the essence that the process of discussing the findings is an open, ongoing, developmental and collective process of reflection and creation, involving the multiplicity of actors that have stakes in the evaluation.

This process implies operationalizing several rounds of feedback loops where findings are discussed and interpreted as soon as they are collected (real-time provision of feedback). The idea is to optimize the use of the evaluation, which, in highly complex and dynamic contexts, requires a timely flow of the data gathered in order to accrue them for learning and informing decision-making.

Decision-making can be done at the strategic and operational level in order to adapt strategies and actions, anticipate trends and future scenarios and develop new innovations to channel the desired transformation of the system. Indeed, in a genuine exercise of triple-loop learning (learn how to learn), it may imply questioning the whole theory of transformation. This may even lead to changing or transforming the purpose of the organization (see section titled "Systems learning and transformative adaptation" in Chapter 4).

Business mindfulness implies questioning everything, through an evaluative mindset, even if what the organization is doing is meaningful in the larger context of the transformation. The process of business mindfulness connects the organization—and the people that work in/for the organization—to the large system, to life. Are we doing the right thing? How do we know what is right? What does the system need now?

In this context, transforming a system requires transforming the organization. A systemic evaluation can be an organizational transformation tool that helps to transform the culture of the organization towards a culture of impact. Systemically approached, evaluation is a tool of organizational consciousness. It may help in leaving behind the mechanistic conceptualization of a traditional profit-orientated organization in favour of an organic, adaptive and living organization that changes and adapts its own behaviours for driving the transition towards the new business paradigm.

Notes

1 This Chinese farmer story is contained in Alan Watts' book, *Eastern Wisdom, Modern Life: Collected talks 1960–1969*, published by New World Library.
2 Shen, C.Y. & Midgley, G. (2007). Toward a Buddhist Systems methodology 1: comparison between Buddhist and systems theories. *Systemic Practice & Action Research*, 20, 167–194.
3 Russon, C. (2008). An Eastern paradigm of evaluation. *Journal of Multidisciplinary Evaluation*, 5(10), 71–77.
4 Russon, C. & Russon, K. (2009). The Insight Evaluation approach. *Journal of Multidisciplinary Evaluation*, 6(12), 205–209.
5 Russon, C. (2019). Methods for collecting data based upon an Eastern paradigm of evaluation. *Journal of Multidisciplinary Evaluation*, 15(32).
6 Simon Sinek explains, in his best-selling book *Start with Why*, how to formulate a purpose statement based on a simple format: "To ____ so that _____". The first blank space represents your contribution and the second the impact of your contribution.
7 Patton, Michael Quinn and Blandin Foundation (2014). Mountain of Accountability: Pursuing mission through learning, exploration and development. Grand Rapids, MN: Blandin Foundation, blandinfoundation.org.a
8 Mayne, J. (2011). Contribution analysis: Addressing cause and effect. In K. Forss, M. Marra and R. Schwartz (Eds.), *Evaluating the Complex*, Transaction Publishers; Piscataway, New Jersey.
9 Based on www.unilever.com/about/who-we-are/our-strategy/ (retrieved August 10 2020).
10 Campbell, D.T. (1976). *Assessing the impact of planned social change*. Hanover, NH: The Public Affairs Center, Dartmouth College.
11 TEEB (2018). *TEEB for Agriculture & Food: Scientific and Economic Foundations*. Geneva: UN Environment.
12 In evaluation, this linear thinking is called the logical framework approach, which is the dominant approach applied since the 1970s and used for planning, managing and evaluating programmes, projects and initiatives in the development cooperation sector.

13 In this article, evaluator Hummelbrunner explains the limitations of the logical framework approach. Hummelbrunner, R. (2010). Beyond Logframe: Critique, variations and alternatives. In N. Fujita (Ed.), *Beyond Logframe: Using systems concepts in evaluation.* Tokyo: Foundation for Advanced Studies on International Development, pp. 1–33.

14 Patton, M.Q. (2020). *Blue Marble Evaluation: Principles and premises.* Guilford Press.

15 In his book *Principles-focused Evaluation* (Guilford Press, 2017), Michael Quinn Patton highlights the utility and relevance of evaluating principles as a rudder to navigate the uncertainties, turbulence, and emergent challenges of complex dynamic environments. The Blue Marble Evaluation approach is, in fact, a principles-focused approach to evaluating global systems transformation.

16 Setting a tailor-based methodological mix is consistent with the theory of methodological pluralism, which is constructed in critical systems thinking (Shen & Midgley 2007).

17 These implications are adapted from Patton's implications of the Bricolage Methods Principle of the *Blue Marble Evaluation* (Guilford Press, 2020).

18 Dichter, S. et al. (2015). The power of lean data. *Stanford Social Innovation Review.*

19 Meadows, D. (2015). *Thinking in Systems: A primer.* Chelsea Green.

20 Maitlis, S. (2005). The social processes of organizational sensemaking. *Academy of Management Review*, 48, 21–49.

References

Campbell, D.T. (1976). *Assessing the Impact of Planned Social Change.* Hanover, NH: The Public Affairs Center, Dartmouth College.

Dichter, S. et al. (2015). The power of lean data. *Stanford Social Innovation Review.*

Garfield, J.L. (1995). *The Fundamental Wisdom of the Middle Way: Nagarjuna's Mulamadhyamakakarija.* Oxford University Press.

Hummelbrunner, R. (2010). Beyond Logframe: critique, variations and alternatives. In N. Fujita (Ed.), *Beyond Logframe: Using systems concepts in evaluation.* Tokyo: Foundation for Advanced Studies on International Development.

Macy, J. (1991). *Mutual Causality in Buddhism and General Systems Theory: The Dharma of natural systems.* State University of New York Press.

Maitlis, S. (2005). The social processes of organizational sensemaking. *Academy of Management Review*, 48, 21–49.

Mayne, J. (2011). Contribution analysis: Addressing cause and effect. In *Evaluating the Complex*, K. Forss, M. Marra and R. Schwartz (Eds.), *Transaction*; Piscataway, New Jersey.

Midgley, G. & Shen, C.Y. (2007). Toward a Buddhist Systems methodology 2: An exploratory, questioning approach. *Systemic Practice & Action Research*, 20, 195–210.

Patton, M.Q. (2019). *Blue Marble Evaluation: Premises and principles.* Guilford Press.

Shen, C.Y. & Midgley, G. (2007). Toward a Buddhist Systems methodology 1: Comparison between Buddhist and systems theories. *Systemic Practice & Action Research*, 20, 167–194.

Watts, A. (2006). *Eastern Wisdom, Modern Life: Collected talks 1960–1969.* New World Library.

Index

Page numbers in *italics* refer to figures, those in **bold** indicate tables.

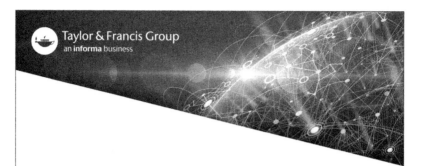

Printed in the United States
by Baker & Taylor Publisher Services